REMEMBERING SIM[

REMEMBERING SIMPLIFIED HANZI

*How not to forget the meaning
and writing of Chinese characters*

Book 2

James W. Heisig

Timothy W. Richardson

University of Hawai'i Press
HONOLULU

25 24 23 22 21   6 5 4

Library of Congress Cataloging-in-Publication Data

Heisig, James W., 1944- Remembering simplified Hanzi : book 1 : how not to forget
    the meaning and writing of Chinese characters / James W. Heisig, Timothy W.
    Richardson.
        p. cm. Includes indexes. ISBN 978-0-8248-3323-7 (pbk. : alk. paper)
        1. Chinese Characters. 2. Chinese language--Study and teaching. I. Richardson,
    Timothy W. II. Title. III. Title: How not to forget the meaning and writing of
    Chinese characters.
PL1171.H45 2008 495.1'07—dc22   2008033030

Remembering Simplified Hanzi: Book 2
ISBN 978-0-8248-3655-9

The typesetting for this book was done at the Nanzan Institute for Religion and Culture.

University of Hawai'i Press books are printed on acid-free paper and meet the guidelines
for permanence and durability of the Council on Library Resources.

CONTENTS

INTRODUCTION

THIS IS THE second of two volumes designed to help students with the meaning and writing of the 3,000 most frequently used simplified Chinese characters. A parallel set of volumes has been prepared for traditional characters. Although there is considerable overlap in the selection and arrangement of the characters, as well as in the mnemonic devices employed, you are advised to stick with one set of books or the other. As we explained in the Introduction to Book 1, combining your learning of traditional and simplified characters is likely to slow down progress and create confusion. That Introduction also provides further details about the approach followed in these books and the rationale behind it.

HOW TO USE THIS BOOK

From the start, our working assumption was that Book 1 and Book 2 would be studied *sequentially*. Each book would introduce half of the most important 3,000 characters in the Chinese language. The idea was that since the 1,000 most frequently used characters were to be introduced in Book 1, learners would complete that volume before passing on to the second. Many, if not most, students will find this preferable.

However, as we weighed the options for organizing the remaining 1,500 characters for Book 2, we realized that others may prefer the more exacting, but also more rationally satisfying, approach of studying the two volumes *simultaneously*. We have adjusted the Introduction to Book 1 to clarify the reasons why this is so, but a word of explanation is in order here.

As each new primitive was presented in Book 1, most of the characters (among the 1,500 selected for the first volume) that could be learned at that point were introduced. The lessons of Book 2 have been designed as extensions of that principle. Thus, nearly all of the 1,500 characters of Book 2 are placed in the lessons in which they *would have appeared* if we had combined everything into a single volume. This means that students who wish to do so can treat the corresponding lessons of Books 1 and 2 as single units.

Having said this, we hasten to add a note of caution: Book 1 was designed to progress from complete stories to short plots to the simple listing of a character's primitive elements. In this way, the student gradually gains independence

1

from the imagination of the authors and develops a knack for creating stories based on personal memories and learning preferences. Book 2 disregards this progression. Even in the early pages, one will find mere plots and listings of elements where the lessons of Book 1 would have given more information. Occasionally we supply a fuller story to clarify the connotation of a key word or to help with a particularly challenging character—or sometimes simply because we cannot resist the temptation. But these are the exception.

Accordingly, if you wish to study the books simultaneously, you may want to get several lessons into Book 1 before you crack Book 2, and then return to those lessons to pick up the new characters.

COMPOUNDS, POSTSCRIPTS, INDEXES

The 55 lessons of this book are followed by a short special section with "compounds" or characters that are best learned in pairs. A final section contains two "postscripts" that we strongly urge you not to skip over.

The Indexes of Book 2 differ slightly from those of Book 1. Index 1 gives a hand-drawn character and its pronunciation for each frame in Book 2. The other four Indexes are comprehensive. That is, they cover the relevant information from both volumes. This will make it easier for you to navigate all 3,000 characters without the need to consult the Indexes from Book 1.

It bears repeating that the pronunciations given in the Indexes are given as an aid should you need to consult a dictionary. Nothing further is said about them in these volumes, and no examples of their use are provided. As we recommended in the Introduction to Book 1, it is best to study the writing and meaning of the characters separately from their pronunciation.

ON CHARACTERS AND THEIR KEY WORDS

Finding unique English key words for 3,000 different Chinese characters was challenging in the extreme. Often there is more than one ordinary character in Chinese corresponding to a single word in English. At times this left us no choice but to stretch the limits of standard English ever so slightly, employing common phrases or even neologisms in order to avoid the duplication of key words. In any case, if you follow the guidance given along the way about preserving a distinct connotation for each key word and heeding its part of speech, these hurdles will be easy to hop over.

Although we do not draw attention to the fact in each case, a relatively small number of the characters presented in the lessons are "bound forms." That is, much like the "compounds" that are given their own section, these characters are always used in combination with others. The Chinese equivalents of "trumpet," "glaze," and "universe," for example, are usually considered to be two-character compounds. Nevertheless, our policy has been to assign each individual character its own key word on the assumption that when the time comes for students to learn compounds, they will find it a straightforward task. Take "trumpet," for instance: the character with that key word (FRAME 1501) is often paired in a compound with that for "flared horn" (2652) to designate what English simply calls a "trumpet."

Remember, too, that while some key words carry clear and discrete connotations, others can only approximate the range of meanings and nuances covered by a character. A broader awareness of what individual characters convey can only be acquired by encountering them in context over time.

A final note of caution: We urge you to avoid dismissing certain characters as not being very useful simply because their key words are not ones you run into very often. "Lambsquarters" and "water caltrops" are not part of everyday English vocabulary, and never appear in personal or family names. Things are different in the world of the characters. It is safe to assume that if a character appears in these books, you will need it to gain proficiency in Chinese.

ACKNOWLEDGMENTS

The authors would like to reiterate their thanks to Robert Roche for his insight, encouragement, and generous assistance over the long years this project has been in the works. The staff and fellows of the Nanzan Institute for Religion and Culture in Nagoya, Japan, made our task a lot easier and provided just the right atmosphere for collaboration. Thanks, too, to Brigham Young University–Hawaii for its support of the project. Tsu-Pin Huang, Yifen Beus, and Pao-Ho Wan assisted us with their expertise on numerous occasions. Pat Crosby, Keith Leber, and Nadine Little of University of Hawai'i Press deserve mention for patiently seeing this book through its editing and production. A special word of appreciation is due Helen Richardson and the Richardson children. Without their willingness to make do without a husband and father for weeks at a time, concentrated periods of work in Japan over the past several years would not have been possible.

Finally, we wish to acknowledge the many readers who have sent us their comments, reactions, and suggestions since the appearance of Book 1. Their feedback has not only made for important improvements; it has confirmed our confidence that we are on the right track.

James W. Heisig
Timothy W. Richardson
15 July 2011

Lessons

LESSON 1

As explained in the Introduction, the lessons of Book 2 are organized according to the characters and primitives introduced in their corresponding lesson in Book 1. With that, we start Book 2 off with a blast:

1501   trumpet [N.]

叭丶   Since the character *eight* depicts an open expanse that begins in the heavens and covers the earth, it is just right for the character that shows the Angel Gabriel pressing his *mouth* against the **trumpet** to announce the end of time—or in this case, the end of Lesson 1. [5]

丿   叩   叩   叭   叭丶

LESSON 2

THERE ARE only two new characters we can make with the elements from Lesson 2 of Book 1.

1502	mutter
咕	Since we already used the image of an *ancient* tombstone in Lesson 2 of Book 1 and we have the *mouth* on the left, we need only think of someone trying to **mutter** something to us. Perhaps it's someone that would like to be let out. [8]

口　　咕

1503	gall bladder
胆	*Flesh . . . daybreak.* [9]

月　　胆

LESSON 3

1504

咱

we (inclusive)

Mouth . . . nostrils. Chinese is one of those languages (Indonesian is another) that have two different ways of expressing "**we**," one including the person or persons spoken to, the other excluding them. We will meet the latter in FRAME 2945. [9]

口　咱

1505

肿

swollen

Flesh . . . middle. [8]

月　肿

1506

串

string together

This character looks like a doodle of a shish kebab. Can you see the skewer used to **string together** those tasty little tidbits for grilling over the fire? Identifying a character by its shape rather than by its primitive elements is something we have shied away from, but we think you will agree this one merits treating as an exception. [7]

口　吕　串

❖ We will stay with *shish kebab* for the primitive meaning.

1507

吓

terrify

Mouth . . . below. [6]

口　吓

1508   overspread [v.]

罩   Just as awnings, clouds, and bedspreads cover things, the *net* in
      this character is used to **overspread** an *eminent* person, prob-
      ably the only way to capture his attention. [13]

罒　罩

LESSON 4

1509	beast

兽　*Horns . . . brains . . . floor . . . mouth.* [11]

⸜　甾　単　兽

1510	hubbub

嚚　So what is all the **hubbub** about? Instead of the four *mouths* munching away on a *chihuahua* that appears in FRAME 249, here they are enjoying—a *head!* [18]

叩　嚪　嚚

LESSON 5

YOU WILL NOTICE that in most cases only the primitive elements are given below, without any detailed story or story plot. Book 1 progresses from full stories to simple plots to component elements. The idea is to gradually turn more and more of the creative work over to the learner. If you feel you are not quite ready to venture off on your own at this point but still want to study the two books together, you might hold off on the lessons of Book 2 until later, when you are more comfortable with inventing your own images and stories.

1511		stand straight

矗

When your gym teacher tells you to "Stop slouching and **stand straight**," the words are spoken with such force that they echo around the gymnasium: "*Straight . . . straight . . . straight.*" [24]

直　直　矗

1513		invert

颠

True . . . head. [16]

真　颠

1513		strengthen

巩

I-beam . . . ordinary. [6]

工　巩

1514		talkative

叨

Mouth . . . dagger. [5]

口　叨

1515		scrape [v.]

刮

Tongue . . . saber. [8]

舌　刮

1516		stare at
盯	*Eyeballs . . . spike.* [7]	

目　盯

1517		rebuke [v.]
呵	*Mouth . . . can.* [8]	

口　呵

LESSON 6

1518	father's sister
姑	Woman . . . ancient. [8]
	女　姑

1519	baby
嬰	Two oysters . . . woman. [11]
	贝　赑　嬰

1520	nanny
姆	Woman . . . mother. [8]
	女　姆

1521	cautious
兢	Overcome . . . overcome. [14]
	克　兢

LESSON 7

1522	**exert oneself**

奮 *St. Bernard dog . . . rice field.* [8]

大 奮

1523	**press from both sides**

夹 Think of those "bulldog clips" that **press from both sides** to hold papers together. This clip is made up of a pair of *animal horns* set in place below the *ceiling*, and what they are holding together is our old friend, the *St. Bernard dog*. First you draw the *ceiling* and then the *animal horns*. Next, you insert the *St. Bernard dog*, putting his head through a hole in the *ceiling* and placing his body between the *animal horns* that **press from both sides** to hold him secure. This "*St. Bernard clip*" sure is a lot cheaper than building a doghouse out in the back yard. [6]

一 ニ 프 뽀 夹

1524	**cheek**

颊 *Press from both sides . . . head.* [12]

夹 颊

1525	**toilet**

厕 *Cliff . . . rule.* [8]

厂 厕

1526	**big**

硕 To remember this character, you need only think of those **big** *stone heads* found in Mesoamerica or on Easter Island. [11]

石　硕

1527	lay brick

砌　　*Stone . . . cut.* [9]

石　砌

1528	whistle [N.]

哨　　*Mouth . . . candle.* [10]

口　哨

1529	sway [V.]

晃　　*Sun . . . ray.* [10]

日　晃

LESSON 8

1530		tears
泪	*Water . . . eyeballs.* [8]	
	氵　泪	

1531		discharge [v.]
泄	*Water . . . generation.* [8]	
	氵　泄	

1532		moor [v.]
泊	*Water . . . dove.* [8]	
	氵　泊	

1533		soak
沾	*Water . . . tell fortunes.* When you hear this key word, think of how a thundershower **soaks** you to the skin, not of something left to **soak** overnight in a marinade. [8]	
	氵　沾	

1534		insignificant
渺	This key word connotes small or trifling. Its elements: *tears . . . few.* [12]	
	氵　泪　渺	

1535		get rid of
汰	*Water . . . overly.* [7]	

汉 汰

1536 chant

咏

The *mouth* of a monk as he **chants** his sutra opens up *eternity* for a moment, transporting one to a realm where the rules of everyday life have been suspended. [8]

口 咏

1537 gland

腺

Flesh . . . spring. [13]

月 腺

1538 Lu

鲁

Fish . . . sun. This character is a common surname. [12]

鱼 鲁

1539 level [ADJ.]

坦

The key word can refer both to **level** land and to those calm and composed people who always seem to keep themselves on an even keel. The elements: *soil . . . daybreak.* [8]

土 坦

1540 dam [N.]

坝

Soil . . . shellfish. [7]

土 坝

1541 bank [N.]

涯

The **bank** shown here is a *cliff* of *bricks* meant to hold back the *water.* [11]

汁 汇 涯

1542 newborn ^(N.)

娃

Woman . . . bricks. This rather peculiar combination of elements gives us the character for **newborns** of all kinds, human and animal. [9]

女 娃

1543 elbow ^(N.)

肘

Flesh . . . glue. [7]

月 肘

1544 obstruct

碍

Stone . . . daybreak . . . glue. [13]

石 碍

1545 take by force

夺

Whereas *burglars* (FRAME 365) appropriate another's property clandestinely, robbers and muggers prefer to confront their victims and **take by force** what is not theirs. The primitive elements: *St. Bernard dog . . . glued to.* [6]

大 夺

1546 scorch

灼

Fire . . . ladle. [7]

火 灼

1547 stir-fry ^(V.)

炒

Fire . . . few. [8]

火　炒

1548   cooking stove

灶　　*Fire . . . soil.* [7]

火　灶

LESSON 9

1549   mile

哩   *Mouth . . . computer.* [10]

口   哩

1550   smidgen

厘   *Cliff . . . computer.* [9]

厂   厘

1551   carp[(N.)]

鲤   *Fish . . . computer.* [15]

鱼   鲤

1552   Hey!

嘿   *Mouth . . . black.* [15]

口   嘿

1553   treat with smoke

熏   If you look closely at this character, you will see that it begins with the character for *thousand*, but holds off writing the final stroke until it is needed for *black*. [14]

丿   二   千   币   币   币   車   車

重   重   熏

1554	cinnabar red
丹	*Hood ... a drop ... one*. This character, commonly used for the color red, is also an essential ingredient in Chinese alchemy. Note that the first stroke of *hood* curves slightly outward. [4]

丿 刀 月 丹

1555	shining
炯	*Fire . . . extraterrestrial*. Consult FRAME 188 for this second primitive. [9]

火 炯

1556	part of the day
晌	*Sun ... orientation*. [10]

日 晌

1557	trickle [v.]
淌	*Water ... esteem*. [11]

氵 淌

1558	calm [ADJ.]
宁	*House ... spike*. [5]

宀 宁

1559	widowed
寡	*House ... ceiling ... nose ... tool ... dagger*. This character is easy enough to parse into its primitive elements, as long as you take care to note how the final stroke of *nose* is extended so it can double up as the first stroke of *tool*. The real challenge comes when you try to put all the pieces together. You will need to muster the imagination of a crime scene investigator to figure out who used what to make whom **widowed**. [14]

宀　宾　寡

1560	boisterous
喧	*Mouth . . . proclaim.* [12]

口　喧

LESSON 10

1561		shed (N.)
棚	*Tree . . . companion.* [12]	
	才　棚	

1562		cypress
柏	*Tree . . . dove.* [9]	
	才　柏	

1563		plain (ADJ.)
朴	*Tree . . . magic wand.* [6]	
	才　朴	

1564		flouds
朵	Since English does not have a "measure word" or "classifier" for flowers and clouds to go with this character, we shall just have to invent one: **flouds**. Its primitives are: *wind . . . tree.* [6]	
	几　朵	

1565		thick stick
杠	*Tree . . . I-beam.* Don't think of shillelagh or truncheon here, but of a **thick stick** used for less violent purposes. [7]	
	才　杠	

1566		chair
椅	*Tree . . . strange.* [12]	

木 椅

1567

櫻   **cherry**

The *baby* on this particular *tree* is a ripe, red **cherry** just waiting to be picked. [15]

木 櫻

1568   **treetops**

梢   *Tree . . . candle.* [11]

木 梢

1569   **prevent**

杜   *Tree . . . soil.* [7]

木 杜

1570   **outstanding**

杰   *Tree . . . cooking fire.* [8]

木 杰

1571   **paulownia**

桐   Since you probably don't know what a **paulownia** *tree* is, we shall let the key word suggest the phrase "the Little Brothers of St. **Paulownia**." It is a short step to associate the *tree* with the *monks* to its right. (For the curious, the name of this oriental *tree* really comes from a Russian princess, Anna Pavlovna.) [10]

木 桐

1572   **Song**

宋   This character refers to the **Song** Dynasty (960–1279). Its elements: *house . . . tree.* [7]

宀　宋

1573

cassia-bark tree

桂

The bark of the **cassia-bark tree**, akin to that of the cinnamon tree, is used as a spice. Its elements: *tree . . . bricks.* [10]

木　桂

1574

drench

淋

Water . . . woods. [11]

氵　淋

1575

burn [v.]

焚

Woods . . . fire. [12]

林　焚

1576

side room

厢

Cliff . . . one another. [11]

厂　厢

1577

obscure [ADJ./V.]

昧

Sun . . . not yet. [9]

日　昧

1578

vermilion

朱

That red-orange color we call vermilion is found in nature during the fall when the leaves lose their sugar and begin to change color. This character depicts the very last leaf on a tree in the fall (the *drop* hung on the first stroke), the leaf that has *not yet* fallen as it one day must. Look at its color—**vermilion**. (Well, not really. The truth is, **vermilion** is made from a mercuric sulfide, but we're sure you will agree that autumn leaves are a lot easier to work with.) [6]

ノ　朱

1579		tree trunk
株	*Tree . . . vermilion.* [10]	

木　株

1580		bud (v.)
萌	*Flowers . . . bright.* [11]	

艹　萌

1581		careless
苟	*Flowers . . . sentence.* [8]	

艹　苟

1582		exacting
苛	*Flowers . . . can.* [8]	

艹　苛

1583		edible root
萝	*Flowers . . . silk gauze.* [11]	

艹　萝

1584		membrane
膜	*Flesh . . . graveyard.* [14]	

月　膜

1585		sunset

暮 *Graveyard . . . sun.* [14]

艹　苗　莫　暮

1586		solitary

寞 *House . . . graveyard/nobody.* We have included the key-word meaning of the second primitive as an alternative you might find useful. Remember, this is always a possibility. [13]

宀　寞

LESSON 11

IF YOU ARE going through these Lessons in tandem with Book 1, you will probably have noticed that the new characters presented here are arranged in the same order they would have had in Book 1, namely, the order in which the primitive elements, or characters serving as primitive elements, have been introduced.

1587		cat
猫	*Pack of wild dogs . . . tomato seedling.* [11]	
	犭 猫	

1588		narrow (ADJ.)
狭	*Pack of wild dogs . . . press from both sides.* [9]	
	犭 狭	

1589		raccoon dog
狸	*Pack of wild dogs . . . computer.* [10]	
	犭 狸	

1590		just like
犹	*Pack of wild dogs . . . Frankenpooch.* [7]	
	犭 犹	

1591		ignite
燃	*Fire . . . sort of thing.* [16]	
	火 燃	

1592 curse [v.]

咒 *Chatterbox ... wind.* [8]

叩　咒

1593 sniff [v.]

嗅 *Mouth ... stinking.* [13]

口　嗅

1594 jail

牢 *House ... cow.* [7]

宀　牢

1595 dude

牡 We already met a character to which we assigned the key word *male* (FRAME 741), but there are certain animals that use a different character for gender identification of the masculine variety. Animals like the **dude** deer (also known as the stag), the **dude** horse (alias, the stallion) and the **dude** cow (a.k.a, the bull) use it. It is composed of the primitive elements *cow* and *soil.* [7]

牛　牡

1596 constitution

宪 The key word refers to the fundamental guiding principles of a government or other organization. Its elements: *House ... before.* [9]

宀　宪

1597 succor [v.]

赞 An Oxford don is drowning in the local swimming pool and calls out "**Succor! Succor!**" After consulting their dictionaries, the lifeguards proceed to save the poor chap. Now instead of the typical lifesaver you find at poolside, they grab a giant *oyster* they have trained to swim out, grab hold of drowning swimmers, and drag them back to safety. When you launch it into the deep, you throw it like a discus and shout, *"Before! Before!"* to warn people to get out of the way, obviously a courtesy inherited from the golf course. [16]

先　　䇮　　赞
　　　　　　　贝

1598	umbrella
伞	*Umbrella . . . animal horns . . . needle.* This is the full character from which the primitive element *umbrella* was derived. [6]
	人　仐　伞

1599	abode
舍	*Meeting . . . ancient.* [8]
	人　舍

1600	wha?
啥	This character is a colloquial abbreviation, often used in Internet communications, for the ordinary compound meaning "What?" Its elements: *mouth . . . abode.* [11]
	口　啥

1601	in agreement
洽	*Water . . . fit.* [9]
	氵　洽

1602	thriving
旺	When a *king* is **thriving**, the *sun* should be shining on his kingdom, but more often than not, it is just shining on HIM. As legends around the world remind us, what invariably happens to *kings* **thriving** at the expense of others is that they get consumed by their own selfishness—or, in the case of this character, *sun*-burned to a crisp until they decide that their subjects should be **thriving**, too. [8]

日　旺

1603	green jade
碧	Jewel . . . dove . . . stone. [14]

王　珀　碧

1604	trivial
琐	Ball . . . small . . . shellfish. [11]

王　珍　琐

1605	tearful
汪	Water . . . jewels. [7]

氵　汪

1606	crooked
枉	Tree . . . king. This character usually applies to someone who bends the rules or perverts the law. [8]

木　枉

1607	pearl
珠	Jewel . . . vermilion. [10]

王　珠

1608	shocking
噩	King . . . . four mouths. [16]

一　丁　可　罒　平　罪　噩　噩

| 1609 | plug ^(N.) |

栓

This character can be used for everything from bottle-stoppers to fire hydrants, but not for electrical plugs. The elements: *tree . . . whole*. [10]

木　栓

| 1610 | pillar |

柱

Tree . . . candlestick. [9]

木　柱

| 1611 | key |

钥

Metal . . . moon. [9]

钅　钥

| 1612 | drill ^(N./V.) |

钻

This key word for this character refers to the machine **drill** and has nothing to do with mental or physical exercises. Its elements: *metal . . . tell fortunes*. [10]

钅　钻

| 1613 | paper money |

钞

Metal . . . few. [9]

钅　钞

| 1614 | lock ^(N./V.) |

锁

Metal . . . small . . . shell. [12]

钅　钅"　锁

1615		put up for sale
销	*Metal . . . candle.* [12]	
	钅 钅 销	

1616		gong
锣	*Metal . . . silk gauze.* [13]	
	钅 锣	

LESSON 13

1617

compel

迫

To **compel** people to go somewhere they really don't want to go, the unscrupulous don't think twice about *white*washing the *road* to make it more appealing. [8]

白　迫

1618

resituate

迁

The key word has to do with changing the location of something or other. Be careful not to confuse with the character for *relocate* (FRAME 1398). The elements you have to work with are: *road . . . thousand*. [6]

千　迁

1619

press (v.)

逼

Wealth . . . road. The key word is used to describe the action of hounding someone or forcing them to do something. [12]

畐　逼

1620

far away

辽

-ed . . . road. [5]

了　辽

1621

make the rounds

逻

The police ordered to **make the rounds** take their orders rather too literally, wrapping the *roads* round and round with *silk gauze*. [11]

罗　逻

1622　　　　　　　　　　　　　　　　　　　　　　　flaunt

逞　*Submit . . . road.* [10]

呈　逞

1623　　　　　　　　　　　　　　　　　　　　　　　rails

轨　*Car . . . baseball team.* The kind of **rails** this character refers to are those used for train tracks, not for banisters. [6]

车　轨

1624　　　　　　　　　　　　　　　　　　　　　　　flatten

轧　*Car . . . fishhook.* [5]

车　轧

1625　　　　　　　　　　　　　　　　　　　　　　　spokes

辐　*Car . . . wealth.* [13]

车　辐

1626　　　　　　　　　　　　　　　　　　　　　chain [N.]

链　*Metal . . . one after another.* [12]

钅　链

1627　　　　　　　　　　　　　　　　　　　　　sauté [V.]

煎　*In front . . . cooking fire.* [13]

前　煎

1628	figure of speech

喻

Analogies, similes, metaphors, and other **figures of speech** often serve a biting wit, depicted colorfully here as a *slaughter-house mouth*. Nice **figure of speech**, eh? [12]

口　喻

1629	elm

榆

Tree . . . slaughterhouse. [13]

木　榆

1630	upper limb

胳

Flesh . . . each. [10]

月　胳

1631	skyscraper

厦

Cliff . . . summer. [12]

厂　厦

LESSON 14

As we do frequently in Book 1, from this point on we will occasionally assign new primitive meanings to characters you have already learned with a different key-word meaning. In many cases, some of the characters in which this new meaning is used will not appear until a later lesson. Each new primitive meaning will get its own frame, marked with the usual symbol (❖). The number in curly brackets refers to the frame number of the original character. We will introduce one such example in this lesson.

1632 牽	lead along
	St. Bernard dog . . . crown . . . cow. [9]

大　产　牽

1634 暈	dizzy
	Sun . . . chariot. [10]

日　暈

1633 渾	muddled
	Water . . . chariot. You may find it useful to pay attention to the "mud" in **muddled** in order to take advantage of the double meaning that allows this character to be associated with both turbid water and confused ideas. [9]

氵　渾

1635 炕	brick-heated bed
	Fire . . . whirlwind. [8]

火　炕

❖ {325}   Eiffel Tower

高 You will recall that in Book 1 we learned primitive meanings for
the abbreviated forms of this character. Here we add a primitive meaning for the full character, one that should be easy to
associate: **Eiffel Tower**. [10]

1636   ointment

膏 *Eiffel Tower . . . flesh.* Note how the topmost primitive here is
condensed to make room for the primitive under it. [14]

高 膏

1637   honest

淳 *Water . . . enjoy.* [11]

氵 淳

1638   go smoothly

亨 *Tall . . . -ed.* These primitives present something of a challenge.
Begin with a situation that comes to mind when you hear the key
word, **go smoothly**. Say, an interview. Your friend, a 7-foot-*tall*
high-school basketball star, is being interviewed for entrance
into an Ivy League school where he hopes to pursue a career in
nuclear medicine, despite academic grades in the lower half of
the alphabet. When he comes out, you ask him, "How'd it go?"
To which he replies, "Duh. I tink it **go**-*ed* **smoothly**." [7]

亠 亨

1639   hum ⁽ᵛ·⁾

哼 *Mouth . . . go smoothly.* [10]

口 哼

1640	whale
鲸	The **whale** swallows a whole school of *fish*, who turn their new abode into a proper little *fish-capital*. [16]

鱼　鲸

1641	shell [N.]
壳	*Soldier . . . crown . . . wind.* The **shell** of this character is different from the primitive element used for sea*shells*. [7]

士　声　壳

1642	spotless
洁	*Water . . . aerosol can.* [9]

氵　洁

LESSON 15

BEGINNING with this lesson, we will be introducing completely new primitive elements not based on characters already learned. Their component parts will all be elements learned in this or a previous lesson.

1643   **small objects**

枚

The key word has been chosen to represent the character's use as a "measure word" for counting coins, paper clips, cuff links, and the like. The elements are: *tree . . . taskmaster.* [8]

木   枚

1644   **herd** (v.)

牧

Rather than go through the time and expense of training dogs to **herd** the *cows* back into the barn at night, we appoint one of the elder *cows* as *taskmaster*, fitting her out with a gown, spectacles, and a whip. [8]

牛   牧

1645   **rose**

玫   *Jewel . . . taskmaster.* [8]

王   玫

1646   **candid**

敦   *Enjoy . . . taskmaster.* [12]

享   敦

1647   **mound**

墩   *Soil . . . candid.* [15]

扌 墩

❖

詹

snitch

The first six strokes of the character show some creature *bound up* by the *animal legs* and suspended over the edge of a *cliff*. It is a picture of the way revenge is taken in the animal kingdom for someone who squealed on his partners (*the words*) and hence was too verbose with the jungle police when it should have remained silent. Hence, the *snitch*. [13]

丶 广 广 詹 詹

1648

瞻

look upward

Eyeballs . . . snitch. [18]

1649

谓

meaning

Words . . . stomach. [11]

讠 谓

1650

询

inquire

Words. . . decameron. [8]

讠 询

1651

讥

deride

Words . . . small table/wind. [4]

讠 讥

1652

罚

penalize

Net . . . words . . . saber. [9]

罒 罚 罚

1653	place an order
订	*Words . . . nail.* Think of the *words* you use to *nail* down your choices as you **place an order** with the waiter. [4]

$$ \text{讠} \quad \text{订} $$

1654	forgive
谅	*Words . . . capitol building.* [10]

$$ \text{讠} \quad \text{谅} $$

❖ {226}	Disneyland
若	It is a short leap from the key-word meaning, *as if,* to the magical world of make-believe, **Disneyland.** [8]

1655	promise [N.]
诺	*Words . . . Disneyland.* [10]

$$ \text{讠} \quad \text{诺} $$

❖	crochet needles
凡	The *hook* and the *needle* easily suggest the little basket of **crochet needles** (or hooks) your grandmother kept next to her rocking chair, where she sat quietly whipping you up a fancy muffler. [3]

$$ \text{乀} \quad \text{凡} $$

1656	interrogate
讯	*Words . . . crochet needles.* [5]

$$ \text{讠} \quad \text{讯} $$

❖	family tree

葉

The element for *generation* placed atop a *tree* naturally gives us the primitive for **family tree**. [9]

世　　葉

1657　　espionage

谍

Words . . . family tree. [11]

讠　　谍

1658　　saucer

碟

Stone . . . family tree. If it is any help, this character is also used in the term for flying **saucers**. [14]

石　　碟

LESSON 16

1659 貳	**II** The use of the Roman numeral II is intended to help capture the sense of a "fraud-proof" writing of the Chinese numeral for "2" in official documents. The primitive elements are: *arrow . . . two . . . shell.* [9] 一　弌　弍　貳
1660 腻	**sick and tired of** *Flesh . . . II.* [13] 月　腻
1661 嘎	**caw** (N.) The **caw** sound is considered a bad omen. Take advantage of this when making your story. *Mouth . . . ceiling . . . nostrils . . . fiesta.* [14] 口　口＾　咟　嘎
1662 域	**domain** If you think of an Internet **domain**, you will not be far from the connotation of this word, which refers to an area of control. The elements are: *land . . . or.* [11] 土　域
1663 栽	**sow** (V.) One way of celebrating *Thanksgiving* is to do something that others will remember at a future *Thanksgiving* dinner—like going out to the garden to **sow** the seeds for a row of cranberry trees. [10]

土 耒 栽

1664

戚

kin

Parade . . . above . . . small. You will remember that we met this final combination of two primitives in FRAME 653. [11]

一 厂 厈 厈 戚

1665

蔑

despise

Flowers . . . net . . . march. Note that because there is nothing actually *marching* under the enclosure for *march*, the horizontal stroke is dropped downward to fill in the space. It is only a matter of aesthetics, so you should not let it bother you too much. [14]

艹 苗 蔑

1666

喊

yell ^(v.)

Mouth . . . salty. [12]

口 喊

1667

濺

splatter ^(v.)

Water . . . cheap. [12]

氵 濺

1668

浇

sprinkle

Water . . . javelin thrower. [9]

氵 浇

1669		astringent

涩　　*Water . . . blade . . . footprint.* [10]

氵　沔　涩

| 1670 | | address ^(N.) |

address ^(N.)

址　　*Soil . . . footprint.* [7]

土　址

| 1671 | | go to |

go to

赴

When you **go to** a new job in a new city, something in you wants to *walk* ahead confidently, with enthusiastic strides. But then something else in you wants you to hold back, like a *divining rod* built into your psyche warning you about rushing in too carelessly. [9]

走　赴

| 1672 | | trip |

trip

趟

This is not an actual **trip** but a "measure word" or "classifier" for **trips** taken. Treat this and other classifiers as nouns when you make your stories. Its elements: *walk . . . esteem.* [15]

走　趟

| 1673 | | dike |

dike

堤

A **dike** is *soil* piled up in advance of a disaster. There is no way of predicting if the great inundation is to *be* or not to *be*, but in either case, the town will be ready. [12]

土　堤

1674

Tianjin

津

Water . . . brush. This character serves as an abbreviation for the important Chinese city of **Tianjin**. [9]

氵　津

1675

keyboard keys

键

Metal . . . build. [13]

钅　律　键

1676

son-in-law

婿

What turns a bachelor into a **son-in-law** (or at least used to) is a *woman* and her dowry, here presented as a small *zoo* (since animals were often used for the purpose in earlier societies) and a *month* away from it all (the "honey*moon*"). [12]

女　妡　婿

LESSON 18

THE TIME has come to roll up your sleeves. Unlike the previous lessons, which were relatively short, many of the following lessons will be considerably longer. In this one you will learn 43 new characters.

| 1677 | | socks |

袜 *Cloak . . . last.* [10]

衤　袜

| 1678 | | decline [v.] |

衰 Refer back to FRAME 403 and the character meaning *grief.* The story recalls the colorful actor, W. C. Fields. It is a little known fact, but as he grew older and began to **decline,** his trademark smirk also started to droop. Plastic surgery being still in its covered wagon days, he had no choice but insert a *walking stick* into his cheeks sideways, and thus maintain his image. [10]

亠　亠　亡　亡　衰

| 1679 | | innermost feelings |

衷 Following on the story from the previous frame, let's say the short, vertical *walking stick* here is not for supporting one's outer frame but one's **innermost feelings.** In the case of W. C. Fields, it sustained the *grief* the actor's fictitious alcoholism was causing those around him. [10]

亠　亡　亩　衷

| 1680 | | ape |

猿 The suspicious politician *Yuan* first encountered in FRAME 404 OF Book 1 is depicted here as an **ape** being hounded by a *pack of wild dogs,* obviously from the opposition party. [13]

犭 猿

1681 **dangle**

吊 *Mouth . . . towel.* [6]

口　吊

1682 **currency**

币 The key word **currency** refers here to money in circulation. Its elements: *eyedropper . . . towel.* [4]

一　币

1683 **handkerchief**

帕 *Towel . . . white.* Compare this character to the primitive element for *white towel* we met in Book 1 (page 166). [8]

巾　帕

1684 **note** [N.]

帖 *Towel . . . tell fortunes.* The key word refers to a memo you leave for someone, not musical annotation. [8]

巾　帖

1685 **sail** [N.]

帆 *Towel . . . ordinary.* [6]

巾　帆

1686 **width of cloth**

幅 *Towel . . . wealth.* [12]

巾　幅

1687		brocade
锦	Gold . . . white towel. [13]	
	钅 锦	

1688		copious
沛	Water . . . market. [8]	
	氵 沛	

1689		persimmon
柿	Tree . . . market. [9]	
	木 柿	

1690		thorn bushes
棘	Thorns alongside thorns. [12]	
	朿 棘	

1691		flower bud
蕾	Flowers . . . thunder. [16]	
	艹 蕾	

1692		taste [v.]
尝	Small . . . crown . . . rising cloud. [9]	
	兴 尝	

1693		altar
坛	Soil . . . rising cloud. [7]	
	土 坛	

1694 枣	jujube

Thorns on *ice.* A **jujube** is a kind of Chinese date sometimes used in traditional medicine for sore throats. [8]

束　枣

1695 吞	gulp down

Heavens . . . mouth. [7]

天　吞

1696 妖	bewitching

Woman . . . die young. [7]

女　妖

1697 沃	fertile

Water . . . die young. Think of this key word as having to do with productive soil. [7]

氵　沃

1698 袄	short Chinese-style coat

Cloak . . . die young. [9]

衤　袄

1699 轿	sedan chair

Traditionally in China, the bride had to leave her family home and go to the groom's home on the wedding day. The bride would sit on a special kind of *cart* known as a **sedan chair,** as the groom and his relatives carried her to her new abode. The *angel* here is, of course, the bride. [10]

车　轿

1700	garbage
垃	Soil . . . vase. [8]

土 垃

1701	weep aloud
啼	Mouth . . . sovereign. [12]

口 啼

1702	fruit stem
蒂	Flowers . . . sovereign. [12]

艹 蒂

1703	100 Chinese acres
顷	You may want to consult FRAME 324 of Book 1 to have a look at the character that means a single *Chinese acre*. The elements here: *spoon . . . head.* [8]

匕 顷

1704	spoon (N.)
匙	Be . . . ancient spoon. [11]

是 匙

1705	well-behaved
乖	Thousand . . . north. [8]

千 乖 乖

❖ For the primitive meaning, think of a particular *goody-goody* from your school days, always ready to please the teachers and the butt of everyone's jokes.

1706	hitch a ride

乘

Goody-goody . . . umbrella. Note how the last two strokes, which we have given as the element for *umbrella*, are drawn the same as the final two strokes in the character for "tree." [10]

乖　乖　乘

1707	leftover (ADJ.)

剩

Try associating this key word with the **leftover** grub in your refrigerator. Its elements: *hitch a ride . . . saber.* [12]

乘　剩

1708	complete (V.)

毕

Compare . . . needle. [6]

比　毕

1709	club (N.)

棍

The **club** depicted in this character is a throwback to the time when discipline was meted out by beating people silly. Here the **club** is an entire *tree* wielded by a tyrannical patriarch on his *descendants* for not eating their Brussels sprouts. [12]

木　棍

1710	in accord

谐

Words . . . all-temperature detergent. As the "chord" in **accord** suggests, the key word connotes things in harmony. [11]

讠　谐

1711	firewood

柴

This (literary) . . . tree. [10]

此 柴

1712 sink ⁽ᵛ·⁾

沦 *Water . . . lifeguard.* [7]

氵 沦

1713 quick-witted

敏 *Every taskmaster* worth his salt needs a repertoire of **quick-witted** retorts. For example, "The last thing I want to do is hurt you. But it's still on my list." [11]

每 敏

1714 mildew ⁽ᴺ·⁾

霉 *Weather . . . every.* [15]

雨 霉

1715 so far

迄 The key word indicates the extent of something in a temporal or spatial sense, but for your story stick with the temporal sense of something that hasn't happened **so far**. *Beg . . . road.* [6]

乞 迄

1716 chop ⁽ᵛ·⁾

砍 *Stone . . . yawn.* Keep distinct from the primitive for *chop* learned in Book 1. [9]

石 砍

1717 hump ⁽ᴺ·⁾

坎 *Soil . . . yawn/lack.* When you speak of "getting over the **hump**," you mean getting yourself past the bumpiest and most difficult

stage of something or making it past the halfway point. As with
an illness, a final exam, or the cold of winter. [7]

土　坎

1718　　　　　　　　　　　　　　　　　　　　　　　　　cook [v.]

炊　　Picture what happens to people who try to **cook** their supper
when they should be taking a nap after a hard day's work. Here
we see a *fire* blazing out of control as a hapless young executive
yawns inattentively. [8]

火　炊

1719　　　　　　　　　　　　　　　　　　　　think highly of

钦　　*Metal . . . yawn.* [9]

钅　钦

LESSON 19

1720 剖	*Muzzle . . . saber.* [10]	cut open
	音 剖	
1721 菩	*Flowers . . . muzzle.* [11]	bodhisattva
	⺾ 菩	
1722 黯	*Black . . . sound.* [21]	tenebrous
	黑 黯	
1723 贏	*Perish . . . mouth . . . flesh . . . oyster . . . ordinary.* [17]	win (v.)
	亡 亡 亡 贏 贏	
1724 芒	*Flowers . . . perish.* [6]	mango
	⺾ 芒	
1725 荒	*Mango . . . flood.* [9]	wasteland
	⺾ 荒	

1726	lie (N.)
谎	Words . . . wasteland. [11]

谎

1727	boundless
茫	Mango . . . water. Note how the water element snuggles in next to the element for perish rather than stand alone on the left as we might expect it to. [9]

艹　氵　茫

1728	workshop
坊	Soil . . . compass. [7]

土　坊

1729	aromatic
芳	Here we see a special compass used to pick out those flowers most suited for making aromatic perfumes. It was originally invented by a bee that had no sense of direction. [7]

艹　芳

1730	call on
访	When you have to call on a dignitary, you have to frame your words with great care. Hence the need for a grammatical compass. [6]

访

1731	silt
淤	Water . . . compass . . . umbrella . . . ice. [11]

氵　淤

1732   stew ^(v.)

熬

Soil . . . release . . . cooking fire. Note how the left half of *release* has to be pressed down in order to squeeze into the space under *soil.* [15]

土   敖   熬

❖   {498}   Magellan

旁

The adventurer Ferdinand **Magellan** is remembered for having been the first person to sail around the world, but scholars of history have forgotten his little-known *side*kick, Pacifica, after whom he would name an entire ocean. [10]

亠   产   旁

1733   upper arm

膀

Flesh . . . Magellan. [14]

月   膀

1734   pound ^(N.)

磅

You have heard of the Rosetta Stone, the ancient Egyptian key to unlocking hieroglyphic writing. Here we have the less known, and, truth be told, historically suspect, *Magellan stone*, which was used to figure out just how much a **pound** really weighed in ancient times. [15]

石   磅

1735   roster

榜

Tree . . . Magellan. [14]

木   榜

1736

sharp

锐   *Metal . . . devil.* [12]

钅   锐

LESSON 20

1737		rainbow
虹	Insect . . . I-beam. [9]	
	虫 虹	

1738		bat (N.)
蝠	The **bat** this character refers to is the flying rodent that hangs around bell towers and damp caves. Its elements: *insect . . . wealth.* [15]	
	虫 蝠	

1739		turbid
浊	Water . . . insect. [9]	
	氵 浊	

1740		locust
蝗	Insect . . . emperor. [15]	
	虫 蝗	

1741		frog
蛙	Insect . . . bricks. [12]	
	虫 蛙	

1742		candle
烛	Fire . . . insect. [10]	
	火 烛	

1743		cocoon
茧	*Flowers . . . insect.* [9]	
	艹 茧	

1744		silkworm
蚕	*The heavens . . . insect.* [10]	
	天 蚕	

1745		placenta
胞	*Part of the body . . . wrap.* [9]	
	月 胞	

1746		cannon
炮	*Fire . . . wrap.* [9]	
	火 炮	

1747		robe [N.]
袍	*Cloak . . . wrap.* [10]	
	衤 袍	

1748		hail [N.]
雹	*Rain . . . wrap.* [13]	
	雨 雹	

1749		unrestrained
豪	*Tiara . . . sow.* [14]	
	亠 豪	

❖

豖

hog-tied

The short stroke in the legs of the *sow* gives us the primitive element meaning **hog-tied**. [8]

豖 豖 豖

1750

啄

peck (v.)

Mouth . . . hog-tied. [11]

口 啄

1751

琢

chisel (v.)

Ball . . . hog-tied. [12]

王 琢

1752

遂

satisfy

Horned sow . . . road. [12]

丷 遂

❖ {525}

家

flophouse

Since we already have a primitive element that means *house*, when the character of the same meaning is used as a primitive element, we will change its meaning to a **flophouse**. [10]

1753

嫁

marry

The primitive on the left makes it clear that this is a character depicting a *woman* who **marries** and moves with her spouse into a new home—in this case, a *flophouse*. [13]

女 嫁

1754

肠

intestines

Part of the body . . . piglets. [7]

月 肠

1755	poplar

杨   *Tree . . . piglets.* [7]

木 杨

1756	scald

烫   During lunch break in the chemistry lab, you are boiling your *soup* in a bowl that you are holding over the large single flame (the full character for *fire*) of a Bunsen burner. Having not yet mastered the basic principles of chemistry, you learn lesson no. 1 the hard way: the bowl, too, gets hot! You drop it on your lap and learn lesson no. 2: hot *soup* **scalds**. [16]

汤 烫

1757	licentious

荡   *Flowers . . . soup.* [9]

艹 荡

1758	ginger

姜   *Sheep . . . woman.* [9]

羊 姜

1759	detailed

详   *Words . . . sheep.* [8]

讠 详

1760	envy^(v.)

羡   *Sheep . . . next.* [12]

羊 羡

1761	railing
栏	Tree . . . orchid. [9]

1762	solely
唯	Mouth . . . turkey. [11]

口 唯

1763	sparrow
雀	Few . . . turkey. Note how the final stroke of *few* doubles up as the first stroke of the *turkey*. [11]

少 雀

1764	pile (N./V.)
堆	Soil . . . turkey. [11]

土 堆

1765	sculpture
雕	Lap/circumference . . . turkey. [16]

周 雕

1766	lop off
截	Thanksgiving . . . turkey. [14]

圡 産 截

1767	all at once
霍	Suddenly, unexpectedly, the week before Thanksgiving it happened: **All at once** a *rain* of *turkeys* fell from the skies, causing havoc in the automobile insurance industry. [16]

雷　霍

1768	feminine
雌	*This (literary) . . . turkey.* [14]

此　雌

1769	apprehensive
焦	*Turkey . . . cooking fire.* [12]

❖ When used as a primitive element, this character will mean pretty much what it looks like: a *roast turkey*.

隹　焦

1770	lay eyes on
瞧	*Eyeballs . . . roast turkey.* [17]

目　瞧

1771	reef
礁	*Stone . . . roast turkey.* [17]

石　礁

1772	banana
蕉	*Flower . . . roast turkey.* [15]

艹　蕉

1773   turn upward

翘

This key word is meant to connote the way things like hair, eyelashes, and puppy dog tails **turn upward**. The elements are: *javelin thrower . . . feathers.* [12]

尧 翘

1774   fall down

塌

The key word can be used for all sorts of things that **fall down**, from rooftops to hairdos. The primitive elements: *soil . . . sun . . . wings.* [13]

土 坍 塌

1775   writing brush

翰

Mist . . . umbrella . . . wings. [16]

卓 斡 翰

❖   headdress

翟

The *feathers* of the *turkey* (with the rest of the bird attached) are used to make a one-of-a-kind **headdress**. [14]

羽 翟

1776   show off (v.)

耀

Ray . . . headdress. [20]

光 耀

1777   jab (v.)

戳

Headdress . . . fiesta. [18]

翟 戳

LESSON 21

As MENTIONED in Lesson 21 of Book 1, from this point on the stroke order will not be given unless it is entirely new, departs from the procedures we have learned so far, or might otherwise cause confusion.

❖ 囚	{551}	dog kennel
	The *pent-in St. Bernard dog* makes the primitive meaning of a **dog kennel** a natural selection. [6]	

1778 咽		throat
	Mouth . . . dog kennel. [9]	

1779 姻		in-law (ADJ.)
	Woman . . . dog kennel. [9]	

1780 墙		wall
	Soil . . . soil . . . animal horns . . . return. [14]	
	扌　 扌　 扌　 圤　 垃　 墙	

1781 旷		expansive
	Sun . . . cave. The key word can be used for both spaces and personalities. [7]	

1782 矿		mine (N.)
	Stone . . . cave. [8]	

1783 庆		celebrate
	Cave . . . St. Bernard dog. [6]	

1784 嘛	**(pause marker)**
	This is a particle that is used within a sentence to mark a pause, drawing attention to what will follow. Its elements: *mouth . . . hemp*. [14]

1785 磨	**grind** (v.)
	Hemp . . . stone. [16]

1786 脏	**dirty**
	Flesh . . . hamlet. [10]

1787 赃	**stolen goods**
	Shellfish . . . hamlet. [10]

1788 桩	**stake** (n.)
	Tree . . . hamlet. As the primitive on the left suggests, this key word refers to the kind of **stake** you drive into the ground. [10]

1789 忠	**loyal**
	Middle . . . heart. [8]

1790 恕	**pardon** (v.)
	Be like . . . heart. [10]

1791 惑	**be bewildered**
	Or . . . heart. [12]

1792 愈	**more and more**
	Slaughterhouse . . . heart. [13]

1793 惠	**favor** (n.)
	One day . . . insect . . . heart. Note how *day* and *insect* overlap. Think of a mayfly or some other *insect* that has a life expectancy of only *one day*, the rest should be easy. You may not be inclined

to do anything special for an insect, but the next time you see a mayfly, put out a saucer of vitamin C to give it a shot at enjoying June and July—just as a **favor**. [12]

一 白 串 車 車 惠

| 1794 | shun |
| 忌 | *Snake . . . heart.* [7] |

| 1795 | troubles |
| 患 | *Shish kebab . . . heart.* [11] |

| 1796 | provoke |
| 惹 | *Disneyland . . . heart.* [12] |

| 1797 | permanent |
| 恒 | *State of mind . . . sunrise, sunset.* Note that this primitive is taken from the explanation in FRAME 195, and has not been used since then. [9] |

| 1798 | realize |
| 悟 | *State of mind . . . I (literary).* As the primitives indicate, this has to do with coming to awareness, not with getting a return on one's investments. [10] |

| 1799 | mourn |
| 悼 | *State of mind . . . eminent.* [11] |

| 1800 | be frightened |
| 惧 | *State of mind . . . tool.* [11] |

| 1801 | prudent |
| 慎 | *State of mind . . . true.* [13] |

1802		indolent
惰	*State of mind . . . left . . . flesh.* [12]	

1803		immense
恢	*State of mind . . . ashes.* [9]	

1804		fearful
惶	*State of mind . . . emperor.* [12]	

1805		recall ^(v.)
忆	*State of mind . . . fishhook.* [4]	

1806		noiseless
悄	*State of mind . . . candle.* [10]	

1807		all of a sudden
恍	*State of mind . . . ray.* [9]	

1808		just right
恰	*State of mind . . . fit.* [9]	

1809		overjoyed
愉	The daily joy of the *slaughterhouse* is to be delivered a fresh load of beef on the hoof. But here the butchers are in an **overjoyed** *state of mind*, presumably because Jurassic Park has closed down and they get first rights to the exotic livestock. [12]	

1810		terror stricken
怔	*State of mind . . . correct.* [8]	

1811		be scared of
怖	*State of mind . . . cloth.* [8]	

1812 慌	nervous
	State of mind . . . wasteland. [12]
1813 愣	dumbfounded
	State of mind . . . net . . . compass. [12]
1814 悦	delighted
	State of mind . . . devil. [10]
1815 憎	loathe
	State of mind . . . increase. [15]
1816 惟	thinking
	State of mind . . . turkey. [11]
1817 悔	be sorry about
	State of mind . . . every. [10]
1818 慕	admire
	Graveyard . . . valentine. [14]
1819 添	augment
	Water . . . heavens . . . valentine. [11]
1820 媳	daughter-in-law
	Woman . . . breath. [13]
1821 熄	put out
	Since this character is used to **put out** lights and fires (but not the cat), its elements remind us of what we do to the candles on a birthday cake: *fire . . . breath.* [14]

1822		secrete
泌	Water . . . certainly. [8]	
1823		Chinese harp
瑟	Two *balls* . . . certainly. [13]	
1824		honey
蜜	House . . . certainly . . . insect. [14]	

LESSON 22

THE 101 CHARACTERS of this lesson make it the longest of the book. The elements introduced in Book 1 at this point leave us no choice. In any case, you will want to break it up into two or three study sessions.

❖ 我	{588}	miser
	In place of the key-word meaning, *I*, we will assign this character the primitive meaning of an *I*-centered individual, the **miser**. [7]	
1825 蛾		moth
	Insect . . . miser. [13]	
1826 扒		pick pockets (v.)
	Fingers . . . eight. [5]	
1827 扣		button (N./V.)
	Fingers . . . mouth. [6]	
1828 拍		racquet
	Fingers . . . dove/white. [8]	
1829 啪		clapping sound
	The sound a rifle makes or the applause of an audience are both covered by this key word, **clapping sound**. The elements are: *mouth . . . racquet.* [11]	
1830 扑		pounce on
	Fingers . . . magic wand. [5]	
1831 拘		detain
	Fingers . . . sentence. [8]	

1832	damage [(v.)]
损	*Fingers . . . employee.* [10]

1833	pioneer [(v.)]
拓	This key word can refer to opening up new territory in both the geographical and figurative senses. *Fingers . . . rocks.* [8]

1834	carry over the shoulder
扛	*Fingers . . . I-beam.* [6]

1835	prick [(v.)]
扎	*Fingers . . . fishhook.* [4]

1836	thumb
拇	*Fingers . . . mother.* [8]

1837	bring to
捎	*Fingers . . . candle.* [10]

1838	copy [(v.)]
抄	*Fingers . . . few.* Anything one **copies** by hand is covered by this character; copying things by machine is not. [7]

1839	pad [(N./v.)]
垫	*Clench . . . soil.* [9]

1840	earnest
挚	*Clench . . hand.* [10]

1841	pinch [(v.)]
捏	*Fingers . . . sun . . . soil.* [10]

1842 拧	tweak (v.) *Fingers . . . calm.* [8]
1843 抹	smear on *Fingers . . . last.* For the sense of this key word, think of when you **smear on** sunscreen lotion. [8]
1844 摸	grope *Fingers . . . graveyard.* The primitives nicely suggest "to **grope** around in the dark." [13]
1845 描	describe *Fingers . . . tomato seedling.* [11]
1846 挑	foment *Fingers . . . portent.* [9]
1847 扰	harass *Fingers . . . Frankenpooch.* [7]
1848 搞	engage in *Fingers . . . Eiffel Tower.* [13]
1849 拴	tether *Fingers . . . whole.* [9]
1850 拾	tidy up *Fingers . . . fit.* [9]
1851 搭	put up The key word means to **put up** a structure, like a tent or a small shed. Its elements are: *finger . . . flowers . . . fit.* You may recall that we already met the combination of elements on the right in FRAME 264 of Book 1. [12]

1852	pillage (v.)
掠	Fingers . . . capital. [11]

1853	wipe away
拭	Fingers . . . style [9]

1854	chafe
挠	Fingers . . . javelin thrower. The sense of the key word is to scratch or abrade. [9]

1855	yank (v.)
扯	Fingers . . . footprint. [7]

1856	bump into
撞	Think of billiard balls that you persuade with a cue stick to bump into each other on a pool table. Only—to your utter surprise—you find that the balls exchange greetings as they bump into each other. "Hello, long time no see. How ya doin' there, 9-ball?" If you can picture a juvenile forming a bridge with his fingers to guide the cue stick to the cue ball, you should have no trouble with this one. [15]

1857	handpick
摘	Fingers . . . antique. The sense of this key word is to gather or pick by hand, not the more figurative sense to single out for special treatment. [14]

1858	drag (v.)
拖	Fingers . . . reclining . . . scorpion. Take care to create an image for this key word that does not conflict with the one you used for the primitive element of the same meaning. [8]

1859	publicize
扬	Fingers . . . piglets. [6]

1860 拦	impede *Fingers . . . orchid.* [8]
1861 搓	massage ^(v.) *Fingers . . . fall short of.* [12]
1862 捆	lash together *Fingers . . . trapped.* In case you had any doubts, this character does not refer to engaging in communal flagellation but to the binding of things into a bundle. [10]
1863 扩	enlarge *Fingers . . . cave.* [6]
1864 撼	joggle ^(v.) *Fingers . . . feel.* [16]
1865 挟	coerce *Fingers . . . press from both sides.* [9]
❖ 亶	Mr. Hyde The *top hat* that *returns* at *daybreak* is none other than **Mr. Hyde** *returning* to his daytime identity as Dr. Jekyll. [13] 亠　亩　亶
1866 擅	act without authority *Fingers . . . Mr. Hyde.* [16]
1867 颤	tremble *Mr. Hyde . . . head.* [19]

1868	take precautions against
戒	The *two hands* being waved about furiously in a *fiesta* belong to the security guards who are advising people to **take precautions against** getting run over by the floats or getting knocked on the head by a butterfingered twirler's baton. [7]

1869	weapon
械	*Tree . . . take precautions against.* [11]

1870	warn
诫	*Words . . . take precautions against.* [9]

1871	rude
莽	*Flowers . . . chihuahua . . . two hands.* [10]

❖	haystack
卉	The *two hands* here are fumbling around in the **haystack** looking for a *needle*. (Or, if you prefer to see the primitive as a drawing of three *needles*, you end up having to look for the **haystack** in the *needles*. Now that's a switch!) [5]

十 卉

1872	dash [v.]
奔	*St. Bernard dog . . . haystack.* [8]

❖	local-yokel chowder
贲	Living too far from the ocean to rely on a steady supply of *clams*, the local yokels of Hayseed County have invented something they like to call "*clam* helper." Take two small *stacks* of premium-quality *hay*, add two bushels of fresh spuds, and a dash of salt to taste. Boil in a hogshead cask for four hours or until the hay is completely dissolved. Take this "*clam*-helper" mix and pour into a bowl with a single frozen *clam* at the bottom. Voilà—le **local-yokel chowder**. Serves one. [9]

<table>
<tr><td colspan="2" align="center">亠 贲</td></tr>
</table>

1873 喷	spurt (v.) *Mouth . . . local-yokel chowder.* [12]
1874 愤	indignation *State of mind . . . local-yokel chowder.* [12]
1875 材	stuff (N.) This character is used for materials for teaching, construction, and all sorts of other things. Its elements: *tree . . . genie.* [7]
1876 荐	recommend *Flowers . . . deposit.* [9]
1877 孕	pregnant *Only then/fist . . . child.* [5]
1878 扔	throw away *Fingers . . . fist.* [5]
1879 携	take along *Fingers . . . turkey . . . fist.* [13] <div align="center">扌 推 携</div>
1880 圾	trash (N.) *Soil . . . outstretched hands.* [6]
1881 梗	stalk (N.) *Tree . . . even more.* [11]

1882	sigh [v.]
叹	Mouth . . . crotch/right hand. [5]

1883	fork [N.]
叉	Crotch/right hand . . . drop of. [3]

1884	authority
权	Tree . . . crotch. [6]

1885	outlaw [N.]
寇	The final stroke of the character for *finish* (the first seven strokes) wraps itself around the primitives for *magic wand* and *crotch* to give us the character for **outlaw**. [11]

1886	knock [v.]
敲	Eiffel Tower . . . magic wand . . . crotch. [14]

1887	rumble [N./v.]
轰	Car . . . pair. [8]

1888	beach [N.]
滩	Water . . . difficult. Alternatively, you may read the primitive elements as *Han* . . . *turkey*. [13]

1889	resolute
毅	Standing up . . . sow . . . missile. The final stroke of *standing up* doubles up with the first stroke of *sow*. [15]

1890	limb
肢	Flesh . . . branch. With *flesh* as a component of the character, it should be clear that this key word refers to a **limb** of a body, of course, not of a tree. [8]

1891 妓	prostitute
Woman . . . branch. [7]	

1892 歧	fork in the road
Footprint . . . branch. [8]	

1893 翅	fins
Branch . . . wings. [10]	

1894 淑	graceful
Water . . . uncle. [11]	

1895 椒	spice plant
Tree . . . uncle. [12]	

1896 盾	shield (N.)
Drag . . . ten . . . eyeballs. [9]	

1897 贩	peddler
Shells . . . against. [8]	

1898 扳	tug (V.)
Fingers . . . against. [7]	

1899 烁	luminous
Fire . . . music. [9]	

1900 觅	try to find
Vulture . . . see. [8]	

1901 妥	appropriate (ADJ.)
Vulture . . . woman. [7]	

❖

豸

leopard

This primitive represents a **leopard** by combining the *claw* with the first part of the element for a *sow*. Note how the final stroke of *claw* is turned and lengthened to double up with the first stroke of *sow*.

Actually, this primitive derives from the character in the following frame. [7]

⼂　⼂　⼂　豸　豸　豸

1902

豹

leopard

Leopard . . . ladle. [10]

1903

貌

mien

Leopard . . . dove . . . human legs. [14]

1904

睬

notice (v.)

Eyeball . . . pick. [13]

1905

允

consent (v.)

The card affirming that you **consent** to have your body parts harvested in case of sudden death usually refers to organs, but this fellow—obviously a professional basketball player at the peak of his career—stipulates that only his *elbows* and *human legs* are to be donated to science. [4]

1906

宏

magnificent

House . . . by one's side . . . elbow. [7]

1907

垒

baseball base

Baseball bases, of course, are used in the national sport of the United States. The elements: *elbows everywhere . . . soil.* [9]

1908	fetus
胎	*Part of the body . . . platform.* [9]

1909	negligent
怠	*Platform . . . heart.* [9]

1910	cheerful
怡	*State of mind . . . platform.* [9]

1911	smelt (v.)
冶	*Ice . . . platform.* [7]

1912	elevate
抬	*Fingers . . . platform.* [8]

1913	cease
罢	*Net . . . go.* [10]

1914	put in order
摆	*Fingers . . . cease.* [13]

1915	mislay
丢	*Thousand . . . walls.* [6]

1916	bring about
致	*Until . . . taskmaster.* The sense of the key word is to cause something to happen. [10]

1917	forsake
弃	*Infant . . . two hands.* [7]

1918	remove
撤	*Fingers . . . education . . . taskmaster.* [15]

1919	sulfur
硫	Stone . . . baby Moses. [12]

1920	glaze (N.)
琉	Jewel . . . baby Moses. [11]

1921	sparse
疏	Zoo . . . baby Moses. You will note that the primitive for *zoo* looks slightly different from the form you learned in Book 1 (疋). In order to fit it on the left, the strokes have to be cramped together, as shown below. [12]

⁊   ⁊   疋   疋   正   疏

1922	veggies
蔬	The key word refers to vegetables, but should be kept distinct from the character of that name (FRAME 666). Its primitives: *flowers . . . sparse.* [15]

1923	cross out
勾	Cast. This is the only case of a character that could have been included in Book 1 when we introduced it as a primitive (page 226). [4]

1924	ditch (N.)
沟	Water . . . cast. [7]

1925	hook (N./V.)
钩	Metal . . . cast. Be sure not to confuse this key word with the primitive element of the same meaning. [9]

1926	crumble
崩	Mountain . . . companion. The key word has to do with the collapse of large structures, not with what happens to cookies or bread. [11]

1927	rock
岩	Mountain . . . stone. [8]

1928	precipitous
峭	Mountain . . . candle. [10]

1929	rugged
崎	Mountain . . . strange. The key word refers to the terrain, not to a character trait. [11]

1930	cliff
崖	Mountain . . . cliff . . . bricks. This is the full character from which we derived the primitive element of the same name. [11]

1931	brilliant
灿	Fire . . . mountain. [7]

1932	charcoal
炭	Mountain . . . ashes. [9]

1933	carbon
碳	Stone . . . charcoal. [14]

1934	(rhetorical question)
岂	The key word is meant to indicate the device Chinese uses to put a **rhetorical question**. Its primitive elements: *mountain . . . snake*. [6]

1935	triumphant
凯	*Mountain . . . snake . . . small table.* The left side of the character is broken up into primitive elements that you will probably find more manageable than the key word of the character "*(rhetorical question)*." [8]

1936	gorge [N.]
峡	*Mountains . . . press from both sides.* [9]

1937	Cui
崔	The key word associated with this character is a family name often associated with Cui Jian, a man honored as the father of Chinese rock music. The elements: *mountain . . . turkey*. [11]
	❖ When used as a primitive element, this character will mean a *pterodactyl*. (Though scientists classify it as a kind of winged lizard, we know from this character that it is actually a distant cousin of the *turkey* that hovers around the *mountains* in search of its prey.)

1938	wreck [V.]
摧	*Fingers . . . pterodactyl.* [14]

❖	mountain goat
屵	A pair of *animal horns* on the top, a "tail" on the bottom, and a *mountain* depict a **mountain goat**. [6]

ﾑ　ﾑ　屵　屵

1939 逆	go against
	The *mountain goat* in this character rebels at the idea of being driven along the *road* to the farm. Everything in its nature **goes against** leaving the rocky hills where it feels at home. [9]

1940 溯	go upstream
	Water . . . mountain goat . . . moon. A secondary sense of this key word is to trace something back to its origins. [13]

1941 塑	plastic (N.)
	Mountain goat . . . moon . . . soil. [13]

1942 盼	await hopefully
	Eyeball . . . part. [9]

1943 颁	promulgate
	Part . . . head. [10]

1944 芬	essence
	Flowers . . . part. The meaning of this key word has nothing to do with the goal of a phenomenological reduction, but with the sweet-smelling fragrance of plants and herbs extracted in order to disguise the olfactory truth. [7]

1945 扮	play the part of
	Fingers . . . part. [7]

1946 岔	diverge
	Part . . . mountain. [7]

1947 颂	extol
	Public . . . head. [10]

1948	litigate
讼	*Words ... public.* [6]

1949	trundle (v.)
滚	*Water ... top hat and scarf ... public.* If it's any help, this is one of the Chinese characters that figures in the compound word for rock 'n' roll (or more accurately, "oscillate 'n' **trundle**"). [13]

1950	elderly man
翁	*Public ... feathers.* [10]

1951	buzzing (N.)
嗡	*Mouth ... elderly man.* [13]

1952	abundant
裕	This character shows the typical *cloak* of *valley* folk, which, unlike the tailor-made, high-fashion overcoats of city folk, is loose fitting and free-form. Hence the key word's meaning of **abundant**. [12]

1953	banyan
榕	*Tree ... contain.* [14]

1954	fuse (v.)
熔	*Fire ... contain.* [14]

LESSON 24

1955 裳	raiment *Outhouse . . . clothing.* [14]
1956 掌	palm of the hand *Outhouse . . . hand.* [12]
1957 撑	prop up *Fingers . . . palm of the hand.* [15]
1958 膛	chest *Flesh . . . main room.* [15]
1959 颇	quite *Covering . . . head.* [11]
1960 坡	slope (N.) *Soil . . . covering.* [8]
1961 披	drape over the shoulder (V.) *Fingers . . . covering.* [8]
1962 菠	spinach *Flowers . . . waves.* [11]
1963 歼	annihilate *Bones . . . thousand.* [7]
1964 殖	breed (V.) *Bones . . . straight.* [12]

1965 殊	dissimilar
Bones . . . vermilion. [10]	

1966 残	incomplete
Bones . . . float. [9]	

1967 咧	grin (v.)
Mouth . . . lines up. [9]	

1968 裂	crack (v.)
Line up . . . clothes. [12]	

1969 毙	die a violent death
Compare . . . death. [10]	

1970 耿	dedicated
Ear . . . fire. [10]	

1971 辑	edit
Car . . . mouth . . . ear. [13]	

1972 耻	shame (n.)
Ear . . . footprint/stop. [10]	

1973 摄	take a photo
Fingers . . . ear . . . pair. [13]	

1974 聪	smart
Ear . . . general. [15]	

1975 娶	take a wife
Take . . . woman. Compare this character for what a woman does when she *marries* into a family (FRAME 1753). [11]	

1976 蔓	creeping vine *Flowers . . . mandala.* [14]
1977 肤	skin (N.) *Flesh . . . husband.* [8]
1978 扶	lend a hand *Fingers . . . husband.* [7]
1979 潜	submerge *Water . . . replace.* [15]
1980 卧	for sleeping *Feudal official . . . magic wand.* This character is used in many words having to do with sleep—things like bedrooms and Pullman cars. [8]

❖ 爿	bunk beds This character shows the left side of a tree that has been unevenly split down the middle. (The right side shows up in FRAME 988.) If you stare at it for a few seconds, you will see the **bunk beds** in no time. The stroke order of this character may surprise you, even though it follows the rules. [4]

ㄴ　ㅐ　ㅢ　爿

1981 藏	hide (V.) The primitive on the top tells us that whatever it is this character wants to **hide** will be covered with *flowers.* The items to be hidden are, of course, *bunk beds,* and the reason for the camouflage is that they are being used on a float in the famous Rose Bowl *Parade* to allow Sleeping Beauty, stretched out on the top *bunk,* to appear to be resting on a blanket of *flowers.* (Note that the final stroke of *bunk beds* doubles up with the second stroke of *parade.*) Let us hope she stays asleep, because the only "prince" around to awaken her is a *feudal official* dressed in tights and twirling a baton. [17]

艹 艹 艹 艹 荋 菔 藏

1982 splendid

熙

The first primitive looks like *underling*, except for the tiny little *mouth* in the middle—much as you would expect of a particularly fawning, bootlicking, toadying *underling* who responds to every suggestion of the boss with the exclamation, "**Splendid!**" without every venturing an opinion of his own. In this case, the boss has him roast a *snakeskin* belt and shoes over a *cooking fire* and eat them for supper. "**Splendid!**" the poor fellow exclaims as he takes his first bite.

The drawing order is pretty much as you would expect, but we give it here to reinforce it all the same. [14]

一 丁 古 𦥑 臣 𦥑 熙

1983 merit [N.]

勋

See if you can design in your head a **merit** badge acknowledging those *employees* with sufficient entrepreneurial *muscle* to carry the weight of company business during an economic downturn. [9]

1984 inferior

劣

Few . . . muscles. [6]

1985 recruit [V.]

募

Graveyard . . . muscle. Note that the final stroke of *graveyard* has to be moved slightly to make enough room for what comes underneath. [12]

1986 advise

劝

Crotch . . . muscle. [4]

1987 plunder [V.]

劫

Go . . . muscle. [7]

1988 抛	toss [v.]
	Fingers . . . baseball (team) . . . muscle. [7]

1989 胁	threaten
	Flesh . . . sweat. [8]

1990 怒	anger [N.]
	Slave . . . heart. [9]

1991 茄	eggplant
	Flowers . . . add. [8]

1992 彻	thorough
	Queue . . . cut. [7]

1993 征	solicit
	Queue . . . correct. [8]

1994 惩	chasten
	Solicit . . . heart. [12]

1995 徒	follower
	Queue . . . walk. [10]

1996 徊	undecided
	Queue . . . return. [9]

1997 役	service
	Queue . . . missile. This is the character used, for example, for military **service**. [7]

1998 循	comply with
	Queue . . . shield. [12]

1999	the other
彼	*Queue . . . covering.* [8]

2000	develop
衍	*Boulevard . . . water.* [9]

2001	weight
衡	To simplify what is located on the *boulevard*, think of a *St. Bernard dog* with a *fish* in its mouth, which accounts for the disappearance of the *fish's* "tail." [16]

2002	title
衔	*Boulevard . . . gold.* The **title** this character refers to is one having to do with rank or office. [11]

LESSON 25

2003 禿	**bald** *Wild rice . . . wind.* [7]
2004 頹	**decrepit** *Bald . . . head.* [13]
2005 秒	**seconds** The reference here is to **seconds** of time, not to second helpings. The elements: *wild rice . . . few.* [9]
2006 稍	**a little** (ADV.) *Wild rice . . . candle.* The key word carries the sense of "slightly" or "to a small degree." [12]
2007 穌	**rise again** The sense of the key word is to revive or be restored to life. The elements are *fish . . . wild rice.* Note that in combination with the character for *Jerusalem* we will learn later (FRAME 2738), it transliterates the name of Jesus. [13]
2008 稿	**draft** (N.) The key word connotes the preliminary composition of a plan or manuscript. Its elements: *wild rice . . . Eiffel Tower.* [15]
2009 稠	**dense** *Wild rice . . . lap/circumference.* [13]
2010 穎	**clever** *Spoon . . . wild rice . . . head.* [13]

2011	crops
稼	*Wild rice . . . flophouse.* [15]

2012	tax
税	*Wild rice . . . devil.* [12]

2013	immature
稚	*Wild rice . . . turkey.* [13]

2014	fungus
菌	*Flowers . . . pent in . . . wild rice.* [11]

2015	ear of grain
穗	*Wild rice . . . favor.* [17]

2016	confidential
秘	*Wild rice . . . certainly.* [10]

2017	private (ADJ.)
私	*Wild rice . . . elbow.* [7]

2018	order (N.)
秩	This key word has nothing to do with a command, but refers to a condition or state, as in the expression "in good **order**." The elements: *wild rice . . . lose.* [10]

2019	shovel (N.)
锹	*Metal . . . autumn.* [14]

2020	pear
梨	*Profit . . . tree.* [11]

2021	plow (N.)
犁	*Profit . . . cow.* [11]

2022	wilt
萎	*Flowers . . . committee.* [11]

❖	Rumpelbrella
黍	Rumpelstiltskin, you will recall, used a spinning wheel to turn straw into gold. Here we find his eccentric brother, **Rumpelbrella**, whose magical *umbrella* can turn *wild rice* into *snowflakes*. [12]

禾　　禿　　黍

2023	sticky
黏	*Rumpelbrella . . . tell fortunes.* [17]

2024	host (N.)
黎	The key word has nothing to do with taking care of guests. It is a literary way of referring to masses of people. Take note of the placing of the elements: *Rumpelbrella . . . bound up . . . eyedropper.* [15]

禾　　利　　黎

❖	Baron von Rumpelbrella
桼	Here we meet the unscrupulous uncle of *Rumpelbrella,* who managed to weasel out of his nephew the blueprints to the magical umbrella that turns wild rice into *snowflakes.* He adapted the technology to turn *trees* into *snowflakes* and amassed billions by "developing" the rain forest of the Amazon into a mega-resort for winter sports. **Baron von Rumpelbrella** and his entire empire are now under investigation by Interpol. [11]

木　　夫　　桼

2025	knees
膝	*Flesh . . . Baron von Rumpelbrella.* [15]

2026	wall paint
漆	*Water . . . Baron von Rumpelbrella.* [14]

2027	rust [N./V.]
锈	*Metal . . . elegant.* [12]

2028	squint [V.]
眯	*Eyeballs . . . rice.* [11]

2029	batter
糊	**Batter** is usually made with great care to get just the right ingredients in just the right proportion, but *rice* **batter** (the source of the rarely served *rice* pancakes) is made by throwing all the ingredients into a large pot from across the room—the more *recklessly*, the better the **batter**. [15]

2030	glue [V.]
粘	*Rice . . . tell fortunes.* Take care not to confuse with the primitive of the same meaning. [11]

2031	of great depth
奥	*Drop . . . helmet . . . rice . . . St. Bernard dog.* Consult FRAME 188 in Book 1 for the combination of the first two primitives. [12]

冂　宑　奥

2032	deep inlet
澳	*Water . . . of great depth.* [15]

2033	remorseful
懊	*State of mind . . . of great depth.* [15]

2034	chrysanthemum
菊	*Flower . . . bound up . . . rice.* [11]

2035	abyss
渊	*Water . . . crutches . . . rice.* [11]

氵　氵丿　氵丿丨　渊

❖	decapitation
汧	The three *drops of water* on the left are for cleaning up the mess that the heavy *sword*, dripping with blood (the two *drops* on either side of the *sword*) has left after relieving some unfortunate creature of its head. Be sure not to confuse the right side with the primitive element we learned for *sweat.* [7]

氵　氿　氿　氿

2036	fine millet
粱	*Decapitation . . . rice.* [13]

2037	roof beam
梁	*Decapitation . . . tree.* [11]

2038	rough
糙	*Rice . . . create.* The key word refers to the texture of things, as of something **rough** to the touch. [16]

2039	grain
粒	*Rice . . . vase.* As the primitive on the left suggests, **grain** here refers to granules, not to a pattern in wood. [11]

2040	cake
糕	*Rice . . . sheep . . . cooking fire.* [16]

❖ 敝 **shredder**

Ignoring for a moment the way this element is actually drawn, the left side looks like something with a *hood* that has *rice* coming out the top and bottom. Actually, those are just little pieces of paper spewing out in all directions from a document shredder. The familiar *taskmaster* standing off to the right gives the character its name. In his attempt to get just the right "look" to identify with his job, he ran his suit, shirt, and tie briefly through the **shredder**. [11]

丶　丷　冂　肖　肖　尚　敝

2041 蔽 **shelter** [N].

Flowers . . . shredder. [14]

2042 憋 **suppress**

Shredder . . . heart. [15]

2043 撇 **cast aside**

Fingers . . . shredder. [14]

2044 弊 **fraud**

Shredder . . . two hands. [14]

2045 莱 **lambsquarters**

The primitive elements that make up this character, *flowers* and *come*, are easier than the key word, which is not likely to be familiar to any but the botanically inclined. **Lambsquarters** is, in fact, a plant similar to the pigweed. The character is used mainly for its phonetic value in rendering foreign names. [10]

艹　莱

2046 搂 **cuddle**

Fingers . . . bride. [12]

2047	construct
筑	*Bamboo . . . strengthen.* [12]
2048	bamboo basket
筿	*Bamboo . . . silk gauze.* [14]
2049	stupid
笨	*Bamboo . . . notebook.* [11]
2050	tube
筒	*Bamboo . . . monk.* [12]
2051	arrow
箭	*Bamboo . . . in front.* In settling on a particular connotation for this key word, take care not to confuse it with the primitive for *arrow,* which does not appear in this character of the same name. [15]
2052	sift
篩	*Bamboo . . . teacher.* [12]
2053	tendon
筋	*Bamboo . . . part of the body . . . power.* [12]

LESSON 26

IT SHOULD come as no surprise that this lesson, which brings us to the primitive element for *person*, is rather long—59 characters in all. You may recall the advice given in FRAME 793 about selecting a particularly colorful acquaintance or member of your family for using in all the stories that involve the *person*.

2054	V
伍	As with II in FRAME 1659, the key word represents the writing of the number "5" for official documents. The elements: *person . . . five.* [6]
2055	animosity
仇	*Person . . . baseball (team).* [4]
2056	start (v.)
倡	*Person . . . prosperous.* [10]
2057	father's older brother
伯	*Person . . . dove.* [7]
2058	mid-
仲	The key word is used in phrases like **mid**summer and **mid**autumn. Its elements: *person . . . middle.* [6]
2059	servant
仆	*Person . . . magic wand.* [4]
2060	estimate (v.)
估	*Person . . . ancient.* [7]

2061 侦	detect
Person . . . chaste. Hint: associate the key word with the work **detect**ives do. [8]	
2062 俱	altogether (ADV.)
Person . . . tool. [10]	
2063 佑	bless
Person . . . right. [7]	
2064 佐	assistant
Person . . . left. [7]	
2065 侧	lateral (ADJ.)
Person . . . rule. [8]	
2066 亿	one hundred million
Person . . . fishhook. [3]	
2067 仔	meticulous
Person . . . child. [5]	
2068 倚	count on
Person . . . strange. [10]	
2069 俏	comely
Person . . . candle. [9]	
2070 佳	superb
Person . . . bricks. [8]	
2071 侍	serve
Person . . . Buddhist temple. [8]	

2072	mate (N.)
伙	Person . . . fire. Let the key word **mate** suggest a partner or associate. [6]

2073	if
倘	Person . . . esteem. [10]

2074	stay overnight
宿	House . . . person . . . hundred. [11]

2075	bend over
伏	Person . . . chihuahua. [6]

2076	wrapping cloth
袱	Cloak . . . bend over. [11]

2077	steal (V.)
偷	Person . . . slaughterhouse. [11]

2078	repay
偿	Person . . . taste. [11]

2079	fell
伐	Person . . . fiesta. Hint: recall the German legend of the English missionary, Saint Boniface, who **felled** the sacred oak tree dedicated to Thor at Geismar (in lower Hessia), occasioning a great fiesta for the Christians in the neighborhood to mark the defeat of their pagan competition. Be sure to fit your special person into the story if you use it. [6]

2080	wear at the waist
佩	Person . . . wind . . . ceiling . . . towel. Think of things like guns and swords that a swashbuckler might **wear at the waist**. [8]

2081 侨	**live abroad** *Person . . . angel.* [8]
2082 倾	**incline** (v.) Take this key word in its literal sense of to lean to one side. The elements: *person . . . 100 Chinese acres.* [10]
2083 伦	**human relationships** *Person . . . lifeguard.* [6]
2084 侮	**insult** (v.) *Person . . . every.* [9]
2085 倍	**times** *Person . . . muzzle.* Think of this character as referring to the number of occurrences of an event. [10]
2086 仿	**mimic** (v.) *Person . . . compass.* [6]
2087 傲	**haughty** *Person . . . soil . . . release.* The combination of the two elements on the right previously appeared in *stew* (FRAME 1732). [13]
2088 僧	**Buddhist monk** *Person . . . increase.* [14]
2089 囚	**prisoner** *Pent in . . . person.* [5]
2090 悠	**without haste** *Person . . . walking stick . . . taskmaster . . . heart.* [11]

2091 侄	nephew
	Person . . . until. [8]

2092 仙	immortal (N.)
	Person . . . mountain. [5]

2093 傍	close to
	Person . . . Magellan. [12]

2094 催	prod (V.)
	Person . . . pterodactyl. [13]

2095 俗	custom
	Person . . . valley. [9]

2096 侠	chivalrous person
	Person . . . press from both sides. [8]

2097 俄	Russia
	Person . . . miser [9]

2098 聚	assemble
	The top you will recognize as the full character for *take*. With a little ingenuity you can doodle the other six strokes into a group of three *persons*, each of them slightly bent out of shape (see FRAME 847). The reason is that they have had their parts "re-**assembled**" as they **assemble** in a crowded hall. Just one of the inherent dangers of attending a rock concert. [14]
	取　取　聚　聚　聚　聚

2099 符	symbol
	Bamboo . . . pay. [11]

2100 贷	loan (N.) *Substitute for . . . shells.* [9]
2101 荷	Holland This character on its own is used as an abbreviation for the Netherlands, although its pronunciation relies on the older name: **Holland**. *Flowers . . . whatwhichwhowherewhy?.* [10]
2102 杖	cane *Tree . . . 100 Chinese inches.* This character has the same meaning as the primitive element we have called *walking stick*, so be sure to keep the two distinct. [7]
2103 仗	battle (N.) *Person . . . 100 Chinese inches.* [5]
2104 丛	thicket *Assembly line . . . floor.* [5]
2105 耸	shrug (V.) *Assembly line . . . ear.* [10]
2106 挫	frustrate *Fingers . . . sit.* [10]
2107 诬	charge falsely *Words . . . witch.* [9]
2108 葛	kudzu *Flowers . . . siesta.* [12]
2109 褐	brown *Cloak . . . siesta.* [14]

2110		use up
竭	*Vase . . . siesta.* [14]	

2111		take a rest
歇	*Siesta . . . yawn.* [13]	

2112		reveal
揭	Gingerly lift up with your *fingers* the sombrero of that fellow over there leaning against the wall for a *siesta*, to **reveal** that it is actually an entire family taking a communal rest from the labors of the day. [12]	

2113 淫	promiscuous
	Water . . . vulture . . . porter. [11]

2114 凭	proof
	Appoint . . . wind. The key word refers to evidence, not to alcohol content. [8]

2115 挺	erect (ADJ.)
	Fingers . . . royal court. [9]

2116 赎	redeem
	Shellfish . . . sell. [12]

2117 瓦	tile
	The **tile** in this character combines four primitive elements: *ceiling . . . plow . . . fishhook . . .* and *drop of.* Since the drawing is a little unexpected, be sure to arrange your story to fit the stroke order. [4]

一　丆　瓦　瓦

2118 瓷	porcelain
	Secondary . . . tile. [10]

2119 拟	simulate
	Fingers . . . by means of. [7]

2120 瓶	bottle (N.)
	Puzzle . . . tile. [10]

2121 宫	palace
	Here a **palace** is composed of *house* and *spine*. [10]

2122 铝	aluminium
	Metal . . . spine. [11]

2123 萤	firefly
	Greenhouse . . . insect. [11]

芦　萤

2124 莹	lustrous
	Greenhouse . . . jade. [10]

芦　莹

2125 蒙	Mongolia
	As with Los Angeles and England (FRAMES 315 and 1323), this frame shows us the first character in the fuller compound for the proper noun. Its component primitives: *greenhouse . . . ceiling . . . sow.* [13]

芦　芦　蒙

2126 朦	dim (ADJ.)
	Moon . . . Mongolia. [17]

月　朦

2127 捞	scoop up
	Fingers . . . labor. [10]

LESSON 28

2128 旋	whirl [v.] A *banner* . . . *zoo*. Hint: think of a merry-go-round. [11]
2129 吻	kiss [v.] *Mouth* . . . *knot*. [7]
2130 匆	hurriedly Think of tying a *knot* in your shoelaces so **hurriedly** that when your *eyedropper* falls out of your shirt pocket it gets tangled up in it. Makes it a little hard to put the drops in. [5] ノ　勹　匀　匆　匆
2131 葱	onion *Flowers* . . . *hurriedly* . . . *heart*. [12]
2132 锡	tin *Metal* . . . *easy*. [13]
2133 惕	watchful *State of mind* . . . *easy*. [11]
2134 卢	Louvre *Magic wand* . . . *flag*. This character is used in the phonetic transcription of the Musée du **Louvre** in Paris. [5]
2135 屉	drawer The key word here refers to a **drawer** *in a piece of furniture*. Its elements: *flag* . . . *generation*. [8]

2136 屑	bits
	The sense of the key word is fragments, as in the phrase "**bits** and pieces." The elements: *flag . . . candle.* [10]

2137 尿	urine
	That rather special kind of *water* we call **urine** is used by many animals as a kind of *flag* to mark off their territory. [7]

2138 犀	rhinoceros
	Lacking a proper charging **rhinoceros** for the annual 4th of July parade, the townspeople put a *cow* on a bicycle with a patriotic *flag* attached to it and a little tape recorder playing "*Snowflakes keep falling on my head.*" [12]

2139 迟	tardy
	Flag . . . eyedropper . . . road. Note that the element for *ruler* differs slightly from the first two elements in this character. [7]

2140 刷	brush (N./V.)
	Flag . . . towel . . . saber. This character and its key word need to be kept distinct from the primitive element for *brush* learned in Book 1. [8]

2141 漏	leak (V.)
	Water . . . flag . . . rain. [14]

2142 屁	fart (N.)
	Flag . . . compare. [7]

2143 屈	knuckle under
	Flag . . . exit. The key word is a colloquialism meaning to submit or yield. [8]

2144 掘	excavate
	Fingers . . . knuckle under. [11]

2145 **footwear**

履 *Flag . . . queue . . . double back.* [15]

2146 **excrement**

屎 *Flag . . . rice.* [9]

2147 **time and again**

屡 *Flag . . . bride.* [12]

2148 **folding screen**

屏 *Flag . . . puzzle.* [9]

2149 **eyebrows**

眉 Over the *eyes* we see a *flag* divided into two colors. This is because the **eyebrows** are painted different colors, one of them red and the other blue. [9]

2150 **flatter**

媚 *Woman . . . eyebrows.* [12]

2151 **daylight**

昼 *Ruler . . . daybreak.* [9]

2152 **enlighten**

启 *Door . . . mouth.* [7]

2153 **shoulder** (N.)

肩 *Door . . . moon.* [8]

2154 **jealous of**

妒 *Woman . . . door.* [7]

2155		stove
炉	*Fire . . . door.* [8]	

2156		reeds
芦	*Flowers . . . door.* [7]	

2157		fan [N.]
扇	*Door . . . feathers.* [10]	

2158 奈	can't help but
	St. Bernard dog . . . altar. [8]

2159 款	funds
	Soldier . . . altar . . . yawn. The key word here refers to sums of money. [12]

2160 凜	chilly
	Ice . . . top hat . . . return . . . altar. [15]

2161 崇	evil spirit
	Exit . . . altar. [10]

2162 祝	wish well
	Altar . . . teenager. The meaning of the key word is to **wish** someone **well**. [9]

2163 祥	propitious
	Altar . . . sheep. [10]

❖ 尉	Cardinal Richelieu
	From your reading of "The Three Musketeers," you may remember **Cardinal Richelieu** as the ambitious and high-ranking churchman who wielded political power second only to the king himself. The character symbolizes this by showing a *flag* that has been spread over and *glued* to an *altar*. [11]

尸　尽　尉

2164 蔚	luxuriant
	Flowers . . . Cardinal Richelieu. [14]

2165	console (v.)
慰	*Cardinal Richelieu . . . heart.* [15]

2166	garlic
蒜	The character for **garlic** shows two full-sized *altars* side by side under a nosegay of *flowers*. [13]

2167	palm tree
棕	*Tree . . . religion.* [12]

2168	universe
宙	*House . . . sprout.* [8]

2169	axle
轴	*Car . . . sprout.* [9]

2170	sleeve
袖	*Cloak . . . sprout.* [10]

2171	temple
庙	*Cave . . . sprout.* Be sure to keep this character distinct from that for a *Buddhist temple* (FRAME 169). [8]

2172	flute
笛	*Bamboo . . . sprout.* [11]

2173	fall due
届	*Flag . . . sprout.* Think of things that **fall due**, like a debt with a date of expiration. [8]

2174	groan
呻	*Mouth . . . monkey.* [8]

2175 坤	female
	Soil . . . monkey. [8]

2176 审	painstaking
	House . . . monkey. [8]

2177 婶	auntie
	Woman . . . painstaking. [11]

2178 畅	smooth
	To get the sense of this key word, think of something without bumps or obstructions, perhaps something like the tail of a *monkey* or a *piglet*. [8]

2179 巢	nest [N.]
	Stream . . . fruit. [11]

2180 棵	flora
	Tree . . . fruit. This is another one of those "measure words" we have run into occasionally. This one is used for green, non-fauna living things like trees and grasses. [12]

2181 裸	naked
	Cloak . . . fruit. [13]

2182 裹	envelop
	The basic idea of this key word is to encase something completely with a covering. Its elements: *top hat and scarf . . . fruit.* Observe how the primitive for *fruit* detaches the final two strokes of the "tree," as in the primitive element for a *wooden pole*, and shortens the vertical center stroke. [14]

亠　東　裹

LESSON 30

2183 析	analyze *Tree . . . tomahawk.* [8]
2184 晰	distinct *Sun . . . analyze.* If it is any help, the father of modern philosophy, René Descartes, based his thought on the search for "clear and **distinct** ideas." [12]
2185 芹	celery *Flowers . . . tomahawk.* [7]
2186 祈	supplicate *Altar . . . tomahawk.* [8]
2187 欣	elated *Tomahawk . . . yawn.* [8]
2188 掀	uncover *Fingers . . . elated .* [11]
2189 惭	conscience stricken *State of mind . . . hew.* [11]
2190 崭	towering *Mountain . . . hew.* [11]
2191 浙	Zhejiang Province *Water . . . discount.* [10]

2192 誓	vow (N./V.)
	Discount . . . words. [14]
2193 拆	take apart
	Fingers . . . reprimand. [8]
2194 炸	blow up
	Fire . . . saw. The key word refers not to what you do to a balloon, but what will happen to a balloon if you do it too much. [9]
2195 诈	swindle
	Words . . . saw. [7]
2196 归	come back
	Saber . . . broom. [5]
❖ 刍	hairnet
	The **hairnet** used here has *bound up* the wayward bristles of an old *broom* of a coiffeur and reshaped it (with a pink ribbon to make it a little more stylish). [5]

⺈   刍

2197 皱	wrinkles
	Hairnet . . . covering. [10]
2198 煞	goblin
	Hairnet . . . taskmaster . . . cooking fire. [13]
2199 趋	hasten
	Walk . . . hairnet. [12]

2200	chick
雏	Hairnet . . . turkey. [13]

❖	dunce
寻	It should not be hard to work the primitive elements—*broom* . . . *crown* . . . *crotch*—into a colorful image of the class **dunce** (especially if you ever had to play the role yourself). [7]

ヨ 彐 寻

2201	immerse
浸	Water . . . dunce. [10]

2202	get some shuteye
寝	House . . . turtle . . . dunce. [13]

2203	invade
侵	Person . . . dunce. [9]

2204	stable (ADJ.)
稳	Wild rice . . . anxious. [14]

2205	fend off
挡	Fingers . . . work as. [9]

2206	peel off
剥	Snowman . . . saber. [10]

2207	wield
秉	A *rake* is drawn inside of the primitive for *wild rice*. Note the doubling up. [8]

2208   **wife**

妻   *Needle . . . rake . . . woman.* Although the elements fit together, note the breakdown in stroke order and the shortening of the *rake's* handle. [8]

一   彐   妻   妻

2209   **miserable**

凄   *Ice . . . wife.* [10]

2210   **nimble**

捷   To remember this character, think of the famous calligrapher and founder of the esoteric Buddhist tradition, Kūkai. He is said to have been able to write five poems simultaneously by holding brushes in his mouth, hands, and feet. You do him one better by having your *fingers* fitted out with *ten* small *rakes*. Dip them in ink and watch as they move across the paper all at once with lightning speed, each leaving behind a distinct shape. At first it looks like no more than a smudgy *trail of footprints,* but if you look closely, you will see that they are Chinese characters arranged into a classical poem. Now that is much more **nimble** than Jack and his candlestick! [11]

扌   扩   拦   拝   捗   捗   捷

2211   **solemn**

肅   Obviously what we have here is someone on *crutches* wielding a *rake.* The pair of detached *animal legs* suggests that a garden rodent resting under the leaves has been caught up in the process, squealing its little lungs out and kicking its legs about as the *rake* digs into it. Just why the person is on *crutches,* and what is so **solemn** about it all, are matters we leave to your imagination to sort out. [8]

聿   聿   肅   肅   肅

2212	howl ^(v.)

2212 howl ^(v.)

啸

Mouth . . . solemn. There are lots of ways to **howl** and lots of things that are said to **howl**. No single English word can handle everything from the rushing of the wind to the screaming of a wild animal and the roaring of the sea. But this character does just that. [11]

2213 desolate

萧

Flowers . . . solemn. [11]

2214 double ^(ADJ.)

兼

At the top we have the *animal horns* and the single horizontal stroke to give them something to hang onto. Below that, we see one *rake* with two handles. Finally, we see a pair of strokes splitting away from each of the handles, indicating that they are both splitting under pressure. The composite picture is of someone leading a **double** life and splitting apart at the seams. Take the time to find this sense in the character and it will be easy to remember, despite initial appearances. [10]

丷　丷　当　肀　聿　兼　兼

2215 earn

赚

Shells . . . double. [14]

2216 dislike ^(v.)

嫌

Woman . . . double. [13]

2217 unassuming

谦

Words . . . double. [12]

2218 apology

歉

Double . . . yawn. [14]

2219 廉	inexpensive
	Cave . . . double. [13]

2220 镰	sickle
	Metal . . . inexpensive. [18]

2221 睁	unshut (v.)
	Eyeballs . . . contend. As you might have guessed from the opening primitive element, this character refers to what your eyes do when you open them. [11]

2222 挣	struggle (v.)
	Fingers . . . contend. [9]

2223 筝	Chinese zither
	Bamboo . . . contend. [12]

2224 塘	pool (n.)
	News flash! In a stunning reversal of the history of sport, archaeologists working on a site in central China recently un*earth*ed artifacts confirming that the origins of synchronized swimming go back to the *Tang* Dynasty. The presence of skimpy swimsuits and nose plugs lying at the bottom of what was once a natural *pool* is said to constitute persuasive scientific evidence that they perished in sync. [13]

2225 隶	bondservant
	We already met this combination in Book 1 (FRAME 956), but failed to note that it was, in fact, the **bondservant** who was shoveling *snowflakes* with a *rake*. [8]

2226 逮	arrest (v.)
	Road . . . bondservant. [11]

2227	generous
慷	*State of mind . . . hale.* [14]

2228	chaff
糠	*Rice . . . hale.* [17]

2229	bamboo shoot
笋	*Bamboo . . . overseer.* [10]

2230	mess around
耍	The hint of mischief in the key word is best managed by imagining yourself teasing a *woman* you know by going after her *combs.* You **mess around** with them by soaking them in dye, hair remover, and catnip. [9]

2231	-proof
耐	The key word is a suffix used to indicate "safe from" or "protected against," as in the words rust**proof**, water**proof**, and fire**proof**. It is composed of: *comb . . . glue.* [9]

2232	wheeze
喘	*Mouth . . . prospector.* [12]

2233	conjecture [v.]
揣	*Fingers . . . prospector.* [12]

❖	cadet
曹	The three primitive elements for **cadet** suggest a young recruit going through his "hazing." *One bent day.* What a perfect way to describe this brief, infantile chapter in military training. If you look at the printed form, you can see the young **cadet** standing proud and erect after having passed the initiation ritual, broad at the shoulders and narrow at the waist. [11]

一　厂　両　甫　冉　曲　曹

2234	trough
槽	*Tree . . . cadet.* [15]

2235	meet with
遭	The sense of this key word is a chance encounter, usually negative, as when one **meets with** misfortune or disaster. Its elements: *cadet . . . road.* [14]

2236	messed up
糟	*Rice . . . cadet.* [17]

2237	quiver [v.]
抖	*Fingers . . . Big Dipper.* [7]

LESSON 31

2238	rue^(v.)

State of mind . . . times past. The sense of the key word is to regret the loss of something cherished. [11]

2239	arrange

Fingers . . . times past. [11]

2240	dried meat

Flesh . . . times past. [12]

2241	wax^(n.)

Insect . . . times past. [14]

2242	hunt^(v.)

Pack of wild dogs . . . times past. [11]

2243	swallow^(n.)

This key word refers to the bird, and the elements suggest that a score of them are being boiled in order to be "swallowed" by their human predators. The primitives: *Twenty . . . mouth . . . north . . . cooking fire*. Note how the *mouth* is placed between the two sides of *north*, for which you may find it helpful to revert to the image of *two people sitting on the ground* back to back, as explained in FRAME 454. [16]

廿　甘　莊　燕　燕

2244	screen^(v.)

Caverns . . . cooking fire . . . road. [14]

2245 畔	littoral (N.)
	Rice field . . . half. The key word here is used principally for areas that border a body of water. [10]

2246 拌	blend (V.)
	Fingers . . . half. [8]

2247 叛	betray
	Half . . . against. [9]

2248 券	voucher
	Quarter . . . dagger. [8]

2249 藤	rattan
	Flower . . . moon . . . quarter . . . snowflakes. [18]

2250 鼎	old cooking pot
	Eyeball . . . bunk beds . . . slice. The *eyeball* takes up so much space that the second stroke of *bunk beds* and the first stroke of *slice* need to be shortened. Take particular care with the stroke order here. [13]

目　目　貝　貝　貝　貝　貝

鼎　鼎

2251 芝	sesame
	Flowers . . . sign of Zorro. [6]

2252 贬	devalue
	Shellfish . . . weary. [8]

2253 泛	nonspecific
	Water . . . weary. [7]

2254	askew
歪 *No . . . correct.* [9]	

LESSON 32

2255	rectify
矫	*Dart . . . angel.* [11]
2256	short of stature
矮	*Dart . . . committee.* [13]
❖	crossbow
矢	If you've ever drawn back a **crossbow**, the elements *elbow* and *dart* should be easy enough to associate with this primitive element. [7]
	ム　矢
2257	sigh-ay-ay
唉	*Mouth . . . crossbow.* The key word is meant to simulate the sad, **sighing** sound issuing forth from the *mouth* of a warrior whose *crossbow* has broken down after the expiration of the warranty. **Ay-ay-ay-ay-aaaaaaaaaaay.** [10]
2258	fine dust
埃	*Soil . . . crossbow.* [10]
2259	suffer
挨	*Fingers . . . crossbow.* [10]
2260	cluster [N.]
簇	*Bamboo . . . tribe.* [17]
2261	thatch [N.]
茅	*Flowers . . . spear.* [8]

2262	tangerine
橘	*Tree . . . spear . . . motorcycle helmet . . . animal legs . . . mouth.* You may want to return to FRAME 451 of Book 1 to recall how you combined the final elements into a memorable image. [16]

2263	relax
舒	*Abode . . . bestow.* [12]

2264	view ^(v.)
览	The only difference between this character and that for *be about to* (FRAME 1010) is that the final element here is changed from *sun* to *see*. Think of the familiar advice, "Look before you leap," and adjust it to the key words: "When you *are about to*, first **view** the situation carefully." [9]

❖ Used as a primitive element, this character will take the more concrete meaning of a *magnifying glass*.

2265	take on
揽	*Fingers . . . magnifying glass.* The sense of the key word is to **take on** a task or assume responsibility for something. [12]

2266	kidneys
肾	*Foiled again! . . . part of the body.* [8]

2267	perpendicular
竖	*Foiled again! . . . vase.* The sense of this key word is vertical or upright. [9]

2268	noble
弘	*Bow . . . elbow.* [5]

2269	barbarian

夷

St. Bernard dog . . . bow. Note how the stroke order follows the principles of writing and does not draw the primitive elements separately. [6]

一　弓　夷　夷

2270	maternal aunt

姨

Woman . . . barbarian. [9]

❖	family feud

畺

Two *rice fields*, each of them separated by a stone wall on the north and another on the south (the three *ones*) create an image of the most famous **family feud** in American history, that between the Hatfields and McCoys. [13]

一　畐　畺　畺　畺

2271	dividing line

疆

Bow . . . soil . . . family feud. Think of this key word as referring to a boundary or border. [19]

2272	stiff (ADJ.)

僵

Person . . . family feud. [15]

2273	porridge

粥

Two *bows . . . rice.* [12]

弓　弜　粥

2274	cicada

蟬

Insect . . . list. [14]

2275 禅	**meditation**	This is the character for Chinese **Chan** (or Zen). Its elements are: *altar . . . list.* [12]
2276 沸	**bring to a boil**	*Water . . . dollar sign.* [8]
2277 拂	**caress** (v.)	*Fingers . . . dollar sign.* [8]
2278 剃	**shave** (v.)	*Younger brother . . . saber.* [9]
2279 递	**hand over**	*Younger brother . . . road.* [10]
2280 梯	**ladder**	*Tree . . . younger brother.* [11]
2281 涕	**snot**	The reason *younger brother* can be such a pain in the neck, a thorn, or bothersome pest—in short, such a "snot"—must have something to do with the disgusting drops of *water* that leak from people's nostrils, which is in fact the **snot** this character refers to. [10]
2282 朽	**decayed**	*Tree . . . snare.* As the primitive on the left suggests, this character often applies to wood. The broader sense of the key word, which includes the way people get **decayed** by senility or old age, may be helpful in making your story. [6]
2283 聘	**employ** (v.)	*Ear . . . sprout . . . snare.* [13]

| 2284 | elder sister |

姊

To complement the older brother (FRAME 93) and elder brother (107), we need an older sister (1344) and now an **elder sister**. The combination of elements to the right of *woman* is a rare one, and for that reason special attention should be given to its drawing. The first two strokes on the right are somewhat like a *snare* except that the first stroke is drawn right to left, like *drag*. So think of it as a *snare* you are *dragging* by hand along the ground. The character finishes with what are actually the last two strokes of a *genie*, who has been caught in the *snare* and is wiggling to get free. What all this has to do with your **elder sister** we leave to you to decide. [7]

女　女ー　妁　姊　姊

| 2285 | loss |

亏

The *snare* with an extra horizontal line gives us a snake hook, a *snare* at the end of a long pole used to snag dangerous reptiles. Or, as in this character, to get hold of the slimy broker responsible for the **loss** of your entire life savings. [3]

丂　亏

❖ In line with the key word, this character will mean *snake hook* when used as a primitive.

| 2286 | filthy |

污

Water . . . snake hook. [6]

| 2287 | brag |

夸

St. Bernard dog . . . snake hook. However you choose to relate the two primitives, hold on to that image for the following two frames. [6]

| 2288 | collapse [v.] |

垮

Soil . . . brag. [9]

2289	carry on the arm
挎	*Fingers . . . brag.* [9]

2290	crocodile
鳄	*Fish . . . chatterbox . . . snake hook.* If you are more familiar with *alligators* than **crocodiles**, feel free to adjust the key word accordingly. [17]

2291	stunned
愕	*State of mind . . . chatterbox . . . snake hook.* [12]

LESSON 33

2292 躺	lie down *Somebody . . . esteem.* [15]
2293 躲	dodge (v.) *Somebody . . . flouds.* [13]
2294 躬	stoop (v.) *Somebody . . . bow.* [10]
2295 嗜	hanker *Mouth . . . old man . . . tongue wagging in the mouth.* [13]
2296 姥	maternal grandmother *Woman . . . old man.* [9]
2297 拷	flog *Fingers . . . take an exam.* [9]
2298 屿	islet *Mountain . . . offer.* [6]
2299 暑	summer heat *Sun . . . puppet.* [12]
2300 睹	behold *Eyeballs . . . puppet.* [13]
2301 署	add your John Hancock *Net . . . puppet.* [13]

2302 薯	yam
	Flowers . . . add your John Hancock. [16]

2303 赌	gamble (v.)
	Shells . . . puppet. [12]

2304 奢	extravagant
	St. Bernard dog . . . puppet. [11]

2305 堵	stop up
	Soil . . . puppet. [11]

2306 煮	boil (v.)
	Puppet . . . cooking fire. [12]

2307 诸	various
	Words . . . puppet. [10]

2308 储	put in storage
	Person . . . various [12]

2309 屠	slaughter
	Flag . . . puppet. [11]

2310 棺	coffin
	Tree . . . bureaucrat. [12]

2311 爹	dad
	Father . . . many. [10]

2312 斧	axe
	Father . . . tomahawk. [8]

2313 咬	bite [v.] *Mouth . . . mingle.* [9]
2314 胶	gum *Flesh . . . mingle.* Think of the thick, sticky goo that oozes out of trees and plants, not the stuff you chew on and blow bubbles with before you stick it under your desk. [10]
2315 狡	sly *Pack of wild dogs . . . mingle.* [9]
2316 捉	catch [v.] In learning this character, think of how you **catch** animals or insects. The elements: *fingers . . . lower leg.* [10]
2317 促	urge [v.] *Person . . . lower leg.* [9]
2318 趴	prostrate oneself *Wooden leg . . . eight.* [9]
2319 踏	trample *Wooden leg . . . water . . . sun.* [15]
2320 践	tread on *Wooden leg . . . float.* [12]
2321 跃	leap [v.] *Wooden leg . . . die young.* [11]
2322 蹄	hoof *Wooden leg . . . sovereign.* [16]

2323 踩	step on
	Wooden leg ... pick. [15]

2324 蹦	hop (v.)
	Wooden leg ... crumble. [18]

2325 跌	slump (v.)
	Wooden leg ... lose. Take this key word in the sense in which prices or productivity can fall or **slump**. [12]

2326 踢	kick (v.)
	Wooden leg ... easy. [15]

2327 踪	tracks
	Wooden leg ... religion. These are the impressions that creatures leave behind when they move from one place to another. For the **tracks** of trains and trolleys, you are better off with the character in FRAME 1623. [15]

2328 跨	straddle (v.)
	Wooden leg ... brag. [13]

❖ 枭	wood pulp
	Let this primitive mean **wood pulp**, from the fact that it is one of the many *goods* produced from *trees*. [13]

品   枭

2329 躁	impetuous
	Wooden leg ... wood pulp. [20]

2330 噪	chirping
	Mouth ... wood pulp. You might just ignore the compound primitive altogether and look instead at all the *mouths* around and in the *tree*. [16]

2331 藻	bath
Water . . . wood pulp. [16]	

2332 藻	algae
Flowers . . . bath. [19]	

2333 燥	parched
Fire . . . wood pulp. [17]	

2334 操	exercise [N.]
Fingers . . . wood pulp. [16]	

2335 猾	cunning
Pack of wild dogs . . . skeleton. [12]	

2336 髓	marrow
Skeleton . . . left . . . part of the body . . . road. Note that the primitive elements are drawn in the order given here. [21]	

LESSON 34

2337 陌	*Pinnacle . . . hundred.* [8]	footpath
2338 隙	The key word refers to a gap or a break. Its elements: *pinnacle . . . small . . . spring.* [12]	rift (N.)
2339 陡	*Pinnacle . . . walk.* [9]	steep
2340 陪	*Pinnacle . . . muzzle.* [10]	accompany
2341 障	*Pinnacle . . . chapter.* [13]	barrier
2342 隧	*Pinnacle . . . satisfy.* [14]	tunnel (N.)
2343 陋	*Pinnacle . . . third . . . fishhook.* The drawing order following the primitives. [8]	undesirable
2344 隐	*Pinnacle . . . anxious.* [11]	hidden
2345 陕	*Pinnacle . . . press from both sides.* [8]	Shaanxi Province

Minuteclods

"Listen my children and your shall hear, of the midnight ride of Clod Revere …." The **Minuteclods** were an elite core of militia in the rebel army that fought for liberty from agricultural oppression during the Vegetable Rebellion of 1775 BCE. They are depicted in the primitive as clods of *soil* with tiny *animal legs*. When they join the regiment, they are fitted out with a specially engineered set of long *walking legs* to be ready to march into battle at a minute's notice. [8]

土　夫　夌

2346

mausoleum

陵　　Pinnacle . . . Minuteclods. [10]

2347

edge (N.)

棱　　Tree . . . Minuteclods. [12]

2348

water caltrop

菱　　Flowers . . . Minuteclods. [11]

2349

bully (V.)

凌　　Ice . . . Minuteclods. [10]

---

cauldron

鬲　This is going to be a rather unusual **cauldron**. Beginning from the bottom of the primitive, we see a sturdy *spike* driven into the ground (and hence hiding the "hook" at the end) to serve as a stand for the **cauldron** to rest on. Above is a pair of *animal horns* that are attached to the bottom of the vessel as two of its "legs." The whole thing sits under a large *glass cover* that functions as a steamer lid. Oh, yes, and that *one mouth* refers to the tiny little opening at the top for letting the steam escape—like you might imagine in an ancient pressure cooker. [10]

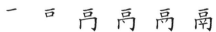

2350	melt
融	*Cauldron . . . insect.* [16]

2351	separate (v.)
隔	*Pinnacle . . . cauldron.* [12]

2352	pilfer
窃	*Hole . . . cut.* [9]

2353	dig (v.)
挖	*Fingers . . . hole . . . fishhook.* [9]

2354	drapes
帘	*Hole . . . towel.* [8]

2355	peep (v.)
窥	The character refers to spying through a **peep**hole, but here we can see a lawyer **peep** through the *regulations* in search of a *hole* for his corrupt client to crawl through. [13]

2356	poor
穷	*Hole . . . muscle.* The key word means having little money, goods, or other means of support. [7]

2357	strait (ADJ.)
窄	This rather antique-sounding word refers to something "not wide." Be sure to keep your image distinct from the one you made for the character that means *narrow* (FRAME 1588). Its elements: *hole . . . saw.* [10]

2358	extract (v.)
榨	*Tree . . . strait.* Think of the physical act of pressing or squeezing to **extract** one thing from another, like juice from oranges. [14]

2359 窟	den
	The key word is used for hideaways of bandits, gangsters, and the like. Its primitives: *hole . . . knuckle under.* [13]

2360 窘	poverty-stricken
	Hole . . . monarch. [12]

2361 窜	scurry
	Hole . . . shish kebab. [12]

2362 腔	body cavity
	Flesh . . . empty. [12]

❖ 咼	esophagus
	Mouth . . . internal. Be sure not to confuse with FRAME 841, which uses the same primitive elements but arranges them differently. Think of the esophagus as reaching deep down from the *mouth* to what's *internal*—in the same direction as the elements. [7]

口　咼

2363 窝	hollow (N.)
	Just as the character for *mouth* could refer to a whole range of things, this one can appear in compounds for things that have a **hollow**—everything from a hornets' nest to a dimple to a fox's lair. Take your pick! *Hole . . . esophagus.* [12]

2364 涡	whirlpool
	Water . . . esophagus. [10]

2365 锅	pot
	Metal . . . esophagus. Be sure to create an image of a cooking **pot** distinct from the *old cooking pot* (FRAME 2250). [12]

2366		misfortune
祸	*Altar . . . esophagus.* [11]	

2367		snail
蜗	*Insect . . . esophagus.* [13]	

2368		visitor
宾	When a brigade of *troops* unexpectedly descends on your *house* for a little R & R, you try to make your **visitors** feel at home, when what you really wish is that they were. [10]	

2369		water's edge
滨	*Water . . . visitor.* [13]	

LESSON 35

2370 绷	**stretch taut** *Thread . . . companion.* [11]
2371 纤	**fiber** This character, which figures in compounds for different kinds of **fiber**, should be associated with the fine and delicate qualities we associate with the word. The elements you have to work with are: *thread . . . thousand.* [6]
2372 绰	**ample** *Thread . . . eminent.* [11]
2373 绍	**acquaint** *Thread . . . summon.* [8]
2374 纱	**yarn** *Thread . . . few.* The primitive on the left is enough to warn us that this character does not refer to tall tales. Be sure to keep your image distinct from that for the primitive of the same meaning. [7]
2375 络	**web** *Thread . . . each.* [9]
2376 绸	**silk fabric** *Thread . . . lap.* [11]
2377 绒	**down** [N.] *Thread . . . fiesta . . . needle.* [9] 纟　纟　纤　绒

2378 绕	go around
	Thread . . . javelin thrower. The key word means to detour or circumvent. [9]

2379 绽	split at the seams
	Thread . . . settle on. [11]

2380 绵	continuous
	If you think of a single, unbroken, **continuous** piece of *thread* being used to make all the *white towels* in your house. It might be efficient, but it could cause problems when it comes to doing the laundry. [11]

2381 缔	conclude
	Let this key word connote what people do when they formalize a treaty, an alliance, an association, and so forth. Its elements are: *thread . . . sovereign.* [12]

2382 纺	spin (v.)
	For the character that means to **spin** *thread* and other fibers, we have the elements: *thread . . . compass.* [7]

2383 缠	wind around
	Thread . . . cave . . . computer. [13]

2384 绘	paint (v.)
	You can **paint** to coat a wall or you can **paint** to create art. This character refers to the latter. *Thread . . . meeting.* [9]

2385 纷	disorderly
	Thread . . . part. [7]

2386 绣	embroidery
	Thread . . . elegant. [10]

2387 缕	in detail
	Thread . . . bride. [12]

2388 缩	shrink ^(v.)
	Thread . . . stay overnight. [14]

2389 纳	let in
	Thread . . . third. The sense of the key word is to admit or receive someone or something. [7]

2390 综	sum up
	Thread . . . religion. [11]

2391 绅	gentry
	Thread . . . monkey. In Chinese nomenclature, the **gentry** was a class of individuals who had passed the bureaucratic examinations. [8]

2392 绪	inception
	Thread . . . puppet. [11]

2393 绞	wring
	Thread . . . mingle. [9]

❖ 爰	migrating ducks
	This primitive is simplicity itself. It depicts bird *claws* (or in this case, duck *claws*) that are joined to one another. Note the extra horizontal stroke in the character for *friend*, which gives the appearance of a "two" in the middle of the character, further emphasizing the togetherness of the **migrating ducks**. [9]

罒　亗　孚　爰　爰

2394		unhurried
缓	*Thread . . . migrating ducks.* [12]	

2395		warm ^(ADJ.)
暖	*Sun . . . migrating ducks.* [13]	

2396		provide assistance
援	*Fingers . . . migrating ducks.* [12]	

❖		canker sore
冐	A *mouth* and *flesh* combine to give us that annoying little ulcer inside the cheek we refer to as a **canker sore**. [7]	

口　冐

2397		tough silk
绢	This character is a literary term referring to thin but **tough silk**. It is made up of the elements for *thread* and *canker sore*. [10]	

2398		contribute
捐	*Fingers . . . canker sore.* [10]	

❖		homing pigeon
敫	You might think here of the first **homing pigeon** in recorded history: the *dove* that Noah *released* from the Ark in search of dry land. The first time, it returned. After seven days, Noah *released* the *dove* again, and this time it came back with an olive branch in its beak. On the third and final flight, it did not return and Noah knew that it had found land. The combination of parts in this primitive element, you may remember, was used with a quite different image in Book 1 (FRAME 497). [13]	

白　舅　敫

2399 缴	shell out
	Thread . . . homing pigeon. [16]

2400 邀	request the presence of
	Homing pigeon . . . road. [16]

2401 缆	cable [N.]
	Thread . . . magnifying glass. [12]

2402 哟	Oh!
	Mouth . . . make an appointment. [9]

2403 颈	neck [N.]
	Spool . . . head. [11]

2404 茎	plant stem
	Flowers . . . spool. [8]

2405 径	trail [N.]
	Queue . . . spool. The key word in this frame should suggest a footpath, not an established overland route. [8]

2406 劲	powerful
	Spool . . . muscle. [7]

❖ 彐	whisk broom
	The **whisk broom** is smaller and more compact than the full-form *broom*. If you take the second, horizontal stroke of broom, bend it upward and draw it first, the rest will follow naturally. Take a moment to trace it out in the order shown below. [3]

𠃍　彑　彐

2407	reason [N.]
缘	Think of this key word as referring to the cause of things. The elements you have to work with are: *thread . . . whisk broom . . . sow.* The final stroke of the *whisk broom* doubles up with the first stroke of the *sow.* [12]

2408	young
幼	*Cocoon . . . muscle.* [5]

2409	creek
溪	*Water . . . vulture . . . cocoon . . . St. Bernard dog.* [13]

2410	secluded
幽	*Mountain . . . two cocoons.* [9]

2411	mysterious
玄	A *top hat* and a *cocoon* combine to create a **mysterious**-looking creature, something out of a science fiction horror movie. [5]

亠　玄

2412	bowstring
弦	What is so *mysterious* about this **bowstring** is that it has been taken from the *bow* and used to string a cello, where it can make music and at the same time still be used by a virtuoso for sending arrows toward their target. Or, from the victim's viewpoint, "killing me softly, with his song." [8]

2413	livestock
畜	*Mysterious . . . rice field.* [10]

2414	save up
蓄	*Flowers . . . livestock.* [13]

❖ 兹	**Mona Lisa**
	Note the doubling up of the element for mysterious here. Now if there is any work of art that qualifies as doubly *mysterious*, it is Da Vinci's **Mona Lisa**. [9]

丷　玄　兹

2415 磁	**magnetism**
	Stone . . . Mona Lisa. Let the key word here refer to the physical quality of certain metals, not to charismatic personalities. [14]

2416 滋	**nourish**
	Water . . . Mona Lisa. [12]

2417 慈	**kindhearted**
	Mona Lisa . . . heart. [13]

2418 累	**tired**
	Rice field . . . floss. [11]

2419 螺	**spiral shell**
	Insect . . . tired. [17]

2420 紫	**purple**
	This (literary) . . . floss. Although you will not meet any examples in these volumes, it may help to think of the "**purple** prose" of those inferior writers who pile clumsy cliches on top of one another from the crack of a rosy-fingered dawn till the fall of the final curtain on a dark and stormy night, or otherwise shamelessly ornament and exaggerate with a complete lack of literary conscience. [12]

2421 繁	**numerous**
	Quick-witted . . . floss. [17]

2422	long-winded
絮	*Be like . . . floss.* [12]

❖	chapel
亠	The *house* with the "cross" on the roof will serve us as a primitive element meaning **chapel**. While we have shied away from using pictographs, we think you will agree that seeing the "cross" as a replacement of the "chimney" atop the *house* is a helpful exception. [4]

$$+ \quad 亠$$

2423	large rope
索	*Chapel . . . floss.* [10]

❖	Sunday school
孛	The *chapel* with the *children* inside becomes a primitive element meaning **Sunday school**. [7]

$$亠 \quad 孛$$

2424	head-hinge
脖	The meaning of this character is actually the "neck," but we adjusted the key word to avoid confusing it with another character we learned for *neck* earlier in this lesson (FRAME 2403). We have adopted a technical term from the little-known classic "Very Gray Anatomy": a **head-hinge**. You may, if you wish, replace it with a term of your own. **Head-stand** and **shoulder-stump** come to mind as possibilities. In any case, its elements are: *flesh . . . Sunday school.* [11]

2425	vibrant
勃	*Sunday school . . . muscle.* [9]

LESSON 36

2426 卸	**unload**
	The left primitive is a union of a *stick horse* and a *footprint*. To the right, the *stamp*. [9]

2427 御	**withstand**
	Queue ... unload. [12]

2428 卵	**nest eggs**
	This character shows a *letter opener* with a couple of *drops* of something or other. The key word should give it away: it has been splattered with **nest eggs** you picked up from a nearby tree. As to what unfortunate creature had its offspring end up on a *letter opener* and what the owner of that desktop weapon had to do with it, these are matters better left to your imagination than to ours. [7]

＇ 𠃌 𠂆 𠂒 𠂔 卯 卵

❖ 孚	**fledglings**
	A *vulture* and a *child* combine to create a rather gruesome image of an aerie full of **fledglings**. [7]

爫 孚

2429 孵	**hatch** [v.]
	Nest eggs ... fledglings. [14]

2430 乳	**breast**
	Fledglings ... fishhook. [8]

2431	float [v.]
浮	Water . . . fledglings. [10]

2432	captive
俘	Person . . . fledglings. [9]

2433	pomegranate
榴	Tree . . . stay. [14]

2434	grandfather
爷	Father . . . chop. [6]

2435	doubt [v.]
疑	The existential state in which one **doubts** everyone and everything is depicted here as *someone sitting on the ground* in the middle of a *zoo* with a *dart* in the bottom and a *chop* in th hand. Now how in the world did I ever get here? Is this real or am I dreaming? [14]

匕   矣   矣^マ   疑

❖ Used as a primitive element, this character will mean a *furled brow*, the kind that shows up when someone is beset by serious doubts.

2436	congeal
凝	Ice . . . furled brow. [16]

2437	exquisite
玲	Jewel . . . orders. [9]

2438	small bell
铃	Metal . . . orders. [10]

2439	pity (v.)
怜	*State of mind . . . orders.* [8]

2440	mountain range
岭	*Mountain . . . orders.* [8]

2441	actor
伶	*Person . . . orders.* [7]

2442	gush (v.)
涌	*Water . . . chop-rack.* [10]

2443	bucket
桶	*Tree . . . chop-rack.* [11]

2444	read aloud
诵	*Words . . . chop-rack.* [9]

2445	model
范	Take your mind off of catwalks and scale airplane kits and think of **model** in the sense of a pattern or example. The elements: *flowers . . . water . . . fingerprint.* [8]

2446	clutch (v.)
扼	*Fingers . . . cliff . . . fingerprint.* [7]

2447	exam paper
卷	*Quarter . . . fingerprint.* [8]

2448	worn out
倦	Few things makes a *person* more **worn out** during the school year than having to sit an *exam paper*. [10]

2449	circle [N.]
圈	The key word refers both to the geometrical object and to a circumscribed group, as in one's "**circle** of friends." Its primitives: *pent in . . . exam paper.* [11]

❖	nameplate
夗	Instead of coming home in the *evening* and fumbling with your keys to open your front door, you simply run your *fingerprint* across your backlit **nameplate** and, presto!—you're in. [5]

夕　夗

2450	resentment
怨	*Nameplate . . . heart.* [9]

2451	winding
宛	*House . . . nameplate.* [8]

❖ Used as a primitive element, this character will mean *mailbox*, from the little *house* with your *nameplate* on it that the postman drops your mail into.

2452	wrist
腕	*Flesh . . . mailbox.* [12]

2453	tactful
婉	*Woman . . . mailbox.* [11]

2454	bowl
碗	*Stone . . . mailbox.* [13]

2455	ash-colored
苍	*Flowers . . . storehouse.* [7]

2456 抢	rob Fingers . . . storehouse. [7]
2457 诡	deceitful Words . . . danger. [8]
2458 跪	kneel Wooden leg . . . danger. [13]

❖

臾

zipper

The *tool* that is made up of two sets of facing *staples* with something between them will mean *zipper* (which is much more convenient for closing your trousers than stapling them). Note that the intervening primitive is drawn after the first set of staples on the left. [10]

丨　丨丨　丨丨　丨丨　臾

2459 與	popular Zipper . . . car. [14]

丨　丨丨　丨丨　丨丨　與

LESSON 37

2460 酌	pour wine *Whiskey bottle . . . ladle.* [10]
2461 酬	reward (N./V.) *Whiskey bottle . . . state.* [13]
2462 酷	brutal *Whiskey bottle . . . declare.* [14]
2463 醇	mellow wine *Whiskey bottle . . . enjoy.* [15]
2464 醋	vinegar *Whiskey bottle . . . times past.* [15]
❖ 㸒	chocolate turtle The **chocolate turtle** is the gooey chocolate-covered candy shaped like a *turtle* that you might have in the *evening* after supper, sitting in your living room with your guests all decked out in formal *evening* attire. All you need to do is think of the *turtle* coming to life when you bite into it. [6] 爿　㸒
2465 醬	thick sauce The character for **thick sauce** also appears in the term for soy **sauce**, so it is one you have probably seen many times already without realizing it. The primitives: *chocolate turtle . . . whiskey bottle.* [13]

2466	award ^(N.)
奖	*Chocolate turtle . . . St. Bernard dog.* [9]

2467	thick liquid
浆	*Chocolate turtle . . . water.* Note that the bottom element uses the full character for *water*. If you return to FRAME 137 in Book 1 and use the story there, it will help. [10]

2468	oar
桨	*Chocolate turtle . . . tree.* [10]

2469	Jiang
蒋	Jiang is the surname of **General**issimo Chiang Kai-shek (or as today's orthography has him, **Jiang** Jieshi), head of the Nationalist Government of the Republic of China until 1975. Conveniently, the primitive elements are: *flowers . . . General.* [12]

❖	foot soldiers
卒	The **foot soldiers** shown here are not your ordinary rank-and-file infantry, but specially manufactured, sophisticated "foot" masseurs for commanding officers. See them march off the *assembly line* in their *top hats* with foot-long *needles* in hand to prick the boils of their superiors. [8}

亠　圶　卒

2470	drunk
醉	*Whiskey bottle . . . foot soldiers.* [15]

2471	shattered
碎	*Stone . . . foot soldiers.* [13]

2472	emerald green
翠	*Feathers . . . foot soldiers.* [14]

2473	unmixed
粹	Rice . . . foot soldiers. The key word connotes something that is pure and unadulterated. [14]

❖	streetwalker
夋	You shouldn't have any trouble associating the character for consent and a pair of walking legs with a streetwalker. (Note that in many character fonts the human legs in consent end up looking more like a pair of animal legs.) [7]

厶　儿　夋

2474	sour
酸	Whiskey bottle . . . streetwalker. [14]

2475	shuttle (N.)
梭	Tree . . . streetwalker. Think back to the original shuttle from which things like space shuttles, airport shuttles, and even shuttlecocks get their names in English, namely the little piece of wood that flies back and forth over the loom. [11]

2476	lofty
峻	Mountain . . . streetwalker. [10]

2477	handsome
俊	Person . . . streetwalker. [9]

2478	found (V.)
奠	The sense of the key word is to establish an institution. Its elements: chieftain . . . St. Bernard dog. [12]

2479	squat (V.)
蹲	Wooden leg . . . chieftain . . . glued to. [19]

| 2480 逗 | tease (v.) |
| Beans . . . road. [10] | |

| 2481 橱 | closet |
| Think of the key word as referring to a cupboard or **closet**, not to a government body. Its elements: *tree . . . kitchen*. [16] | |

| 2482 嘻 | giggling |
| Mouth . . . joyful. [15] | |

| 2483 嘉 | commend |
| Drum . . . add. You might also want to try beginning with the character for *joyful* and simply nudge the element for *mouth* over to make room to complete the character for *add*. [14] | |

| 2484 盟 | alliance |
| Bright . . . dish. [13] | |

| 2485 孟 | Mencius |
| This character is best known as the beginning of the name of one of ancient China's most celebrated philosophers, **Mencius** (385–303 BCE). Its primitives: *child . . . dish*. [8] | |

| 2486 猛 | fierce |
| Pack of wild dogs . . . Mencius. [11] | |

| 2487 盐 | salt (N.) |
| Soil . . . magic wand . . . dish. [10] | |

| 2488 盔 | helmet |
| To avoid confusing this key word with the primitive element of the same name, picture an entirely different kind of **helmet** and associate it forcefully with the elements: *ashes . . . dish*. [11] | |

2489	small box
盒	Fit . . . dish. [11]

2490	flourishing
盛	This key word refers to something that is prospering. Its elements: *turn into . . . dish.* [11]

2491	small cop
盏	Float . . . dish. [10]

2492	master thief
盗	Next . . . dish. [11]

2493	collide with
磕	Stone . . . go . . . dish. [15]

2494	replete
盈	Fist . . . again . . . dish. [9]

2495	basin
盆	Part . . . dish. For the particular connotation of this key word, think of a wash**basin**. [9]

2496	amass
蕴	Flowers . . . thread . . . sun . . . dish. [15]

❖ 小/	bullfighter
	Following up on the story learned back in FRAME 1010, we assign this primitive element the sense of **bullfighter**. [5]

川　小/　小/

2497 鉴	probe ^(v.) *Bullfighter . . . gold.* Take this key word as meaning to delve into or investigate something. [13]
2498 滥	indiscriminate *Water . . . hidden camera.* [13]
❖ 尢	Frankenbowser You will recall the primitive element for the freakish transformation of the little chihuahua into *Frankenpooch* from Book 1 (page 109). Here we see a later and no less ghastly experiment with the larger *St. Bernard dog*, something we like to call the **Frankenbowser**. [3] 丿 尢 尢
2499 尴	abashed *Frankenbowser . . . hidden camera.* [13]
2500 尬	embarrassed *Frankenbowser . . . introduce.* [7]
❖ 尤	Frankenbowser Rex The transformation of the first stroke of *Frankenbowser* into a *crown* gives us the *crowning* experiment of the mad scientist: a creature that can stand shoulder to shoulder with the fiercest beasts of the Jurassic age—the **Frankenbowser Rex**. [4] 宀 尣 尤
2501 沈	Shen *Water . . . Frankenbowser Rex.* [7]
2502 枕	pillow *Tree . . . Frankenbowser Rex.* [8]

2503 耽	indulge in
	Ear . . . Frankenbowser Rex. [10]

2504 衅	quarrel [N.]
	Blood . . . half. [11]

2505 垦	reclaim
	Silver . . . soil. [9]

2506 狠	ruthless
	Pack of wild dogs . . . silver. [9]

2507 恳	wholeheartedly
	Silver . . . heart. [10]

2508 艰	arduous
	Crotch . . . silver. [8]

2509 爵	upper crust
	Vulture . . . net . . . silver . . . glued to. Europeans are not the only ones with a history of nobility, peerage, and aristocracy. China, too, had its **upper crust.** [17]

2510 嚼	chew [V.]
	Mouth . . . upper crust. [20]

2511 卿	minister
	Letter opener . . . silver. Be sure to locate the primitive for *silver* INSIDE the *letter opener.* The key word refers to a high-ranking government official in Chinese history. [10]

2512 恨	hate [V.]
	State of mind . . . silver. [9]

2513 朗	lucent
Halo . . . moon. [10]	

2514 狼	wolf
Pack of wild dogs . . . halo. [10]	

2515 粮	provisions
Rice . . . halo. [13]	

2516 酿	brew [v.]
Whiskey bottle . . . halo. [14]	

2517 饥	starving
Food . . . small table. [5]	

2518 饶	spare [v.]
Food . . . javelin thrower. [9]	

2519 饰	ornaments
Food . . . reclining . . . towel. [8]	

2520 饮	beverage
Food . . . yawn. [7]	

2521 蚀	eat away
Food . . . insect. [9]	

2522 饱	sated
Food . . . wrap. [8]	

2523 馒	bread
Food . . . mandala. [14]	

2524	cookie
饼	Food . . . puzzle. [9]

2525	dumpling
饺	Food . . . mingle. [9]

2526	hungry
饿	Food . . . miser. [10]

2527	irrigate
溉	Water . . . since. [12]

2528	incensed
慨	State of mind . . . since. Be sure you put the accent of the key word on the second syllable. [12]

LESSON 38

2529 苹	apple *Flowers . . . water lily.* [8]
2530 萍	duckweed *Apple . . . water.* The small aquatic plant known as **duckweed** gets its name from the fact that it is a culinary delicacy for ducks, who are known to bob for it at Halloween parties. [11] 艹　氵　萍
2531 秤	scale (N.) The sense of the key word is a **scale** for weighing. The elements: *wild rice . . . water lily.* Do not confuse with the primitive of the same name. [10]
2532 淆	confuse *Water . . . sheaf . . . possess.* [11]
2533 艾	Chinese mugwort Beneath the *flowers* at the top, we see a *sheaf*, giving us a **Chinese mugwort**, one of the herbs used in the heat therapy known as moxibustion. [5]
2534 哎	Good grief! *Mouth . . . Chinese mugwort.* [8]
2535 赵	Zhao *Walk . . . sheaf.* The key word is a common surname. [9]
2536 攀	climb (V.) *Woods* with two *sheaves . . . St. Bernard dog . . . hand.* [19]

木　杴　梺　樊　攀

2537 刹	brake ^(v.) *Kill . . . saber.* [8]
2538 枫	maple *Tree . . . windstorm.* [8]
2539 钢	steel *Metal . . . ridge of a hill.* [9]
2540 岗	hillock *Mountain . . . ridge of a hill.* [7]
2541 纲	guidelines *Thread . . . ridge of a hill.* [7]

2542

屯　　　　　　　　　　　　stockpile ^(v.)

One . . . pit . . . fishhook. [4]

一　　凵　　屯

❖ The primitive meaning of this character is *earthworm*, which is more colorful than the key word. If you think of trying to *stockpile* a shipment of *earthworms*, you should have all you need.

2543 吨	ton *Mouth . . . earthworm.* [7]
2544 顿	pause ^(N./V.) *Earthworm . . . head.* [10]

2545 纯	unadulterated
	Thread . . . earthworm. Be sure to keep this key word distinct from the character for *unmixed* (FRAME 2398); both words carry the sense of "pure." [7]

2546 齿	teeth
	Footprint . . . person . . . pit. [8]

2547 龄	length of service
	This key word can refer to things like one's **length of service** in the military and to the time a ship has been in use. Its elements: *teeth . . . orders.* [13]

2548 汹	turbulent
	The meaning of this character can be literal or metaphorical. The elements are: *water . . . cruel.* [7]

2549 篱	fence
	Bamboo . . . leave. [16]

2550 仪	rite
	Person . . . righteousness. Take care not to confuse this key word with *ceremony* (FRAME 902), which has a similar meaning. [5]

2551 辜	crime
	Ancient . . . chili pepper. [12]

2552 辞	phraseology
	Tongue . . . chili pepper. [13]

2553 宰	butcher (v.)
	House . . . chili pepper. This key word means to slaughter or dress animals and also to fleece unsuspecting customers. [10]

2554	differentiate
辨	Two *chili peppers* . . . *saber*. [16]

辛　剃　辨

2555	braid [N.]
辫	Two *chili peppers* . . . *thread*. [17]

2556	arm [N.]
臂	*Hot sauce* . . . *flesh*. [17]

2557	split [V.]
劈	*Hot sauce* . . . *dagger*. [15]

2558	analogy
譬	*Hot sauce* . . . *words*. [20]

2559	out-of-the-way
僻	Picture whoever it is you chose to represent the primitive for *person* as having been secluded to an **out-of-the-way** place. As it turns out, she had been going too heavy on the *hot sauce* and the results had led to unpleasant odors coming from both ends that did not go down well in good company. [15]

2560	entangle
纠	*Thread* . . . *cornucopia*. [5]

2561	cough [V.]
咳	*Mouth* . . . *acorn*. [9]

2562	cry out
嚷	*Mouth* . . . *pigeon coop*. [20]

2563		inlay [v.]
镶	*Metal . . . pigeon coop.* [22]	
2564		stronghold
塞	*Hamster cage . . . soil.* [13]	
2565		stockade
寨	*Hamster cage . . . pole.* [14]	

LESSON 39

2566 晴	sunny *Sun . . . telescope/blue or green.* [12]
2567 猜	guess (v.) *Pack of wild dogs . . . telescope.* [11]
2568 靖	pacify *Vase . . . telescope.* [13]
2569 债	debt *Person . . . responsibility.* [10]
2570 牲	domestic animal *Cow . . . cell.* [9]
2571 隆	impressive *Pinnacle . . . walking legs . . . ceiling . . . cell.* [11]
2572 腥	fishy smell *Flesh . . . star.* [13]
2573 猩	orangutan *Pack of wild dogs . . . star.* [12]
2574 醒	awaken *Whiskey bottle . . . star.* [16]
2575 寿	longevity *Bushes . . . glue. Note how the final stroke of bushes slants to the left to make room for the glue.* [7]

❖ The meaning of the character will change to a *long, gray beard* when it is used as a primitive element.

2576	farmland
畴	*Rice field . . . long, gray beard.* [12]

2577	large waves
涛	*Water . . . long, gray beard.* [10]

2578	cast [v.]
铸	Aside from giving it a shape, another reason to **cast** *metal* is to give it a longer life. In this case, the proof lies in the *long, gray beard* a particular piece of *metal* is sporting. [12]

2579	pray
祷	*Altar . . . long, gray beard.* [11]

2580	make arrangements
筹	*Bamboo . . . long, gray beard.* [13]

2581	contract [N.]
契	*Bushes . . . sword . . . St. Bernard dog.* [9]

2582	adore
拜	*Hand . . . ceiling . . . bushes.* [9]

❖	briar
夆	Think here of the hordes of would-be princes who perished on the **briar** *bushes*—or at least ended up with bloody *walking legs*—trying to make their way to Sleeping Beauty. The image of the sharply pointed **briars** will serve you well in the characters that follow. [7]

夂 夅 夆

2583 锋	**cutting edge**
	Metal . . . briar. This character can be used for the sharp point of an implement or for its finely honed **cutting edge**. [12]

2584 逢	**chance upon**
	Briar . . . road. [10]

2585 缝	**sew**
	Thread . . . chance upon. [13]

2586 蓬	**disheveled**
	If it is true that the rain falls on the good and the wicked alike without discrimination, the same can be said of *flowers* blowing about in the spring breeze: they *chance upon* all heads equally, the sheveled and the **disheveled** alike. Another reason not to worry about whether your hair is combed or not. [13]

2587 篷	**awning**
	Bamboo . . . chance upon. [16]

2588 蜂	**bee**
	Insect . . . briar. [13]

2589 峰	**peak** [N.]
	Mountain . . . briar. [10]

2590 瞎	**visionless**
	We chose this key word to keep the character distinct from the normal word for *blind* (FRAME 491). Its elements are: *eyeballs . . . harm.* [15]

2591 辖	**administer**
	To **administer** something means to be in control of it. The difficulties begin when one is trying to **administer** more than one thing at the same time. For example, if you are doing your busi-

ness on a cellphone while driving your *car*, you are sure to end up doing *harm* to both tasks. [14]

2592	breach [N.]
豁	*Harm . . . valley.* [17]

2593	Korea
韩	*Mist . . . briar patch.* [12]

2594	disobey
违	*Briar patch . . . road.* [7]

2595	latitude
纬	*Thread . . . briar patch.* The **latitude** this key word refers to is the opposite of longitude. [7]

2596	play an instrument
奏	*Bonsai . . . heavens.* [9]

2597	gather together
凑	This key word can be used when people **gather together** as well as when people **gather together** things. The elements: *ice . . . play an instrument.* [11]

2598	Qin
秦	*Bonzai . . . wild rice.* **Qin** Shi Huang was the founder and first emperor of the **Qin** Dynasty. He undertook huge projects (the Great Wall, the Terra-Cotta Warriors, etc.) at the expense of many lives. Take care not to confuse this character with the one we learned just above in FRAME 2596. [10]

2599	foolish
蠢	*Springtime . . . two insects.* [21]

❖ 圣	scarecrow
	The *crotch* and *cornstalk* combine to give us a **scarecrow**. [5]
	又　圣

2600 泽	swamp [N.]
	Water . . . scarecrow. [8]

2601 译	translate
	Words . . . scarecrow. [7]

2602 择	select [V.]
	Fingers . . . scarecrow. [8]

2603 捧	carry in both hands
	Fingers . . . proffer. [11]

2604 砖	brick
	Stone . . . corncob pipe. Be sure to make an image that keeps this key word distinct from the primitive of the same meaning. [9]

2605 唾	saliva
	Mouth . . . droop. [11]

LESSON 40

2606	recite
吟	As we have already learned characters for *poem* (FRAME 355) and *song* (FRAME 476), it is important to give this key word an image all its own. Its elements are the same as those in FRAME 1245; only their position has changed: *mouth . . . clock*. [7]

2607	greedy
贪	*Clock . . . shells.* [8]

2608	stringed instrument
琴	A pair of *jewels . . . clock*. [12]

2609	refine
炼	You **refine** things when you submit them to *fire*. This applies to a range of things from metals to milk (when you pasteurize it). Here you are trying the process out on an old *covered rickshaw*, hoping that the *fire* will perform some alchemical magic and transmute your *rickshaw* into a miniature figurine of pure gold. At least it's worth a try.... [9]

2610	bask
晒	*Sun . . . Old West.* [10]

2611	spill ^(v.)
洒	*Water . . . Old West.* [9]

2612	perch ^(v.)
栖	*Tree . . . Old West.* [10]

2613	chestnut
栗	*Old West . . . tree.* Be sure to keep the character in this frame distinct from that of the previous frame—the primitive elements are the same! [10]

2614	sacrifice (v.)
牺	Like the character in FRAME 910, this one can be used for *animal sacrifices,* but it can also mean to **sacrifice** something for the sake of something else of higher value. Its elements: *cow . . . Old West.* [10]

2615	deep pool
潭	The *Old West* and *sunflower* paint for us a picture of a lonesome cowboy roaming aimlessly and daydreaming of his Daisy Belle as he plucks the petals off a *sunflower.* "She loves me, she loves me not. She loves me..." Little does he notice the *water* gathering at his feet as he stumbles and falls into a **deep pool.**

Be careful to keep the right side of this character distinct from the character for "ticket" (FRAME 1256). [15] |

2616	overturn
覆	*Old West . . . queue . . . double back.* Be sure to take this key word in its literal sense of turning something over or upsetting it. [18]

2617	flutter (v.)
飘	*Ticket . . . windstorm.* [15]

2618	donate
献	*South . . . chihuahua.* [13]

LESSON 41

2619 阔	broad *Gate . . . lively.* [12]
2620 润	moisten *Water . . . gate . . . jewel.* [10]
2621 阁	cabinet The key word here refers to a government **cabinet**. Its elements: *gate . . . each.* [9]
2622 搁	put aside *Fingers . . . cabinet.* [12]
2623 闹	stir up trouble *Gate . . . market.* [8]
2624 阅	peruse *Gate . . . devil.* [10]
2625 闷	stuffy Take the key word in its literal sense of insufficiently ventilated or hard-to-breathe air. The primitives: *gate . . . heart.* [7]
2626 闭	close (v.) *Gate . . . genie.* [6]
2627 闪	flash (v.) *Gate . . . person.* [5]

2628		valve
阀	*Gate . . . fell.* [9]	

2629		floodgate
闸	*Gate . . . radish.* [8]	

2630		explicate
阐	*Gate . . . list.* [11]	

2631		ravine
涧	*Water . . . interval.* [10]	

2632		humble (ADJ.)
菲	*Flowers . . . jail cell.* [11]	

2633		lifetime
辈	*Jail cell . . . car.* [12]	

2634		sad
悲	*Jail cell . . . heart.* [12]	

2635		irresolute
徘	*Queue . . . jail cell.* [11]	

2636		gullet
喉	*Mouth . . . marquis.* [12]	

2637		monkey
猴	*Pack of wild dogs . . . marquis.* [12]	

2638 肝	liver
	Flesh . . . clothesline. [7]

2639 刊	publication
	This character refers to the finished product, not to the process of preparing it. Its elements: *clothesline . . . saber.* [5]

2640 奸	adultery
	Woman . . . clothesline. [6]

2641 汗	sweat ^(N.)
	Water . . . clothesline. [6]

2642 杆	shaft
	The *dry tree* is a special botanical wonder, found only in a certain region within the deserts of central Australia (we are sworn to secrecy on the precise location), so named because it is able to survive the periodic droughts that claim all other vegetation. The locals have discovered that if they carve a long **shaft** from the *tree,* it will lead them to underground wells. [7]

2643 轩	veranda
	Car . . . clothesline. [7]

2644 罕	rarely
	Paper punch . . . clothesline. [7]

2645 竿	pole
	Bamboo . . . clothesline. [9]

2646		bold
悍	*State of mind . . . drought.* [10]	

2647		plead
吁	*Mouth . . . clothing conveyor.* [6]	

2648		smear (v.)
涂	*Water . . . scale.* [10]	

2649		recount (v.)
叙	*Scale . . . crotch.* The meaning of the key word is to narrate or give an account. [9]	

2650		slowly
徐	*Queue . . . scale.* [10]	

2651		slanting
斜	*Scale . . . Big Dipper.* [11]	

2652		flared horn
喇	*Mouth . . . bundle . . . saber.* [12]	

2653		hack (v.)
嗽	The key word here refers to the way people cough who have been smoking so long their lungs never quite seem to clear. It has nothing to do with cutting things up or breaking into computer systems. Its elements: *mouth . . . bundle . . . yawn.* [14]	

2654		rely on
赖	*Bundle . . . defeated.* [13]	

2655		lazy
懒	*State of mind . . . rely on.* [16]	

2656	tender [ADJ.]
嫩	*Woman . . . bundle . . . taskmaster.* [14]
2657	director
董	*Flowers . . . heavy.* [12]

LESSON 43

2658 疗	cure (v.) *Sickness . . . -ed.* [7]
2659 痰	phlegm *Sickness . . . inflammation.* [13]
2660 症	disease *Sickness . . . correct.* [10]
2661 疼	hurt (v.) *Sickness . . . winter.* [10]
2662 痒	itch (v.) *Sickness . . . sheep.* [11]
2663 瘫	paralysis *Sickness . . . difficult.* [15]
2664 疫	epidemic *Sickness . . . missile.* [9]
2665 癌	cancer *Sickness . . . goods . . . mountain.* [17]
2666 疲	fatigued *Sickness . . . covering.* [10]
2667 痴	idiotic *Sickness . . . know.* [13]

2668 瘤	tumor
	Sickness . . . stay. [15]

2669 疮	sore (N.)
	Sickness . . . storehouse. [9]

2670 疾	rapid
	Be sure to keep this character distinct from *quick* (FRAME 1289). Picture a succession of poison *darts* (the sort that inflict *sickness*) flying out **rapid**-fire from a blowgun, so that "**rapid**-fire" can conjure up the proper image. [10]

2671 瘾	addiction
	Sickness . . . hidden. [16]

2672 痕	trace (N.)
	Sickness . . . silver. [11]

2673 汇	converge
	Water . . . box. [5]

2674 框	rectangular frame
	Tree . . . box . . . jewel. This character can be used in words referring to the **rectangular frames** around pictures, windows, doors, and the like. [10]

2675 筐	rectangular basket
	Bamboo . . . box . . . king. Nowadays this character can be used for baskets of various shapes, but formerly it was associated with **rectangular baskets** woven of bamboo strips. [12]

竹　竺　筐　筐

2676	smash [v.]
砸	Stone . . . box . . . towel. [10]

2677	artisan
匠	Box . . . tomahawk. [6]

2678	bandit
匪	Box . . . jail cell. [10]

2679	keep out of sight
匿	Box . . . Disneyland. [10]

2680	pocket
兜	This character is composed of a *dove* flapping about between two facing *boxes*, and a pair of *human legs*. [11]

白   泊   泊ク   兜

2681	gigantic
巨	If you look at this character ignoring the order in which its strokes are written, you see a *box* with another *box* turned around and placed inside of it. In the fierce competition to hold the Guinness World Record for the world's largest *box*, someone has put the previous record holder's *box* inside a *box* so **gigantic** that it takes up an entire city block. [4]

一   큭   彐   巨

    ❖ In line with the key word, this character will mean a *giant* when used as a primitive. Some fairy-tale *giant* you remember from your childhood, like the one in "Jack and the Beanstalk," should do nicely.

2682	cupboard
柜	Tree . . . giant. [8]

2683 渠	canal
	Water . . . giant . . . tree. [11]

2684 拒	refuse [v.]
	Fingers . . . giant. [7]

2685 矩	square [N.]
	Dart . . . giant. [9]

2686 距	distance
	Wooden leg . . . giant. [11]

2687 殴	hit [v.]
	Region . . . missile. [8]

2688 呕	vomit [v.]
	Mouth . . . region. [7]

2689 躯	human body
	Somebody . . . region. [11]

2690 昂	hold one's head high
	Sun . . . stamp collection. [8]

2691 抑	curb [v.]
	The sense of the key word is to restrain, as in "to **curb** one's emotions." The elements: *fingers . . . stamp collection.* [7]

2692 葵	large-flowered plants
	Flowers . . . teepee . . . heavens. [12]

❖ 登	{1301}	stepladder

The character for *ascend* learned in Book 1 will serve us here as a primitive element with the meaning of a **stepladder**. [12]

2693 瞪	glare [v.]

Eyeball . . . stepladder. [17]

2694 凳	bench

Stepladder . . . small table. [14]

2695 澄	transparent

Water . . . stepladder. [15]

❖ 尞	pup tent

The *St. Bernard dog* and its overlap with the element for *teepee* suggest the meaning of this primitive element: a **pup tent**. The combination of *sun* and *small* at the bottom can be seen as a little opening or flap through which the *sun* shines in the morning to let you know it's time to get up. [12]

大　大　尤　杏　尞

2696 僚	coworker

Person . . . pup tent. [14]

2697 拨	allocate

Fingers . . . courier. [8]

2698 泼	splash [v.]

Water . . . courier. [8]

❖ 友	seeing-eye chihuahua

The combination of the elements for a *chihuahua* and *friend* combine to give us the **seeing-eye chihuahua**. The only thing you have to watch out for is the stroke order. Take care not to confuse with the primitive for *courier* which appears in the previous two frames. If it helps, the profession of a **seeing-eye chihuahua** is often one taken up by aging *couriers* who cannot fetch and carry things very well any more, but are not content to just collect their pensions and live off society. Hence the absence of the first half-stroke (see FRAME 1302). [5]

友 友

2699	pull out
拔	*Fingers . . . seeing-eye chihuahua.* [8]

2700	fir tree
杉	*Tree . . . rooster tail.* [7]

2701	well-mannered
彬	*Tree . . . fir tree.* Make sure your image of this character's key word is kept distinct from the one you have for *well-behaved* (FRAME 1705). [11]

2702	shirt
衫	*Cloak . . . rooster tail.* [8]

2703	manifest (ADJ.)
彰	*Chapter . . . rooster tail.* [14]

2704	puffy
膨	*Flesh . . . drum . . . rooster tail.* As is obvious from the primitive on the left, this character refers to the condition of being bloated or swollen, not to being pompous or running short of breath. [16]

2705	seep
渗	*Water . . . brawl.* [11]

2706	diagnose
诊	*Words . . . cocktail.* This key word should be taken in its medical sense. [7]

2707	take advantage of
趁	You **take advantage of** the fine weather by leaving the bar and taking your daily *cocktail* for a *walk*. [12]

❖	kiddie cocktail
翏	Instead of the cutesy umbrella that usually comes with your Shirley Temple, this **kiddie cocktail** sports a not-so-cutesy pair of mechanical flapping *wings*, which splatter the contents of the *cocktail* over everyone—to the great delight of the **kiddies**. [11]

羽羽   翏

2708	deserted
寥	House . . . kiddie cocktail. [14]

2709	wrong (ADJ.)
谬	Words . . . kiddie cocktail. [13]

2710	small shovel
铲	Metal . . . products. [11]

2711	Samoa
萨	This character is used phonetically in many names, including that for the country of **Samoa**, for which it provides the first character. Its elements: *flowers . . . pinnacle . . . products.* [11]

2712	Liu
刘	Highlander . . . saber. [6]

2713	tomb
坟	Soil . . . Highlander. [7]

2714	design (N.)
纹	Thread . . . Highlander. The sense of the key word is a pattern, like the kind you might find on your dinnerware. [7]

2715	abstain from food
斋	Highlander . . . comb. [10]

2716	speck

斑 *Highlander* between two *balls*. [12]

王　玨　斑

2717	pharmaceutical [N.]

剂 When you think of the key word **pharmaceutical**, you think of chemical compounds used as medicines (though the key word is broader in scope). In China, as in the West, one of the oldest principles behind the mixtures was "homeopathy," that is, the idea that the medication should produce symptoms that are *identical* to those of the malady, or at least as similar to them as possible. This includes medicines in all forms and chemical agents and mixtures of many kinds. All you need do is imagine the pharmacist cutting up his herbs with a long shining *saber* and you have the complete picture for a **pharmaceutical**. [8]

2718	squeeze [V.]

挤 *Fingers . . . identical.* [9]

2719	backbone

脊 *Person . . . sparkler . . . flesh.* [10]

2720	letter

函 The key word for this character refers to **letters** sent in correspondence, not to the symbols of the alphabet. Its elements: *-ed . . . sparkler . . . pit.* [8]

⁀　了　函

2721	culvert

涵 *Water . . . letter.* [11]

2722 映	reflect
	Sun . . . center. The key word refers to what mirrors and shiny objects do, not to any contemplative activity. [9]

2723 殃	calamity
	Bones . . . center. [9]

2724 秧	youngling
	Wild rice . . . center. [10]

2725 焕	glowing
	Fire . . . Victorian lady. [11]

2726 肥	plump
	Flesh . . . mosaic. [8]

2727 爬	crawl (v.)
	Claw . . . mosaic. [8]

2728 疤	scar (N.)
	Sickness . . . mosaic. [9]

LESSON 45

2729 甜	sugary
	The *tongue* that speaks *sweet* words is typical of the many things in life that can be described as **sugary**. As long as you stick to the positive connotations of the term, even your special sweetie qualifies. Note that here we have reverted to the key word meaning of the element 甘. From the following frame, we will revert to its primitive meaning. [11]

2730 嵌	set (v.)
	Mountain . . . wicker basket . . . yawn. [12]

2731 钳	pliers
	Metal . . . wicker basket. [10]

2732 媒	matchmaker
	Woman . . . such and such. [12]

2733 煤	coal
	Fire . . . such and such. [13]

2734 谋	scheme (v.)
	Words . . . such and such. [11]

2735 棋	chess
	Tree . . . hamper. [12]

2736 欺	dupe
	Hamper . . . yawn. [12]

2737 旗	flag (N.)
	Banner . . . hamper. Be sure you create an image of a **flag** as different as possible from the one you use for the primitive element of the same meaning. [14]

2738 嘶	hoarse
	Mouth . . . Sphinx. [15]

2739 撕	rip (V.)
	Fingers . . . Sphinx. [15]

❖ 其	{1338} Hercules
	The abstract key word *tremendously* does not suggest a consistent image. We will therefore replace it with the figure of Hercules, remembered for his *tremendously* arduous tasks. [9]

2740 堪	tolerate
	Soil . . . Hercules. [12]

2741 勘	survey (V.)
	Hercules . . . muscle. [11]

2742 遣	dispatch (V.)
	Purse . . . maestro . . . road. Remember to draw the element for *road* in *dispatch* last. [13]

2743 谴	censure (V.)
	Words . . . dispatch. [15]

2744 囊	sack (N.)
	This character is exactly the same as the primitive for *pigeon coop*, except that a *purse* and a *crown* are tucked inside of the *top hat*. Pay attention to the opening stroke order and you will see how the fourth stroke of the *purse* is also used in draw-

ing the *top hat,* and the last stroke doubles up with the second stroke of the *crown.* [22]

一　　　二　　　丰　　　声　　　囊

2745　　　　　　　　　　　　　　　　　　　　　　　　burst [v.]

溃　　*Water . . . expensive.* [12]

LESSON 46

2746 宜	**fitting** (ADJ.) Take this key word in its sense of suitable or appropriate. The elements are: *house . . . shelves.* [8]
2747 谊	**friendship** *Words . . . fitting.* [10]
2748 租	**rent** (N./V.) *Wild rice . . . shelves.* [10]
2749 粗	**coarse** *Rice . . . shelves* [11]
2750 阻	**block** (V.) *Pinnacle . . . shelves.* [7]
2751 桑	**mulberry tree** *Crotches everywhere . . . tree.* [10]
2752 嗓	**voicebox** *Mouth . . . mulberry tree.* [13]
2753 叠	**heap** (V.) *Crotches, chrotches everywhere . . . crown . . . shelves.* [13]
2754 锄	**hoe** (N./V.) *Metal . . . assist.* [12]
2755 碰	**bump** (V.) *Person . . . side by side.* [13]

2756	musical score
谱	*Words . . . universal.* [13]

2757	kettle
壶	*Soldier . . . crown . . . profession.* [10]

2758	bore a hole
凿	The element for *profession* at the top and for *pit* at the bottom will be familiar to you. The remaining five-stroke form standing in the middle that looks like *animal horns* on a *clothesline* is probably easier to remember as the currency symbol for the Chinese yuan: ¥). Incidentally, you have seen this final shape before where it was part of a larger primitive (FRAMES 1259 and 2618). [12]

2759	wet
湿	*Water . . . sun . . . profession.* [12]

2760	mute (ADJ.)
哑	*Mouth . . . Asia.* [9]

2761	promote
晋	*Asia . . . sun.* Take care not to confuse this character with the one for *universal* (FRAME 1348). [10]

2762	fool (V.)
哄	*Mouth . . . together.* [9]

2763	deluge
洪	Think of the **deluge** here as a great flood, not as a heavy downpour. The elements: *water . . . together.* [9]

2764	warm by a fire
烘	*Fire . . . together.* [10]

2765 戴	have on
	Chinese distinguishes between major items of clothing, which people "wear" and accessories like glasses, hats, and bracelets, which they **have on**. *Thanksgiving . . . brains . . . together.* [17]

2766 翼	wings
	Wings . . . brains . . . together. This is the character from which we derived the primitive of the same meaning. [17]

2767 恭	respectful
	Together . . . valentine. [10]

2768 拱	arch (N./V.)
	Fingers . . . together. [9]

2769 撰	compose
	Think here of what you do when you **compose** a term paper. The primitives are: *fingers . . .* two *snakeskins . . . together.* [15]

2770 糞	dung
	Rice . . . together. [12]

2771 殿	ceremonial hall
	Flag . . . together . . . missile. [13]

2772 暴	violent
	Sun . . . together . . . snowflakes. [15] 曰　異　暴

2773 瀑	waterfall
	Water . . . violent. [18]

2774		explode
爆	*Fire . . . violent.* [19]	

2775	hug ^(v.)
拥	*Fingers . . . rack/utilize.* [8]

2776	put to work
佣	*Person . . . rack.* [7]

2777	fling ^(v.)
甩	Think of this character as a *rack* of "tails" of various beasts. [5]

2778	mediocre
庸	*Cave . . . rake . . . rack.* The only thing you have to watch out for here is the handle of the *rake*, which is drawn last. [11]

庐 庐 庐 庸

2779	touch ^(v.)
触	*Safe . . . insect.* The sense of this key word is to bring the skin into contact with something, in this case an office *safe*. [13]

2780	crab ^(N.)
蟹	*Untie . . . insect.* [19]

2781	lax
懈	People are said to be **lax** when they are negligent of their duties. The character suggests that they are in a *state of mind* that has *untied* itself from the real world. [16]

2782	Vol.
册	This character is similar to the primitive for *tome* learned in Book 1 (page 344), but the drawing is quite different. [5]

刀　刀刀　刑刑

2783	delete
删	*Vol. . . . saber.* [7]

2784	palisade
栅	Here we have a very special **Palisade** Park. Now a **palisade** fence is usually made of stakes driven into the ground, but here it is made of *trees* lined up and joined to one another by *Vols.* of an encyclopedia spread open and attached to a trunk on each side. That way, when people stop for a rest on their walk through **Palisade** Park, they can not only enjoy the shade of the *tree* but further their education at the same time. [9]

2785	coral
珊	*Jewel . . . Vol.* [9]

2786	everywhere
遍	*Book cover . . . road.* [12]

2787	partial
偏	*Person . . . book cover.* The sense of the key word is that of having a bias or preference for someone or something. [11]

LESSON 48

| 2788 抵 | resist |
| Fingers . . . calling card. [8] | |

| 2789 氓 | hoodlum |
| Perish . . . people. [8] | |

| 2790 哺 | breastfeed |
| Mouth . . . dog tag. [10] | |

| 2791 浦 | river mouth |
| Water . . . dog tag. [10] | |

| 2792 蒲 | cattail |
| Conveniently, **cattails** are found in the wetlands and around *river mouths*. Think of the furry *flowers* of the **cattails** as belonging to actual cats submerged under the water, and watch what happens when you try to pull one up! [13] | |

| 2793 薄 | slight ^(ADJ.) |
| The character for **slight** needs an image of something thin and frail: like a *cattail glued to* the hindquarters of your pet Siamese, who lost hers in an alley brawl. [16] | |

| 2794 铺 | shop ^(N.) |
| Metal . . . dog tag. [12] | |

| 2795 捕 | capture |
| Fingers . . . dog tag. [10] | |

2796 敷	apply
	Dog tag . . . release. This key word refers to what you do when you slap on powders, ointments, and other things. Also, step back to FRAME 1732 to remind yourself of how the left half of the element for *release* gets compressed. [15]

2797 膊	shoulder to wrist
	Flesh . . . gummed label. [14]

2798 傅	mentor
	Person . . . gummed label. [12]

2799 缚	bind fast
	Thread . . . gummed label. [13]

2800 簿	register [N.]
	Bamboo . . . water . . . gummed label. [19]

2801 郁	depressed
	Possess . . . city walls. [8]

2802 郭	outer walls
	Enjoy . . . city walls. This is the character on which the primitive meaning *city walls* is based. [10]

2803 廓	limitless
	Cave . . . outer walls. [13]

2804 邓	Deng
	Crotch/right hand . . . city walls. This key word is the family name of **Deng** Xiaoping, a famous leader of the Chinese Communist Party. Known as the architect of "socialism with Chinese characteristics," he led China into what is called a "socialist market economy." [4]

2805	despicable
鄙	*Mouth . . . needle . . . return . . . city walls.* [13]

2806	Jerusalem
耶	Once again, we beg your leave to introduce a key word that draws on the largely phonetic value of a character. In this case, it is the first of four characters used in the transliteration for the city **Jerusalem**. Its elements are *ear . . . city walls*. [8]

2807	post^(v.)
邮	*Sprout . . . city walls.* The key word connotes what you do when you drop a letter into the mailbox. [7]

2808	nation
邦	The *bushes* that appear on the left here are bent because they were planted too close to the *city walls* and cannot grow naturally. All in all, not a bad metaphor for what happens to a **nation** when it closes itself in against the outside world as if it were a fortress that needed guarding. If the *city walls* were torn down, not only would the *bushes* grow straight, the people inside would be able to enjoy them.
	You will remember this combination of primitives from FRAME 1386. We could have placed this character two frames up. Surely you will find it in your heart to forgive this peccadillo on our part. [6]

2809	truss^(v.)
绑	*Thread . . . nation.* [9]

2810	outskirts
郊	*Mingle . . . city walls.* The key word refers to the area outlying a major city, both suburbs as well as the countryside. [8]

2811	neighbor
邻	*Orders . . . city walls.* [7]

2812		hallway
廊	Cave . . . young man. [11]	

2813	satin
缎	*Thread . . . section.* [12]

2814	wily
刁	The elements, in the order of writing, are: *clothes hanger . . . drop of.* Note that the *drop* is drawn lower-left to upper-right, much like the second stroke in the primitive for "ice." [2]

2815	hold in the mouth
叼	*Mouth . . . wily.* [5]

2816	calcium
钙	*Metal . . . correct . . . clothes hanger.* Observe how the final stroke of *correct* runs on to the element for *clothes hanger.* [10]

2817	ardent
殷	*Drag . . . white . . . clothes hanger . . . missile.* As unfamiliar as the left side of this character looks, if you draw it in the order of the primitives, it is really quite simple. [10]

丿　尸　身　殷

2818	attend to
伺	*Person . . . take charge of.* The key word connotes to serve or wait upon, not to pay attention to. [7]

2819	rear (v.)
饲	*Food . . . take charge of.* The key word refers to what you do when you raise animals. [8]

2820	liner
舶	The type of *boat* connoted by this key word is a large ocean-going **liner**. Work with the elements *boat* and *dove* to make a distinct image from other kinds of boats and ships. [11]

2821	warship
舰	*Boat . . . see.* [10]

2822	navigate
航	*Boat . . . whirlwind.* [10]

2823	rudder
舵	*Boat . . . it.* [11]

2824	ship's cabin
舱	*Boat . . . storehouse.* [10]

2825	light boat
艇	*Boat . . . royal court.* [12]

2826	along (PREP.)
沿	*Water . . . belch.* The key word is used in phrases such as "**along** the beach." [8]

2827	lead (N.)
铅	*Metal . . . belch* [10]

2828	fox
狐	*Pack of wild dogs . . . melon.* [8]

2829	petal
瓣	Two *chili peppers . . . melon.* [19]
	辛 瓜 瓣

2830 溢	**brim over**
	Water . . . benefit. Avoid using the image you had for *overflow* (FRAME 725), although the meaning is basically the same. [13]
2831 隘	**pass** (N.)
	Pinnacle . . . benefit. [12]
2832 霞	**red sky**
	As that bit of folk wisdom about the *weather* goes, "**Red sky** at night—sailor's delight; **red sky** in the morning—sailor's warning." What about the day? Just because no one has ever seen a **red sky** in the daytime is no reason not to have a proverb about it. We'll get you started and you can finish it as you wish: "**Red sky** in the day—your *braces*... [17]
2833 氨	**ammonia**
	Air . . . peaceful. [10]
2834 氧	**oxygen**
	Air . . . sheep. [10]
2835 氛	**atmosphere**
	Air . . . part. [8]
2836 氢	**hydrogen**
	Air . . . spool. [9]
2837 氯	**chlorine**
	Air . . . snowman. [12]

2838		tyrant
霸	Rain . . . leather . . . flesh. [21]	
2839		boots
靴	Leather . . . transform. [13]	
2840		whip (N./V.)
鞭	Leather . . . convenient. [18]	
2841		bow respectfully
鞠	Leather . . . bound up . . . rice. [17]	

2842 芽	sprout (N.)
	Flowers . . . tusk. Be careful not to confuse this character with the primitive of the same meaning we learned in Book 1. [7]

2843 讶	surprised
	Words . . . tusk. [6]

2844 雅	polished
	The key word **polished** describes persons who are cultured or sophisticated. The elements: *tusk . . . turkey.* [12]

2845 邪	wicked
	Tusk . . . city walls. [6]

2846 悉	be informed
	Droppings . . . heart. [11]

2847 毯	blanket (N.)
	Fur . . . inflammation. [12]

2848 毫	milli-
	Tiara . . . fur. This character figures in words like **millimeter**, **milligram**, and **millisecond**. [11]

❖ 耒	Christmas tree
	The first stroke of this character, the *ceiling*, cuts into the element for *not yet* because the **Christmas tree** you brought home to decorate turned out to be too large for the living room and was *not yet* ready to be decorated. So you cut a hole in the *ceiling* and let the top protrude out of the floor of the upstairs

bedroom. Too bad the angel won't be able to look down on the lights and tinsel this year. [6]

一 耒

2849	consume
耗	*Christmas tree . . . fur.* [10]

2850	till (v.)
耕	*Christmas tree . . . well.* [10]

2851	records
籍	*Bamboo . . . Christmas tree . . . times past.* The key word refers to official documents or registries. [20]

2852	in disorder
藉	*Flowers . . . Christmas tree . . . times past.* [17]

2853	be afraid of
畏	*Brains . . . barrette.* [9]

2854	Hello...
喂	*Mouth . . . be afraid of.* For reasons we can only imagine, Chinese has combined these elements into the word one uses in answering the telephone. [12]

2855	bloated
胀	*Flesh . . . long.* [9]

2856	tent
帐	*Towel . . . long.* [8]

LESSON 52

2857 誉	**reputation**
	Excitement . . . words. [13]
2858 剑	**saber**
	Hootenanny . . . saber. This is the character from which the primitive of the same name was derived in Book 1. [9]
2859 敛	**restrain**
	Hootenanny . . . taskmaster. [11]
2860 捡	**pick up** (v.)
	Fingers . . . hootenanny. The character means to **pick up** small objects with one's *fingers.* [10]
2861 俭	**thrifty**
	Person . . . hootenanny. [9]
2862 签	**sign** (v.)
	To qualify for the annual *hootenanny* competition in Shandong, West Virginia, contestants must first shimmy up a twelve-foot stalk of *bamboo*, brush in mouth, to **sign** their names on a ledger at the top. [13]
2863 鹏	**roc**
	The **roc**, the mythical *bird* of prey so large that it could destroy the ship of Sinbad the Sailor, only wreaks destruction because it cannot find a suitable *companion*. Where are the bird psychologists when you need them? [13]

2864	twitter [v.]
鸣	*Mouth . . . bird.* As the elements make obvious, this character literally means to make *bird* sounds. [8]

2865	swan
鸿	*Yangtze . . . bird.* [11]

2866	oriole
莺	*Greenhouse . . . bird.* [10]

2867	pigeon
鸽	*Fit . . . bird.* [11]

2868	crane
鹤	The element on the right is, of course, the *bird*. But take care with the one on the left. It has the "chimney" on the *house* doubled up with the first stroke of the *turkey*. You might think of this as a *turkey house* (or *turkey pen*). Now the **crane** is distinguished from the rest of the *birds* in the *turkey house* because it is the one that is always "craning" its neck out the top and looking around to tell the short-necked fowl what is going on elsewhere in the barnyard. [15]

2869	magpie
鹊	*Times past . . . bird.* [13]

2870	gull
鸥	*Region . . . bird.* [9]

2871	goose
鹅	As it turns out, this character is the "fowl" half of the compound for Mother **Goose**. Its primitive elements: *miser . . . bird.* [12]

2872	raven
鸦	*Tusk . . . bird.* Scientific classifications aside, in ordinary usage the difference between the **raven** and the *crow* in the next frame is that the former tends to sound more literary. [9]

2873	crow
乌	The only difference between this character and that for "bird" is that the third stroke, the little *drop* we identified as the beak, is missing. Clearly this **crow** doesn't have anything to "crow" about.[4]

2874	zoom-zoom
呜	Of all the different sounds this character can represent ono-matopoeically, we have chosen that of an automobile racing past. Or maybe a turbo-powered, road-running *crow*. (Since it doesn't have a beak, we leave it to you to decide where the *mouth* is.) [7]

2875	pound with a pestle
捣	You usually **pound with a pestle** to mix herbs into a medicine, but here your *fingers* are clasped around a gigantic **pestle** with which you **pound** and grind a more challenging concoction: an entire *island*. [10]

扌　扌　扌ʼ　扩　捣　捣

2876	residence
寓	*House . . . Talking Cricket.* [12]

2877	pea-brained
愚	*Talking Cricket . . . heart.* [13]

2878	by chance
偶	*Person . . . Talking Cricket.* [11]

2879	vat
缸	*Tin can . . . I-beam.* [9]

2880	kiln
窑	*Hole . . . tin can.* [11]

❖	stork
雚	Here we have a senile, old *turkey* that thinks it's a **stork**. The element for *chatterbox* refers to the incessant gobbling of the *turkey*, who is doing its best to keep its bundle in its stubby beak while announcing the new arrival to the entire neighborhood. The fragrant *flowers* have been added to improve the odor of the parcel. [17]

艹　　　茻　　　雚

2881	jar
罐	*Tin can . . . stork.* This is the character from which we derived the primitive meaning of our more modern *tin can.* [23]

2882	pour into
灌	*Water . . . stork.* [20]

❖	canteen
匋	A *bound up tin can* gives us a **canteen**. [8]

勹　　匋

2883	pottery
陶	*Pinnacle . . . canteen.* [10]

2884	wash in a container
淘	*Water . . . canteen.* [11]

2885 掏	Fingers . . . canteen. [11]	draw out
2886 谣	Words . . . can opener. [12]	rumor
2887 冤	Crown . . . rabbit. [10]	injustice
2888 挽	Fingers . . . hare. [10]	tow (v.)
2889 勉	Hare . . . muscle. [9]	strive
2890 馋	Food . . . hare . . . ice. [14]	gluttonous
2891 橡	Tree . . . elephant. [15]	rubber tree
2892 豫	Bestow . . . elephant. [15]	pleased

2893	numeral
码	*Stone . . . horse.* The key word refers to all sorts of numerals— phone numbers, page numbers, and so forth. [8]

2894	tame (ADJ./V.)
驯	*Horse . . . flood.* [6]

2895	Matteo
玛	*Jewel . . . horse.* This character is frequently used for its phonetic value in proper names. We choose as an example the name **Matteo**, in tribute to the celebrated sixteenth-century Jesuit scholar, **Matteo** Ricci, whose knowledge of Chinese language and culture helped him build bridges between China and Europe. He is known, among other things, for "A Treatise on Mnemonics," which outlines a method for remembering based on the medieval notion of a "memory palace." [7]

2896	be stationed
驻	*Horse . . . candlestick.* [8]

2897	arrogant
骄	*Horse . . . angel.* [9]

2898	gallop (V.)
驰	*Horse . . . scorpion.* [6]

2899	leech-hopper
蚂	To the best of our knowledge, no **leech-hopper** has ever been found in nature, so you will just have to invent one to capture the sense of this key word, which is used in compounds for various insects like locusts, dragonflies, ants, and, of course, leeches and grasshoppers. Its elements: *insect . . . horse.* [9]

2900	maneuver (v.)
驶	*Horse . . . history.* One who operates vehicles like ships or planes is said to **maneuver** them. [8]

2901	disturb
骚	Note the drawing order. Then think of a carnivorous *insect* clinging to the underbelly of a *horse*, sticking in a *fork*, and gouging out little bits of supper. Picture it sitting at a little table, with a bib on, a glass of wine in hand, and a "Do not **disturb**" sign hanging alongside. [2]

马　马又　马又　骚

2902	drive (v.)
驾	*Add . . . horse.* [8]

2903	donkey
驴	*Horse . . . door.* [7]

2904	take flight
腾	Think of the key word in the sense of something that soars rapidly upward or takes a leap, like the price of a stock or the ascent of an airplane as it **takes flight**. Its elements: *flesh . . . quarter . . . horse.* [13]

2905	mule
骡	*Horse . . . tired.* [17]

2906	trot (v.)
骤	Think here of the Hambletonian Stakes, that prestigious harness race in which the *horses* that *assemble* for the occasion **trot**, pulling drivers riding in open, two-wheeled sulkies. [17]

2907	rush (v.)
闯	Gate . . . horse. This key word means to charge at or storm a barrier. [6]
2908	drive away
驱	Horse . . . region. [7]
2909	refute
驳	Horse . . . sheaves stacked on top of each other. [7]
2910	cheat (v.)
骗	Horse . . . book cover. [12]
2911	bluff (v.)
唬	The primitive to the right is the full character for **tiger**, and thus includes the *wind* (see FRAME 1459). [11]
2912	take captive
虏	Tiger . . . muscle. [8]
2913	despotic
虐	Tiger . . . backward *broom*. [9] 虍 虐 虐 虐
2914	filter (v.)
滤	Water . . . ponder. [13]

LESSON 54

❖ 舛	**sunglasses** The element for *evening* adds a second lens to our *monocle*, giving us *sunglasses,* whose function is, after all, to darken the daylight. [6] 夕　夕ー　夕ㄷ　舛
2915 瞬	**instant** [N.] *Eyeball . . . vulture . . . crown . . . sunglasses.* [17]
❖ 粦	**jack-o'-lantern** Picture a pumpkin at night with *rice* spurting out the top like an eruption of fireworks. The *sunglasses* show that it not just your ordinary run-of-the-mill garden pumpkin, but belongs to the fashionable **jack-o'-lantern** set. [12] 米　粦
2916 麟	**Chinese unicorn** *Deer . . . jack-o'-lantern.* Obviously, the **Chinese** idea of a **unicorn** is very different from the European one. [23]
2917 燐	**phosphorous** *Stone . . . jack-o'-lantern.* [17]
2918 唇	**lips** *Sign of the dragon . . . mouth.* Note the difference in the way the first primitive is drawn in this and the following frame. Here the second stroke is clearly elongated. [10]

2919 辱	disgrace [N./V.]
	Sign of the dragon . . . glue. [10]

2920 震	quake [V.]
	Weather . . . sign of the dragon. [15]

2921 振	vibrate
	Fingers . . . sign of the dragon. [10]

2922 郑	Zheng
	Golden calf . . . city walls. The key word here is another common surname. [8]

2923 掷	hurl
	Fingers . . . Zheng. [11]

2924 魄	vigor
	White . . . ghost. [14]

2925 槐	scholar tree
	Tree . . . ghost. [13]

2926 魅	enchant
	Ghost . . . not yet. [14]

2927 瑰	marvelous
	Jewel . . . ghost. [13]

2928 魂	soul
	Rising cloud . . . ghost. [13]

2929 愧	ashamed
	State of mind . . . ghost. [12]

2930 魁	leader
	Ghost . . . Big Dipper. [12]

2931 胧	hazy
	Moon . . . dragon. [9]

2932 垄	raised path between fields
	One way to keep your *land* marked off from your neighbor's is to build a **raised path between fields** that serves as a kind of natural fence. Another way, is to have a *dragon* sit on the border. "Good fences make good neighbors," as Robert Frost observed, but fearsome *dragons* probably make for even better neighbors. (This character appears frequently in terms related to monopolizing, which suggests an altogether different role for the *dragon*.) [8]

2933 宠	dote on
	If people typically pamper their pet dogs and cats, imagine how they would have to **dote on** a pet *house dragon.* [8]

2934 庞	huge
	Cave . . . dragon. [8]

2935 拢	draw near
	Fingers . . . dragon. [8]

2936 聋	deaf
	Dragon . . . ear. [11]

2937 笼	cage [N.]
	Bamboo . . . dragon. Be sure to come up with an image for **cage** that does not conflict with the element for *hamster cage* we learned in Book 1. [11]

2938 挪	transfer (v.)
	One economical way to **transfer** hardened criminals to *Alcatraz* is to dangle them cuffed by the *fingers* from a long wire attached on one end to the Bay Bridge, and on the other to the dreaded island. Just slide them across San Francisco Bay to the fate that awaits them. [9]

2939 辆	vehicles
	Car . . . yoke. [11]

2940 瞒	dissemble
	The sense of this key word is "to hide the truth from." Its elements: *eyeballs . . . flowers . . . yoke.* [15]

2941 龟	tortoise
	Bound up . . . electricity. Note how the top part of the the final stroke is swallowed up by the second stroke. [7]

❖ 黾	electrical outlet
	The characters for *mouth* and *electricity* combine to give us the primitive for an **electrical outlet**. [8]

口　黾

2942 蝇	flies
	Insect . . . electrical outlet. [14]

2943 绳	rope (N.)
	Thread . . . electrical outlet. [11]

2944 淹	inundate
	Water . . . hang glider. [11]

2945 俺	we (exclusive)
	This character should be taken as forming a pair with *we (inclusive)* (FRAME 1504). There the person or persons spoken to were included; here they are excluded. The elements: *person . . . hang glider.* [10]

2946 钮	push button [N.]
	Metal . . . clown. [9]

2947 羞	shy
	Wool . . . clown. [10]

2948 纽	New York
	As we saw with the character to which we assigned the key word *L.A.* in Book 1, this character is the first in the compound for **New York**. Its primitive elements: *thread . . . clown.* [7]

2949 赫	illustrious
	Crimson . . . crimson. [14]

2950 奕	radiating vitality
	Apple . . . St. Bernard dog. [9]

2951 迹	indication
	Let this key word connote the sort of **indications** or traces detectives look for in compiling their clues. Its elements: *apple . . . road.* [9]

2952 蛮	barbaric
	Apple . . . insect. [12]

2953	**beer**
啤	*Mouth . . . lowly.* This is the character that is followed by the generic character for "liquor" (see FRAME 1126) to give the term for **beer**. [11]

2954	**spleen**
脾	As in the Western tradition where the **spleen** produces black bile or "melancholy," one of the four basic bodily "humors" that affect one's temperament, in Chinese, too, this character is often associated with ill temper. Its component elements: *part of the body . . . lowly.* [12]

2955	**stele**
碑	*Stone . . . lowly.* [13]

2956	**admonish**
嘱	*Mouth . . . belong to.* [15]

2957	**IV**

肆	We assigned this character the meaning of the Roman numeral IV because it is used in bank drafts to avoid the fraud that might occur with the simpler character (FRAME 4). The element to the right, *brush,* is familiar to you.
	
	  The element on the left is a variant of the character we learned for *long* (FRAME 1428). The story starts to get complicated, but the point is, you will have to learn to write the element given here. If it's any help, you can think of the form as a doodle of four (IV) strands of wet hair that you are dangling over your *elbow* to dry. Think of this as you trace the stroke order given below. [13]
	
	  一 丆 二 三 丰 長 肆

❖	**mortar**
臼	The primitive element for a **mortar** (a vessel you use a pestle to crush or grind something in) should not be confused with that for *zipper.* [6]

丿 𠂆 𠂇 𣥂 𦥑 臼

2958

插

insert [v.]

Fingers . . . thousand . . . mortar. [12]

2959

毀

ruin [v.]

The key word easily suggests to demolish or **ruin** a building. They do so by putting *i-beams* into a gigantic *mortar* that is attached to a catapult so they can be heaved at the structure like *missiles.* [13]

白 皀 毀

2960

鼠

mouse

The *mortar* at the top tells us that this **mouse** has a very peculiar-looking head. The rest of its body uses a new combination of pieces we met before. Look closely and you will see a pair of *plows* at the bottom, with "*rain*drops" from the element for *rain* hanging on them, and a *fishhook* for a tail. This is a fun, if unusual character to write, so take your time combining the elements into a memorable image. [13]

臼 𦥔 𦥖 鼡 鼡 鼠

2961

舅

mother's brother

Mortar . . . male. [13]

❖

臽

scoop

Think of an ice-cream **scoop** or something similar to combine the ingredients: a *claw* and a *mortar.* [10]

爫 臽

2962

滔

surging

Water . . . scoop. [13]

2963	unhulled rice
稻	Wild rice . . . scoop. [15]

2964	tread [v.]
蹈	Wooden leg . . . scoop. [17]

❖	cake mixer
叟	Here we see a labor-intensive **cake mixer**: someone sitting down with a large wooden *mortar* resting in the *crotch* of the legs, pounding away at the batter with a *walking stick*. When you use this element, you may, of course, think of a more modern, electric apparatus. [9]

丿　　亻　　𠂉　　𠂉ㄱ　　𠂉ㄱ　　𦥑　　申　　叟

2965	elder brother's wife
嫂	Woman . . . cake mixer. [12]

2966	search [v.]
搜	Fingers . . . cake mixer. [12]

2967	emaciated
瘦	Sickness . . . cake mixer. [14]

2968	vessels
艘	This character is a measure word or classifier for boats and ships. Its elements: *boat . . . cake mixer.* [15]

❖	pothole
臽	When you stop to think about it, a **pothole** is a kind of *mortar* recessed in the middle of a roadway. And, as usually happens to a **pothole** when the road workers are patching it up, it is roped off—or *bound up*—with a little fence and a sign that reads "persons working." [8]

夕 臽

2969

焰

flame [N.]

Think of a solitary **flame** here, the bigger the better, to avoid confusing this character with the simple primitive for *flames* learned in Book 1. Its elements: *fire . . . pothole.* [12]

2970

馅

filling [N.]

The key word for this character refers to the kind of **filling** you put in pies, dumplings, and steamed buns. Its elements: *food . . . pothole.* [16]

2971

陷

get stuck

Pinnacle . . . pothole. [10]

❖

爻爻

stitching

Think of these four xes as the cross-*stitching* you see on those old-fashioned "Home Sweet Home" embroideries. [8]

丿　　乂　　乂　　乂乂　　乂乂
　　　　　乂　　乂　　乂乂

2972

爽

frank [ADJ.]

St. Bernard dog . . . stitching. You may find the stroke order a little unusual. And you needn't worry about our fluffy friend the *St. Bernard* being sewn up into frankfurter meat. The **frank** of this key word simply means "straightforward." [11]

一　　尸　　尹　　爽　　爽

2973

缀

embellish

The *threads* attached to the end of this *stitching* are a fringe-like adornment to further **embellish** the finished product. Note how the four "stitches" are drawn in a different order from that of the previous frame. [11]

纟 纟 纟 纟 纟

❖ Farmer's Almanac

囟 The small box with an antenna coming out the top suggests a handheld electronic device. On the screen, we see only a *sheaf*, indicating that it is in fact a portable **Farmer's Almanac** that can be popped open for consultation as the need arises. [6]

ˊ 冂 冋 囟

2974 thick-headed

傻 Take your time with this character to be sure you have all the elements related to one another: *person . . . Farmer's Almanac . . . animal legs . . . walking legs.* [13]

Compounds

Compounds

THE 26 CHARACTERS brought together here are best learned in pairs or "compounds." The full term and its meaning is given before each set of characters.

蝴蝶 butterfly

2975 蝴	butterfly (front end)
	Since the Chinese word for **butterfly** requires two characters, we may learn them together by taking the first character as the **front end** and the next as the **back end**. The elements you have to work with to remember the **front end** (the head, thorax, and forewings are): *insect . . . recklessly.* [15]

2976 蝶	butterfly (back end)
	And here are the elements for remembering the **butterfly's** **back end** (the abdomen and hind wings): *insect . . . family tree.* [15]

蜘蛛 spider

2977 蜘	spider (front end)
	Insect . . . know. Think of a black widow **spider**. The **front end** is the part that *knows* an intruder is in the neighborhood. [14]

2978 蛛	spider (back end)
	Insect . . . vermilion. The **back end** of the black widow **spider** is the part that has the *vermilion*-colored hourglass shape on its underside. [12]

骆驼 camel

2979 骆	*Horse . . . each.* [9]	camel (front end)
2980 驼	*Horse . . . it.* [8]	camel (back end)

蜻蜓 dragonfly

2981 蜻	*Insect . . . blue or green / telescope.* [14]	dragonfly (front end)
2982 蜓	*Insect . . . royal court.* [12]	dragonfly (back end)

凤凰 phoenix

2983 凤	*Wind . . . crotch.* [4]	male phoenix
2984 凰	*Wind . . . emperor.* [11]	female phoenix

玻璃 glass

2985 玻	*Jewel . . . covering.* [14]	glass (front side)

2986 璃	glass (back side)
Jewel . . . leave. [14]	

橄榄 olive

2987 橄	olive (A)
Tree . . . brave. [15]	

2988 榄	olive (B)
Tree . . . magnifying glass. [13]	

芙蓉 hibiscus

2989 芙	hibiscus (A)
Flowers . . . husband. [7]	

2990 蓉	hibiscus (B)
Flowers . . . contain. [13]	

咖啡 coffee

2991 咖	coffee (first drop)
Mouth . . . add. [8]	

2992 啡	coffee (last drop)
Mouth . . . jail cell. [11]	

葡萄 grapes

2993 葡	grapes (A)
Flowers . . . bound up . . . dog tag. [12]	

2994	grapes (B)
萄	*Flowers . . . canteen.* [11]

蘑菇 mushroom

2995	mushroom (cap)
蘑	*Flowers . . . grind.* [19]
2996	mushroom (stem)
菇	*Flowers . . . father's sister.* [11]

吩咐 instruct

2997	in-
吩	*Mouth . . . part.* [7]
2998	-struct
咐	*Mouth . . . pay.* [8]

乒乓 ping-pong

This combination of characters is used as the informal name for the game of table tennis.

2999	ping
乒	Left-legged *troop.* [6]
3000	pong
乓	Right-legged *troop.* [6]

Postscripts

Postscript

POSTSCRIPT 1

IF YOU HAVE made your way successfully through all 3,000 characters covered in the foregoing lessons, you have every right to heave a great sigh of relief. But before you get too comfortable, there are a couple of Postscripts we would like to add.

First of all, in compiling a list of characters for these books, the primary criterion was frequency of use. At the same time, other considerations persuaded us to allow a small number of characters to slip in that fell just shy of our frequency criteria. Some of them helped reinforce the learning of important primitive elements. Others helped clarify the special method of ordering followed in these pages. Still others were just so simple to learn that we could not resist making an exception of them.

In the process, another group of characters that by virtue of frequency belonged in the lessons had to be set aside. There are eighteen of them in all, and we have gathered them together for you here. Of these, half are used as surnames, some of them very common, and half for various kinds of proper names.

We recommend that you think of the following pages as a first real-world challenge to the skills you have picked up in the course of these two books. Once you have passed this test, a second Postscript awaits you for a final touch.

We begin with the nine surnames. In one case, the romanization of the name is identical to a key word that appears in an earlier lesson but with a different character. It is marked with a "-2".

3001	曹 [11]	Cao
	When used as a primitive element, this character took *cadet* as its meaning (page 126).	
3002	潘 [15]	Pan

3003	谭	[19]	Tan
3004	姚	[9]	Yao-2
3005	薛	[7]	Xue
3006	彭	[12]	Peng
3007	冯	[5]	Feng
3008	魏	[17]	Wei
3009	岳	[8]	Yue

The characters in the next nine frames are often met in proper names. They are presented in no particular order.

3010	莉	[10]	jasmine
	Often used in girls' names.		
3011	湘	[12]	Hunan Province
	An abbreviation for the province's name.		
3012	甸	[7]	outlying areas
3013	沧	[7]	dark blue

3014	穆	[16]	reverent

3015	娜	[10]	*na*

The character is often used to transliterate the sound *na* as it appears in names such as An*na* and Dia*na*.

3016	琼	[12]	fine jade

3017	琳	[12]	gem

3018	钧	[9]	30 catties

An ancient unit of weight amounting to roughly 15 kilograms (see FRAME 856). It often appears in boys' names.

Postscript 2

To END ON a suitably serious note, we have included a special character that does not show up among the nearly 50,000 characters covered in the largest modern dictionaries of the Chinese language. The character, which is reduplicated to refer to a type of noodles famous in Shaanxi Province, is said to be the most complex Chinese character around today and has become the stuff of legend. There is even a mnemonic ditty about its drawing order.

And finally, a story to end all stories . . .

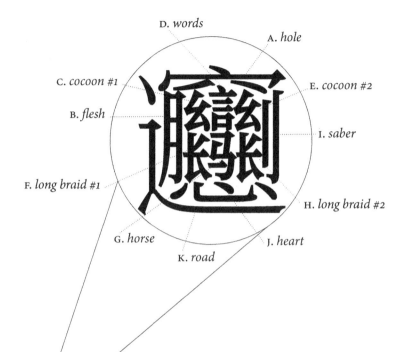

D. *words*

A. *hole*

C. *cocoon #1*

E. *cocoon #2*

B. *flesh*

I. *saber*

F. *long braid #1*

H. *long braid #2*

G. *horse*

J. *heart*

K. *road*

50,001

Biang

Perhaps you have heard of the celebrated Chinese singer and songwriter Flank Chinatra, known throughout the land for such timeless hits as "Hong Kong, Hong Kong," "Strangers in Shanghai" (in the local dialect, "Strangers in the Nai"), and "Mai Wei."

Now the story is told of a strange dream Flank had one night that led to the composition of one of his most famous ballads. Chinatra recalls in his memoirs that he dreamed he was traveling a back *road* that led to the city of Guangzhou astride his magnificent *horse*, **Biang**, who trotted proudly, its tail woven into two *long braids* fluttering in the breeze. Suddenly and without warning his mount collapsed and died. Days passed without anyone appearing on the deserted *road*, and Flank grew weak and disoriented.

On the verge of starvation, and in an act of desperation, he unsheathed his trusty *saber*, cut a *hole* in the *flesh* of the *horse*, and took out the *heart* to eat. Leaning against the carcass, he began to croon a dirge for the poor departed beast. The *words* of the song carried to two *cocoons* nearby, inspiring the beautiful butterflies inside to break out and take flight. Thinking it a good omen, Flank cried out in his sleep: "Fly me to Guangzhou!" He awoke in a cold sweat and immediately put the *words* to paper, forever immortalizing his legendary horse **Biang**.

Don't be surprised if you hear noodle vendors whistling the tune as they slap their **Biang Biang** noodles into shape. [46]

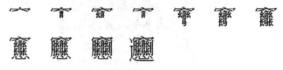

Indexes

INDEX I
Hand-Drawn Characters

This Index presents all the characters in this book in the order of their appearance. They are printed in one of the typical type styles used to teach children how to draw characters with a pen or pencil—the same form used in this book to show proper stroke order. The pronunciation (Mandarin) of the character is given beneath. Some of the characters have multiple pronunciations, which can be found by consulting a dictionary under the pronunciation given here.

叭	咕	胆	咱	肿	串	吓	罩	兽	嚣
bā	*gū*	*dǎn*	*zán*	*zhǒng*	*chuàn*	*xià*	*zhào*	*shòu*	*xiāo*
1501	1502	1503	1504	1505	1506	1507	1508	1509	1510

矗	颠	巩	叨	刮	盯	呵	姑	婴	姆
chù	*diān*	*gǒng*	*dāo*	*guā*	*dīng*	*hē*	*gū*	*yīng*	*mǔ*
1511	1512	1513	1514	1515	1516	1517	1518	1519	1520

兢	奋	夹	颊	厕	硕	砌	哨	晃	泪
jīng	*fèn*	*jiā*	*jiá*	*cè*	*shuò*	*qì*	*shào*	*huàng*	*lèi*
1521	1522	1523	1524	1525	1526	1527	1528	1529	1530

泄	泊	沾	渺	汰	咏	腺	鲁	坦	坝
xiè	*bó*	*zhān*	*miǎo*	*tài*	*yǒng*	*xiàn*	*lǔ*	*tǎn*	*bà*
1531	1532	1533	1534	1535	1536	1537	1538	1539	1540

涯	娃	肘	碍	夺	灼	炒	灶	哩	厘
yá	*wá*	*zhǒu*	*ài*	*duó*	*zhuó*	*chǎo*	*zào*	*lǐ*	*lí*
1541	1542	1543	1544	1545	1546	1547	1548	1549	1550

鲤	嘿	熏	丹	炯	晌	淌	宁	寡	喧
lǐ	*hēi*	*xūn*	*dān*	*jiǒng*	*shǎng*	*tǎng*	*níng*	*guǎ*	*xuān*
1551	1552	1553	1554	1555	1556	1557	1558	1559	1560

棚	柏	朴	朵	杠	椅	樱	梢	杜	杰
péng	*bǎi*	*pǔ*	*duǒ*	*gàng*	*yǐ*	*yīng*	*shāo*	*dù*	*jié*
1561	1562	1563	1564	1565	1566	1567	1568	1569	1570

桐	宋	桂	淋	焚	厢	昧	朱	株	萌
tóng	*Sòng*	*guì*	*lìn*	*fén*	*xiāng*	*mèi*	*zhū*	*zhū*	*méng*
1571	1572	1573	1574	1575	1576	1577	1578	1579	1580
苟	苛	萝	膜	暮	寞	猫	狭	狸	犹
gǒu	*kē*	*luó*	*mó*	*mù*	*mò*	*māo*	*xiá*	*lí*	*yóu*
1581	1582	1583	1584	1585	1586	1587	1588	1589	1590
燃	咒	嗅	牢	牡	宪	赞	伞	舍	啥
rán	*zhòu*	*xiù*	*láo*	*mǔ*	*xiàn*	*zàn*	*sǎn*	*shè*	*shá*
1591	1592	1593	1594	1595	1596	1597	1598	1599	1600
洽	旺	碧	琐	汪	枉	珠	噩	栓	柱
qià	*wàng*	*bì*	*suǒ*	*wāng*	*wǎng*	*zhū*	*è*	*shuān*	*zhù*
1601	1602	1603	1604	1605	1606	1607	1608	1609	1610
钥	钻	钞	锁	销	锣	迫	迁	逼	辽
yào	*zuàn*	*chāo*	*suǒ*	*xiāo*	*luó*	*pò*	*qiān*	*bī*	*liáo*
1611	1612	1613	1614	1615	1616	1617	1618	1619	1620
逻	逞	轨	轧	辐	链	煎	喻	榆	胳
luó	*chěng*	*guǐ*	*yà*	*fú*	*liàn*	*jiān*	*yù*	*yú*	*gē*
1621	1622	1623	1624	1625	1626	1627	1628	1629	1630
厦	牵	浑	晕	炕	膏	淳	亨	哼	鲸
shà	*qiān*	*hún*	*yūn*	*kàng*	*gāo*	*chún*	*hēng*	*hēng*	*jīng*
1631	1632	1633	1634	1635	1636	1637	1638	1639	1640
壳	洁	枚	牧	玫	敦	墩	瞻	谓	询
ké	*jié*	*méi*	*mù*	*méi*	*dūn*	*dūn*	*zhān*	*wèi*	*xún*
1641	1642	1643	1644	1645	1646	1647	1648	1649	1650
讥	罚	订	谅	诺	讯	谍	碟	贰	腻
jī	*fá*	*dìng*	*liàng*	*nuò*	*xùn*	*dié*	*dié*	*èr*	*nì*
1651	1652	1653	1654	1655	1656	1657	1658	1659	1660
嘎	域	栽	戚	蔑	喊	溅	浇	涩	址
gā	*yù*	*zāi*	*qī*	*miè*	*hǎn*	*jiàn*	*jiāo*	*sè*	*zhǐ*
1661	1662	1663	1664	1665	1666	1667	1668	1669	1670
赴	趟	堤	津	键	婿	袜	衰	衷	猿
fù	*tàng*	*dī*	*jīn*	*jiàn*	*xù*	*wà*	*shuāi*	*zhōng*	*yuán*
1671	1672	1673	1674	1675	1676	1677	1678	1679	1680

吊	币	帕	帖	帆	幅	锦	沛	柿	棘
diào	bì	pà	tiě	fān	fú	jǐn	pèi	shì	jí
1681	1682	1683	1684	1685	1686	1687	1688	1689	1690
蕾	尝	坛	枣	吞	妖	沃	袄	轿	垃
lěi	cháng	tán	zǎo	tūn	yāo	wò	ǎo	jiào	lā
1691	1692	1693	1694	1695	1696	1697	1698	1699	1700
啼	蒂	顷	匙	乖	乘	剩	毕	棍	谐
tí	dì	qǐng	chí	guāi	chéng	shèng	bì	gùn	xié
1701	1702	1703	1704	1705	1706	1707	1708	1709	1710
柴	沦	敏	霉	迄	砍	坎	炊	钦	剖
chái	lún	mǐn	méi	qì	kǎn	kǎn	chuī	qīn	pōu
1711	1712	1713	1714	1715	1716	1717	1718	1719	1720
菩	黯	赢	芒	荒	谎	茫	坊	芳	访
pú	àn	yíng	máng	huāng	huǎng	máng	fáng	fāng	fǎng
1721	1722	1723	1724	1725	1726	1727	1728	1729	1730
淦	熬	膀	磅	榜	锐	虹	蝠	浊	蝗
gàn	áo	bǎng	bàng	bǎng	ruì	hóng	fú	zhuó	huáng
1731	1732	1733	1734	1735	1736	1737	1738	1739	1740
蛙	烛	茧	蚕	胞	炮	袍	雹	豪	啄
wā	zhú	jiǎn	cán	bāo	pào	páo	báo	háo	zhuó
1741	1742	1743	1744	1745	1746	1747	1748	1749	1750
琢	遂	嫁	肠	杨	烫	荡	姜	详	羡
zhuó	suì	jià	cháng	yáng	tàng	dàng	jiāng	xiáng	xiàn
1751	1752	1753	1754	1755	1756	1757	1758	1759	1760
栏	唯	雀	堆	雕	截	霍	雌	焦	瞧
lán	wéi	què	duī	diāo	jié	huò	cí	qiáo	jiāo
1761	1762	1763	1764	1765	1766	1767	1768	1769	1770
礁	蕉	翘	塌	翰	耀	戳	咽	姻	墙
jiāo	jiāo	qiào	tā	hàn	yào	chuō	yān	yīn	qiáng
1771	1772	1773	1774	1775	1776	1777	1778	1779	1780
旷	矿	庆	嘛	磨	脏	赃	桩	忠	恕
kuàng	kuàng	qìng	ma5	mó	zāng	zāng	zhuāng	zhōng	shù
1781	1782	1783	1784	1785	1786	1787	1788	1789	1790

惑 huò 1791	愈 yù 1792	惠 huì 1793	忌 jì 1794	患 huàn 1795	惹 rě 1796	恒 héng 1797	悟 wù 1798	悼 dào 1799	惧 jù 1800
慎 shèn 1801	惰 duò 1802	恢 huī 1803	惶 huáng 1804	忆 yì 1805	悄 qiǎo 1806	恍 huǎng 1807	恰 qià 1808	愉 yú 1809	怔 zhēng 1810
怖 bù 1811	慌 huāng 1812	愣 lèng 1813	悦 yuè 1814	憎 zēng 1815	惟 wéi 1816	悔 huǐ 1817	慕 mù 1818	添 tiān 1819	媳 xí 1820
熄 xī 1821	泌 mì 1822	瑟 sè 1823	蜜 mì 1824	蛾 é 1825	扒 pá 1826	扣 kòu 1827	拍 pāi 1828	啪 pā 1829	扑 pū 1830
拘 jū 1831	损 sǔn 1832	拓 tuò 1833	扛 káng 1834	扎 zhā 1835	拇 mǔ 1836	捎 shāo 1837	抄 chāo 1838	垫 diàn 1839	挚 zhì 1840
捏 niē 1841	拧 nǐng 1842	抹 mǒ 1843	摸 mō 1844	描 miáo 1845	挑 tiǎo 1846	扰 rǎo 1847	搞 gǎo 1848	拴 shuān 1849	拾 shí 1850
搭 dā 1851	掠 lüè 1852	拭 shì 1853	挠 náo 1854	扯 chě 1855	撞 zhuàng 1856	摘 zhāi 1857	拖 tuō 1858	扬 yáng 1859	拦 lán 1860
搓 cuō 1861	捆 kǔn 1862	扩 kuò 1863	撼 hàn 1864	挟 xié 1865	擅 shàn 1866	颤 chàn 1867	戒 jiè 1868	械 xiè 1869	诫 jiè 1870
莽 mǎng 1871	奔 bēn 1872	喷 pēn 1873	愤 fèn 1874	材 cái 1875	荐 jiàn 1876	孕 yùn 1877	扔 rēng 1878	携 xié 1879	圾 jī 1880
梗 gěng 1881	叹 tàn 1882	叉 chā 1883	权 quán 1884	寇 kòu 1885	敲 qiāo 1886	轰 hōng 1887	滩 tān 1888	毅 yì 1889	肢 zhī 1890
妓 jì 1891	歧 qí 1892	翅 chì 1893	淑 shū 1894	椒 jiāo 1895	盾 dùn 1896	贩 fàn 1897	扳 bān 1898	烁 shuò 1899	觅 mì 1900

妥	豹	貌	睬	允	宏	垒	胎	怠	怡
tuǒ	*bào*	*mào*	*cǎi*	*yǔn*	*hóng*	*lěi*	*tāi*	*dài*	*yí*
1901	1902	1903	1904	1905	1906	1907	1908	1909	1910
冶	抬	罢	摆	丢	致	弃	撤	硫	琉
yě	*tái*	*bà*	*bǎi*	*diū*	*zhì*	*qì*	*chè*	*liú*	*liú*
1911	1912	1913	1914	1915	1916	1917	1918	1919	1920
疏	蔬	勾	沟	钩	崩	岩	峭	崎	崖
shū	*shū*	*gōu*	*gōu*	*gōu*	*bēng*	*yán*	*qiào*	*qí*	*yá*
1921	1922	1923	1924	1925	1926	1927	1928	1929	1930
灿	炭	碳	岂	凯	峡	崔	摧	逆	溯
càn	*tàn*	*tàn*	*qǐ*	*kǎi*	*xiá*	*cuī*	*cuī*	*nì*	*sù*
1931	1932	1933	1934	1935	1936	1937	1938	1939	1940
塑	盼	颁	芬	扮	岔	颂	讼	滚	翁
sù	*pàn*	*bān*	*fēn*	*bàn*	*chà*	*sòng*	*sòng*	*gǔn*	*wēng*
1941	1942	1943	1944	1945	1946	1947	1948	1949	1950
嗡	裕	榕	熔	裳	掌	撑	膛	颇	坡
wēng	*yù*	*róng*	*róng*	*shang5*	*zhǎng*	*chēng*	*táng*	*pō*	*pō*
1951	1952	1953	1954	1955	1956	1957	1958	1959	1960
披	菠	歼	殖	殊	残	咧	裂	毙	耿
pī	*bō*	*jiān*	*zhí*	*shū*	*cán*	*liě*	*liè*	*bì*	*gěng*
1961	1962	1963	1964	1965	1966	1967	1968	1969	1970
辑	耻	摄	聪	娶	蔓	肤	扶	潜	卧
jí	*chǐ*	*shè*	*cōng*	*qǔ*	*màn*	*fū*	*fú*	*qián*	*wò*
1971	1972	1973	1974	1975	1976	1977	1978	1979	1980
藏	熙	勋	劣	募	劝	劫	抛	胁	怒
cáng	*xī*	*xūn*	*liè*	*mù*	*quàn*	*jié*	*pāo*	*xié*	*nù*
1981	1982	1983	1984	1985	1986	1987	1988	1989	1990
茄	彻	征	惩	徒	徊	役	循	彼	衍
qié	*chè*	*zhēng*	*chéng*	*tú*	*huái*	*yì*	*xún*	*bǐ*	*yǎn*
1991	1992	1993	1994	1995	1996	1997	1998	1999	2000
衡	衔	秃	颓	秒	稍	稣	稿	稠	颖
héng	*xián*	*tū*	*tuí*	*miǎo*	*shāo*	*sū*	*gǎo*	*chóu*	*yǐng*
2001	2002	2003	2004	2005	2006	2007	2008	2009	2010

稼	税	稚	菌	穗	秘	私	秩	锹	梨
jià	shuì	zhì	jùn	suì	mì	sī	zhì	qiāo	lí
2011	2012	2013	2014	2015	2016	2017	2018	2019	2020
犁	萎	黏	黎	膝	漆	锈	眯	糊	粘
lí	wěi	nián	lí	xī	qī	xiù	mī	hú	zhān
2021	2022	2023	2024	2025	2026	2027	2028	2029	2030
奥	澳	懊	菊	渊	梁	梁	糙	粒	糕
ào	ào	ào	jú	yuān	liáng	liáng	cāo	lì	gāo
2031	2032	2033	2034	2035	2036	2037	2038	2039	2040
蔽	憋	撇	弊	莱	搂	筑	箩	笨	筒
bì	biē	piě	bì	lái	lǒu	zhù	luó	bèn	tǒng
2041	2042	2043	2044	2045	2046	2047	2048	2049	2050
箭	筛	筋	伍	仇	倡	伯	仲	仆	估
jiàn	shāi	jīn	wǔ	chóu	chàng	bó	zhòng	pú	gū
2051	2052	2053	2054	2055	2056	2057	2058	2059	2060
侦	俱	佑	佐	侧	亿	仔	倚	俏	佳
zhēn	jù	yòu	zuǒ	cè	yì	zǐ	yǐ	qiào	jiā
2061	2062	2063	2064	2065	2066	2067	2068	2069	2070
侍	伙	倘	宿	伏	袱	偷	偿	伐	佩
shì	huǒ	tǎng	sù	fú	fú	tōu	cháng	fá	pèi
2071	2072	2073	2074	2075	2076	2077	2078	2079	2080
侨	倾	伦	侮	倍	仿	傲	僧	囚	悠
qiáo	qīng	lún	wǔ	bèi	fǎng	ào	sēng	qiú	yōu
2081	2082	2083	2084	2085	2086	2087	2088	2089	2090
侄	仙	傍	催	俗	侠	俄	聚	符	贷
zhí	xiān	bàng	cuī	sú	xiá	é	jù	fú	dài
2091	2092	2093	2094	2095	2096	2097	2098	2099	2100
荷	杖	仗	丛	耸	挫	诬	葛	褐	竭
hé	zhàng	zhàng	cóng	sǒng	cuò	wū	gé	hé	jié
2101	2102	2103	2104	2105	2106	2107	2108	2109	2110
歇	揭	淫	凭	挺	赎	瓦	瓷	拟	瓶
xiē	jiē	yín	píng	tǐng	shú	wǎ	cí	nǐ	píng
2111	2112	2113	2114	2115	2116	2117	2118	2119	2120

宫	铝	萤	莹	蒙	朦	捞	旋	吻	匆
gōng	lǚ	yíng	yíng	méng	méng	lāo	xuán	wěn	cōng
2121	2122	2123	2124	2125	2126	2127	2128	2129	2130
葱	锡	惕	卢	屉	屑	尿	犀	迟	刷
cōng	xī	tì	lú	tì	xiè	niào	xī	chí	shuā
2131	2132	2133	2134	2135	2136	2137	2138	2139	2140
漏	屁	屈	掘	履	屎	屡	屏	眉	媚
lòu	pì	qū	jué	lǚ	shǐ	lǚ	píng	méi	mèi
2141	2142	2143	2144	2145	2146	2147	2148	2149	2150
昼	启	肩	妒	炉	芦	扇	奈	款	凛
zhòu	qǐ	jiān	dù	lú	lú	shàn	nài	kuǎn	lǐn
2151	2152	2153	2154	2155	2156	2157	2158	2159	2160
祟	祝	祥	蔚	慰	蒜	棕	宙	轴	袖
suì	zhù	xiáng	wèi	wèi	suàn	zōng	zhòu	zhóu	xiù
2161	2162	2163	2164	2165	2166	2167	2168	2169	2170
庙	笛	届	呻	坤	审	婶	畅	巢	棵
miào	dí	jiè	shēn	kūn	shěn	shěn	chàng	cháo	kē
2171	2172	2173	2174	2175	2176	2177	2178	2179	2180
裸	裹	析	晰	芹	祈	欣	掀	惭	崭
luǒ	guǒ	xī	xī	qín	qí	xīn	xiān	cán	zhǎn
2181	2182	2183	2184	2185	2186	2187	2188	2189	2190
浙	誓	拆	炸	诈	归	皱	煞	趋	雏
zhè	shì	chāi	zhà	zhà	guī	zhòu	shà	qū	chú
2191	2192	2193	2194	2195	2196	2197	2198	2199	2200
浸	寝	侵	稳	挡	剥	秉	妻	凄	捷
jìn	qǐn	qīn	wěn	dǎng	bō	bǐng	qī	qī	jié
2201	2202	2203	2204	2205	2206	2207	2208	2209	2210
肃	啸	萧	兼	赚	嫌	谦	歉	廉	镰
sù	xiào	xiāo	jiān	zhuàn	xián	qiān	qiàn	lián	lián
2211	2212	2213	2214	2215	2216	2217	2218	2219	2220
睁	挣	筝	塘	隶	逮	慷	糠	笋	耍
zhēng	zhēng	zhēng	táng	lì	dài	kāng	kāng	sǔn	shuǎ
2221	2222	2223	2224	2225	2226	2227	2228	2229	2230

耐	喘	揣	槽	遭	糟	抖	惜	措	腊
nài	chuǎn	chuǎi	cáo	zāo	zāo	dǒu	xī	cuò	là
2231	2232	2233	2234	2235	2236	2237	2238	2239	2240
蜡	猎	燕	遮	畔	拌	叛	券	藤	鼎
là	liè	yàn	zhē	pàn	bàn	pàn	quàn	téng	dǐng
2241	2242	2243	2244	2245	2246	2247	2248	2249	2250
芝	贬	泛	歪	矫	矮	唉	埃	挨	簇
zhī	biǎn	fàn	wāi	jiǎo	ǎi	ài	āi	ái	cù
2251	2252	2253	2254	2255	2256	2257	2258	2259	2260
茅	橘	舒	览	揽	肾	竖	弘	夷	姨
máo	jú	shū	lǎn	lǎn	shèn	shù	hóng	yí	yí
2261	2262	2263	2264	2265	2266	2267	2268	2269	2270
疆	僵	粥	蝉	禅	沸	拂	剃	递	梯
jiāng	jiāng	zhōu	chán	chán	fèi	fú	tì	dì	tī
2271	2272	2273	2274	2275	2276	2277	2278	2279	2280
涕	朽	聘	姊	亏	污	夸	垮	挎	鳄
tì	xiǔ	pìn	zǐ	kuī	wū	kuā	kuǎ	kuà	è
2281	2282	2283	2284	2285	2286	2287	2288	2289	2290
愕	躺	躲	躬	嗜	姥	拷	屿	暑	睹
è	tǎng	duǒ	gōng	shì	lǎo	kǎo	yǔ	shǔ	dǔ
2291	2292	2293	2294	2295	2296	2297	2298	2299	2300
署	薯	赌	奢	堵	煮	诸	储	屠	棺
shǔ	shǔ	dǔ	shē	dǔ	zhǔ	zhū	chǔ	tú	guān
2301	2302	2303	2304	2305	2306	2307	2308	2309	2310
爹	斧	咬	胶	狡	捉	促	趴	踏	践
diē	fǔ	yǎo	jiāo	jiǎo	zhuō	cù	pā	tà	jiàn
2311	2312	2313	2314	2315	2316	2317	2318	2319	2320
跃	蹄	踩	蹦	跌	踢	踪	跨	躁	噪
yuè	tí	cǎi	bèng	diē	tī	zōng	kuà	zào	zào
2321	2322	2323	2324	2325	2326	2327	2328	2329	2330
澡	藻	燥	操	猾	髓	陌	隙	陡	陪
zǎo	zǎo	zào	cāo	huá	suǐ	mò	xì	dǒu	péi
2331	2332	2333	2334	2335	2336	2337	2338	2339	2340

障	隧	陋	隐	陕	陵	棱	菱	凌	融
zhàng	suì	lòu	yǐn	shǎn	líng	léng	líng	líng	róng
2341	2342	2343	2344	2345	2346	2347	2348	2349	2350
隔	窃	挖	帘	窥	穷	窄	榨	窟	窘
gé	qiè	wā	lián	kuī	qióng	zhǎi	zhà	kū	jiǒng
2351	2352	2353	2354	2355	2356	2357	2358	2359	2360
窜	腔	窝	涡	锅	祸	蜗	宾	滨	绷
cuàn	qiāng	wō	wō	guō	huò	wō	bīn	bīn	bēng
2361	2362	2363	2364	2365	2366	2367	2368	2369	2370
纤	绰	绍	纱	络	绸	绒	绕	绽	绵
xiān	chuò	shào	shā	luò	chóu	róng	rào	zhàn	mián
2371	2372	2373	2374	2375	2376	2377	2378	2379	2380
缔	纺	缠	绘	纷	绣	缕	缩	纳	综
dì	fǎng	chán	huì	fēn	xiù	lǚ	suō	nà	zōng
2381	2382	2383	2384	2385	2386	2387	2388	2389	2390
绅	绪	绞	缓	暖	援	绢	捐	缴	邀
shēn	xù	jiǎo	huǎn	nuǎn	yuán	juàn	juān	jiǎo	yāo
2391	2392	2393	2394	2395	2396	2397	2398	2399	2400
缆	哟	颈	茎	径	劲	缘	幼	溪	幽
lǎn	yō	jǐng	jīng	jìng	jìng	yuán	yòu	xī	yōu
2401	2402	2403	2404	2405	2406	2407	2408	2409	2410
玄	弦	畜	蓄	磁	滋	慈	累	螺	紫
xuán	xián	chù	xù	cí	zī	cí	lèi	luó	zǐ
2411	2412	2413	2414	2415	2416	2417	2418	2419	2420
繁	絮	索	脖	勃	卸	御	卵	孵	乳
fán	xù	suǒ	bó	bó	xiè	yù	luǎn	fū	rǔ
2421	2422	2423	2424	2425	2426	2427	2428	2429	2430
浮	俘	榴	爷	疑	凝	玲	铃	怜	岭
fú	fú	liú	yé	yí	níng	líng	líng	lián	lǐng
2431	2432	2433	2434	2435	2436	2437	2438	2439	2440
伶	涌	桶	诵	范	扼	卷	倦	圈	怨
líng	yǒng	tǒng	sòng	fàn	è	juàn	juàn	quān	yuàn
2441	2442	2443	2444	2445	2446	2447	2448	2449	2450

宛	腕	婉	碗	苍	抢	诡	跪	舆	酌
wǎn	wàn	wǎn	wǎn	cāng	qiǎng	guǐ	guì	yú	zhuó
2451	2452	2453	2454	2455	2456	2457	2458	2459	2460
酬	酷	醇	醋	酱	奖	浆	桨	蒋	醉
chóu	kù	chún	cù	jiàng	jiǎng	jiāng	jiǎng	jiǎng	zuì
2461	2462	2463	2464	2465	2466	2467	2468	2469	2470
碎	翠	粹	酸	梭	峻	俊	奠	蹲	逗
suì	cuì	cuì	suān	suō	jùn	jùn	diàn	dūn	dòu
2471	2472	2473	2474	2475	2476	2477	2478	2479	2480
橱	嘻	嘉	盟	孟	猛	盐	盔	盒	盛
chú	xī	jiā	méng	mèng	měng	yán	kuī	hé	shèng
2481	2482	2483	2484	2485	2486	2487	2488	2489	2490
盏	盗	磕	盈	盆	蕴	鉴	滥	尴	尬
zhǎn	dào	kē	yíng	pén	yùn	jiàn	làn	gān	gà
2491	2492	2493	2494	2495	2496	2497	2498	2499	2500
沈	枕	耽	衅	垦	狠	恳	艰	爵	嚼
shěn	zhěn	dān	xìn	kěn	hěn	kěn	jiān	jué	jiáo
2501	2502	2503	2504	2505	2506	2507	2508	2509	2510
卿	恨	朗	狼	粮	酿	饥	饶	饰	饮
qīng	hèn	lǎng	láng	liáng	niàng	jī	ráo	shì	yǐn
2511	2512	2513	2514	2515	2516	2517	2518	2519	2520
蚀	饱	馒	饼	饺	饿	溉	慨	苹	萍
shí	bǎo	mán	bǐng	jiǎo	è	gài	kǎi	píng	píng
2521	2522	2523	2524	2525	2526	2527	2528	2529	2530
秤	淆	艾	哎	赵	攀	刹	枫	钢	岗
chèng	yáo	ài	āi	zhào	pān	shā	fēng	gāng	gǎng
2531	2532	2533	2534	2535	2536	2537	2538	2539	2540
纲	屯	吨	顿	纯	齿	龄	汹	篱	仪
gāng	tún	dūn	dùn	chún	chǐ	líng	xiōng	lí	yí
2541	2542	2543	2544	2545	2546	2547	2548	2549	2550
辜	辞	宰	辨	辫	臂	劈	譬	僻	纠
gū	cí	zǎi	biàn	biàn	bì	pī	pì	pì	jiū
2551	2552	2553	2554	2555	2556	2557	2558	2559	2560

咳	嚷	镶	塞	寨	晴	猜	靖	债	牲
ké	rǎng	xiāng	sài	zhài	qíng	cāi	jìng	zhài	shēng
2561	2562	2563	2564	2565	2566	2567	2568	2569	2570
隆	腥	猩	醒	寿	畴	涛	铸	祷	筹
lóng	xīng	xīng	xǐng	shòu	chóu	tāo	zhù	dǎo	chóu
2571	2572	2573	2574	2575	2576	2577	2578	2579	2580
契	拜	锋	逢	缝	蓬	篷	蜂	峰	瞎
qì	bài	fēng	féng	féng	péng	péng	fēng	fēng	xiā
2581	2582	2583	2584	2585	2586	2587	2588	2589	2590
辖	豁	韩	违	纬	奏	凑	秦	蠢	泽
xiá	huō	hán	wéi	wěi	zòu	còu	qín	chǔn	zé
2591	2592	2593	2594	2595	2596	2597	2598	2599	2600
译	择	捧	砖	唾	吟	贪	琴	炼	晒
yì	zé	pěng	zhuān	tuò	yín	tān	qín	liàn	shài
2601	2602	2603	2604	2605	2606	2607	2608	2609	2610
洒	栖	栗	牺	潭	覆	飘	献	阔	润
sǎ	qī	lì	xī	tán	fù	piāo	xiàn	kuò	rùn
2611	2612	2613	2614	2615	2616	2617	2618	2619	2620
阁	搁	闹	阅	闷	闭	闪	阀	闸	阐
gé	gē	nào	yuè	mēn	bì	shǎn	fá	zhá	chǎn
2621	2622	2623	2624	2625	2626	2627	2628	2629	2630
涧	菲	辈	悲	徘	喉	猴	肝	刊	奸
jiàn	fěi	bèi	bēi	pái	hóu	hóu	gān	kān	jiān
2631	2632	2633	2634	2635	2636	2637	2638	2639	2640
汗	杆	轩	罕	竿	悍	吁	涂	叙	徐
hàn	gǎn	xuān	hǎn	gān	hàn	yù	tú	xù	xú
2641	2642	2643	2644	2645	2646	2647	2648	2649	2650
斜	喇	嗽	赖	懒	嫩	董	疗	痰	症
xié	lǎ	sòu	lài	lǎn	nèn	dǒng	liáo	tán	zhèng
2651	2652	2653	2654	2655	2656	2657	2658	2659	2660
疼	痒	瘫	疫	癌	疲	痴	瘤	疮	疾
téng	yǎng	tān	yì	ái	pí	chī	liú	chuāng	jí
2661	2662	2663	2664	2665	2666	2667	2668	2669	2670

癮	痕	汇	框	筐	砸	匠	匪	匿	兜
yǐn	hén	huì	kuàng	kuāng	zá	jiàng	fěi	nì	dōu
2671	2672	2673	2674	2675	2676	2677	2678	2679	2680
巨	柜	渠	拒	矩	距	殴	呕	躯	昂
jù	guì	qú	jù	jǔ	jù	ōu	ǒu	qū	áng
2681	2682	2683	2684	2685	2686	2687	2688	2689	2690
抑	葵	瞪	凳	澄	僚	拨	泼	拔	杉
yì	kuí	dèng	dèng	chéng	liáo	bō	pō	bá	shān
2691	2692	2693	2694	2695	2696	2697	2698	2699	2700
彬	衫	彰	膨	渗	诊	趁	寥	谬	铲
bīn	shān	zhāng	péng	shèn	zhěn	chèn	liáo	miù	chǎn
2701	2702	2703	2704	2705	2706	2707	2708	2709	2710
萨	刘	坟	纹	斋	斑	剂	挤	脊	函
sà	liú	fén	wén	zhāi	bān	jì	jǐ	jǐ	hán
2711	2712	2713	2714	2715	2716	2717	2718	2719	2720
涵	映	殃	秧	焕	肥	爬	疤	甜	嵌
hán	yìng	yāng	yāng	huàn	féi	pá	bā	tián	qiàn
2721	2722	2723	2724	2725	2726	2727	2728	2729	2730
钳	媒	煤	谋	棋	欺	旗	嘶	撕	堪
qián	méi	méi	móu	qí	qī	qí	sī	sī	kān
2731	2732	2733	2734	2735	2736	2737	2738	2739	2740
勘	遣	谴	囊	溃	宜	谊	租	粗	阻
kān	qiǎn	qiǎn	náng	kuì	yí	yì	zū	cū	zǔ
2741	2742	2743	2744	2745	2746	2747	2748	2749	2750
桑	嗓	叠	锄	碰	谱	壶	凿	湿	哑
sāng	sǎng	dié	chú	pèng	pǔ	hú	záo	shī	yǎ
2751	2752	2753	2754	2755	2756	2757	2758	2759	2760
晋	哄	洪	烘	戴	翼	恭	拱	撰	粪
jìn	hǒng	hóng	hōng	dài	yì	gōng	gǒng	zhuàn	fèn
2761	2762	2763	2764	2765	2766	2767	2768	2769	2770
殿	暴	瀑	爆	拥	佣	甩	庸	触	蟹
diàn	bào	pù	bào	yōng	yōng	shuǎi	yōng	chù	xiè
2771	2772	2773	2774	2775	2776	2777	2778	2779	2780

懈	册	删	栅	珊	遍	偏	抵	氓	哺
xiè	cè	shān	zhà	shān	biàn	piān	dǐ	máng	bǔ
2781	2782	2783	2784	2785	2786	2787	2788	2789	2790
浦	蒲	薄	铺	捕	敷	膊	傅	缚	簿
pǔ	pú	bó	pù	bǔ	fū	bó	fù	fù	bù
2791	2792	2793	2794	2795	2796	2797	2798	2799	2800
郁	郭	廓	邓	鄙	耶	邮	邦	绑	郊
yù	guō	kuò	dèng	bǐ	yē	yóu	bāng	bǎng	jiāo
2801	2802	2803	2804	2805	2806	2807	2808	2809	2810
邻	廊	缎	刁	叼	钙	殷	伺	饲	舶
lín	láng	duàn	diāo	diāo	gài	yīn	cì	sì	bó
2811	2812	2813	2814	2815	2816	2817	2818	2819	2820
舰	航	舵	舱	艇	沿	铅	狐	瓣	溢
jiàn	háng	duò	cāng	tǐng	yán	qiān	hú	bàn	yì
2821	2822	2823	2824	2825	2826	2827	2828	2829	2830
隘	霞	氨	氧	氛	氢	氯	霸	靴	鞭
ài	xiá	ān	yǎng	fēn	qīng	lǜ	bà	xuē	biān
2831	2832	2833	2834	2835	2836	2837	2838	2839	2840
鞠	芽	讶	雅	邪	悉	毯	毫	耗	耕
jū	yá	yà	yǎ	xié	xī	tǎn	háo	hào	gēng
2841	2842	2843	2844	2845	2846	2847	2848	2849	2850
籍	藉	畏	喂	胀	帐	誉	剑	敛	捡
jí	jiè	wèi	wèi	zhàng	zhàng	yù	jiàn	liǎn	jiǎn
2851	2852	2853	2854	2855	2856	2857	2858	2859	2860
俭	签	鹏	鸣	鸿	莺	鸽	鹤	鹊	鸥
jiǎn	qiān	péng	míng	hóng	yīng	gē	hè	què	ōu
2861	2862	2863	2864	2865	2866	2867	2868	2869	2870
鹅	鸦	乌	呜	捣	寓	愚	偶	缸	窑
é	yā	wū	wū	dǎo	yù	yú	ǒu	gāng	yáo
2871	2872	2873	2874	2875	2876	2877	2878	2879	2880
罐	灌	陶	淘	掏	谣	冤	挽	勉	馋
guàn	guàn	táo	táo	tāo	yáo	yuān	wǎn	miǎn	chán
2881	2882	2883	2884	2885	2886	2887	2888	2889	2890

橡	豫	码	驯	玛	驻	骄	驰	蚂	驶
xiàng	yù	mǎ	xún	mǎ	zhù	jiāo	chí	mǎ	shǐ
2891	2892	2893	2894	2895	2896	2897	2898	2899	2900
骚	驾	驴	腾	骡	骤	闯	驱	驳	骗
sāo	jià	lǘ	téng	luó	zhòu	chuǎng	qū	bó	piàn
2901	2902	2903	2904	2905	2906	2907	2908	2909	2910
唬	虏	虐	滤	瞬	麟	磷	唇	辱	震
hǔ	lǔ	nüè	lù	shùn	lín	lín	chún	rǔ	zhèn
2911	2912	2913	2914	2915	2916	2917	2918	2919	2920
振	郑	掷	魄	槐	魅	瑰	魂	愧	魁
zhèn	zhèng	zhì	pò	huái	mèi	guī	hún	kuì	kuí
2921	2922	2923	2924	2925	2926	2927	2928	2929	2930
胧	垄	宠	庞	拢	聋	笼	挪	辆	瞒
lóng	lǒng	chǒng	páng	lǒng	lóng	lóng	nuó	liàng	mán
2931	2932	2933	2934	2935	2936	2937	2938	2939	2940
龟	蝇	绳	淹	俺	钮	羞	纽	赫	奕
guī	yíng	shéng	yān	ǎn	niǔ	xiū	niǔ	hè	yì
2941	2942	2943	2944	2945	2946	2947	2948	2949	2950
迹	蛮	啤	脾	碑	嘱	肆	插	毁	鼠
jì	mán	pí	pí	bēi	zhǔ	sì	chā	huǐ	shǔ
2951	2952	2953	2954	2955	2956	2957	2958	2959	2960
舅	滔	稻	蹈	嫂	搜	瘦	艘	焰	馅
jiù	tāo	dào	dǎo	sǎo	sōu	shòu	sōu	yàn	xiàn
2961	2962	2963	2964	2965	2966	2967	2968	2969	2970
陷	爽	缀	傻	蝴	蝶	蜘	蛛	骆	驼
xiàn	shuǎng	zhuì	shǎ	hú	dié	zhī	zhū	luò	tuó
2971	2972	2973	2974	2975	2976	2977	2978	2979	2980
蜻	蜓	凤	凰	玻	璃	橄	榄	芙	蓉
qīng	tíng	fèng	huáng	bō	lí	gǎn	lǎn	fú	róng
2981	2982	2983	2984	2985	2986	2987	2988	2989	2990
咖	啡	葡	萄	蘑	菇	吩	咐	乒	乓
kā	fēi	pú	táo	mó	gū	fēn	fù	pīng	pāng
2991	2992	2993	2994	2995	2996	2997	2998	2999	3000

曹	潘	谭	姚	薛	彭	冯	魏	岳	莉
cáo	*pān*	*tán*	*yáo*	*xuē*	*péng*	*féng*	*wèi*	*yuè*	*lì*
3001	3002	3003	3004	3005	3006	3007	3008	3009	3010

湘	甸	沧	穆	娜	琼	琳	钧	𰻝
xiāng	*diàn*	*cāng*	*mù*	*nà*	*qióng*	*lín*	*jūn*	*biáng*
3011	3012	3013	3014	3015	3016	3017	3018	50,001

INDEX II

Primitive Elements

This Index lists all the primitive elements used in this book. Characters used as primitives are only listed if the writing is significantly altered. The primitives are arranged according to the number of strokes. The number refers to the page on which the element is first introduced.

1 画	′	丨	㇄	㇄	㇀	㇏	㇆		
	1.31	1.32	1.56	1.56	1.253	1.253	1.349		

2 画	八	勹	丷	ナ	刂	刂	㇇	冂	人
	1.39	1.39	1.40	1.50	1.52	1.52	1.54	1.88	1.115

	儿	冖	二	爻	口	⺀	冫	㇈	乂
	1.115	1.136	1.137	1.159	1.168	1.170	1.170	1.179	1.217

	厂	厶	亻	刂	丂	勹	㇉	阝	卩
	1.221	1.223	1.244	1.279	1.282	1.284	1.284	1.288	1.296

	卩	マ	巴	乂	凵	丩	乛	匸	阝
	1.297	1.297	1.299	1.307	1.308	1.310	1.325	1.330	1.348

3 画	六	屮	少	巛	川	氵	宀	艹	㇌
	1.49	1.62	1.63	1.70	1.70	1.71	1.90	1.100	1.107

	犭	亼	辶	夂	弋	巳	口	忄	扌
	1.108	1.117	1.128	1.132	1.148	1.197	1.205	1.207	1.212

	廾	兀	犬	云	彳	彐	纟	幺	饣
	1.215	1.215	1.216	1.224	1.237	1.267	1.292	1.294	1.304

丰	乡	毛	丷	凡	厶	尢		
1.318	1.333	1.356	1.359	2.44	2.151	2.165		

4画

册	巛	朩	屮	亢	夂	龰	衣	镸
1.60	1.82	1.94	1.112	1.137	1.143	1.155	1.162	1.162
仓	小	殳	罒	云	勾	壬	牜	礻
1.178	1.207	1.220	1.222	1.225	1.226	1.252	1.255	1.260
尹	卄	収	少	宀	臣	旡	主	夬
1.268	1.273	1.280	1.284	1.290	1.299	1.304	1.314	1.326
卬	丷	区	冃	丬	亠	尣		
1.331	1.335	1.357	1.368	2.93	2.154	2.165		

5画

氺	言	丷	戊	戈	疋	足	礻	帀
1.71	1.138	1.142	1.150	1.152	1.157	1.160	1.162	1.167
匆	芦	弗	至	卯	卯	皿	艮	卅
1.198	1.254	1.281	1.294	1.297	1.297	1.301	1.302	1.312
夫	东	疒	癶	参	虫	冊	氐	丰
1.317	1.322	1.330	1.331	1.334	1.339	1.344	1.346	1.349
台	卉	刍	夗	忄	圣	发		
1.350	2.80	2.121	2.158	2.164	2.178	2.190		

6画

圭	叩	刖	吉	戈	戍	聿	畫	衣
1.80	1.111	1.131	1.140	1.150	1.151	1.160	1.160	1.162
束	乔	羊	羑	严	行	庀	关	自
1.168	1.173	1.199	1.200	1.223	1.237	1.256	1.275	1.285
糸	艮	良	函	丑	缶	虍	屰	爿
1.295	1.302	1.303	1.308	1.319	1.361	1.364	2.88	2.160

14画 翟
2.68

17画 雚
2.218

INDEX III

Characters by Number of Strokes

Here you will find all the characters treated in Books 1 and 2, grouped by the number of strokes. Characters within each group are arranged according to first stroke, of which there are five basic types. Their order is the same as the five strokes of the character 札:

⊖	一 *horizontal or* ╱ *rising*
①	│ *vertical or* ┘ *vertical with left hook*
②	ノ ′ *falling to the left*
⊙	丶 ′ *dot or* ╲ *falling to the right*
⊝	ㄴ 乙 ㄱ フ ㄱ ㄑ ㄴ ㄛ ′ *etc., sharp turn*

1 画

⊖	一	1
⊝	乙	95

2 画

⊖	丁	90
	七	7
	二	2
	十	10
	厂	121
①	卜	43
②	乃	625
	九	9
	人	793
	儿	56
	入	693
	八	8
	几	57
	匕	453
⊝	了	101

	刀	83
	刁	2814
	力	732
	又	633

3 画

⊖	万	65
	丈	837
	三	3
	下	46
	于	1281
	土	158
	士	334
	大	113
	寸	166
	工	76
	干	1277
	才	620
	与	1032
	亏	2285
①	上	45
	口	11

	小	109
	山	688
	巾	410
②	丸	42
	久	839
	么	670
	乞	470
	个	258
	亿	2066
	凡	62
	勺	69
	千	39
	及	627
	夕	115
	川	134
⊙	广	556
	之	988
	亡	490
	义	1180
	门	1260
⊝	也	505

	刃	84
	叉	1883
	女	102
	子	97
	尸	882
	己	515
	巳	519
	弓	1013
	习	545
	卫	1112
	乡	1387
	飞	96
	马	1453

4 画

⊖	不	991
	丰	1223
	云	428
	互	681
	五	5

	井	1358
	元	59
	切	85
	区	1295
	友	635
	天	436
	太	131
	夫	726
	专	1236
	尤	240
	屯	2542
	巨	2681
	开	613
	厅	122
	廿	976
	戈	361
	扎	1835
	支	650
	历	737
	木	202
	歹	712

惯	582	竟	487	随	1057	棉	418	越	393
惧	1800	章	447	隐	2344	棋	2735	趋	2199
断	931	粒	2039	颇	1959	棍	1709	辜	2551
旋	2128	粗	2749	颈	2403	棒	1233	逼	1619
族	999	粘	2030	骑	1458	棕	2167	雁	1431
望	493	盖	1137			棘	1690	雄	671
梁	2037	袄	2076	**12 画**		棚	1561	韩	2593
毫	2848	谍	1657	㊀ 募	1985	森	204	颊	1524
涯	1541	谐	1710	博	1381	棱	2347	㋹ 啼	1701
液	873	谋	2734	喜	1135	椁	2180	喂	2854
涵	2721	谓	1649	堤	1673	棺	2310	喇	2652
淯	2532	谎	1726	堪	2740	椅	1566	喉	2636
淋	1574	谜	781	塔	264	植	207	喊	1666
淌	1557	阐	2630	厨	1133	椒	1895	喘	2232
淑	1894	鸿	2865	彭	3006	欺	2736	喝	851
淘	2884	鹿	1462	惑	1791	款	2159	喧	1560
淡	175	麻	561	惠	1793	殖	1964	喻	1628
淤	1731	㋐ 婉	2453	惹	1796	焚	1575	喷	1873
淫	2113	婚	1374	揉	1004	煮	2306	嵌	2730
深	1075	婶	2177	提	598	琢	1751	帽	416
淳	1637	屠	2309	插	2958	琳	3017	幅	1686
渊	2035	巢	2179	握	887	琴	2608	悲	2634
混	458	弹	1019	揣	2233	琼	3016	掌	1956
添	1819	敢	722	揪	770	硫	1919	敞	345
清	1213	淹	2944	揭	2112	确	1363	景	331
渠	2683	综	2390	援	2396	硬	632	晰	2184
凑	2597	绿	1093	搓	1861	翘	1773	晴	2566
渗	2705	绸	2376	搜	2966	联	1471	晶	23
渔	155	维	1082	搭	1851	落	316	暑	2299
渐	930	缀	2973	搂	2046	葛	2108	最	720
焕	2725	绽	2379	搁	2622	葡	2993	畴	2576
兽	1509	绰	2372	搅	601	董	2657	紫	2420
率	1320	绵	2380	揽	2265	葬	716	蛙	1741
痒	2662	绪	2392	散	974	葵	2692	蛛	2978
痕	2672	绩	1216	敬	344	蒂	1702	蜓	2982
盗	2492	绷	2370	斑	2716	蒋	2469	赐	881
眷	984	绳	2943	斯	1339	葱	2131	赏	703
着	536	续	1096	暂	929	裁	401	赔	482
祸	2366	蛋	514	替	728	裂	1968	赋	386
祷	2579	逮	2226	朝	49	趁	2707	赌	2303
窑	2880	隆	2571	期	1336	超	392	赎	2116

INDEX IV

Character Pronunciations

This Index alphabetically lists the pronunciations, with their respective frame numbers, of all the characters treated in Books 1 and 2. Some of the characters have multiple pronunciations, which can be found by consulting a dictionary under the pronunciation given here.

A

ā	阿	1055
ā	啊	1056
āi	哀	403
āi	埃	2258
āi	哎	2534
ái	挨	2259
ái	癌	2665
ǎi	矮	2256
ài	爱	669
ài	碍	1544
ài	唉	2257
ài	艾	2533
ài	隘	2831
ān	安	197
ān	氨	2833
ǎn	俺	2945
àn	案	214
àn	暗	485
àn	按	606
àn	岸	1278
àn	黯	1722
áng	昂	2690
āo	凹	31
áo	熬	1732
ǎo	袄	1698
ào	奥	2031
ào	澳	2032
ào	懊	2033
ào	傲	2087

B

bā	八	8
bā	巴	1326
bā	吧	1329
bā	叭	1501
bā	疤	2728
bá	拔	2699
bǎ	把	1327
bà	爸	1328
bà	坝	1540
bà	罢	1913
bà	霸	2838
bái	白	34
bǎi	百	35
bǎi	柏	1562
bǎi	摆	1914
bài	败	341
bài	拜	2582
bān	班	1009
bān	般	1396
bān	搬	1398
bān	扳	1898
bān	颁	1943
bān	斑	2716
bǎn	板	657
bǎn	版	987
bàn	办	743
bàn	半	980
bàn	伴	981
bàn	扮	1945

bàn	拌	2246
bàn	瓣	2829
bāng	帮	1386
bāng	邦	2808
bǎng	膀	1733
bǎng	榜	1735
bǎng	绑	2809
bàng	棒	1233
bàng	磅	1734
bàng	傍	2093
bāo	包	520
bāo	胞	1745
báo	雹	1748
bǎo	宝	267
bǎo	保	823
bǎo	堡	824
bǎo	饱	2522
bào	抱	589
bào	报	1104
bào	豹	1902
bào	暴	2772
bào	爆	2774
bēi	杯	995
bēi	卑	1496
bēi	悲	2634
bēi	碑	2955
běi	北	454
bèi	贝	52
bèi	备	317
bèi	背	455
bèi	被	711

bèi	倍	2085
bèi	辈	2633
bēn	奔	1872
běn	本	213
bèn	笨	2049
bēng	崩	1926
bēng	绷	2370
bèng	蹦	2324
bī	逼	1619
bí	鼻	617
bǐ	匕	453
bǐ	比	456
bǐ	笔	1423
bǐ	彼	1999
bǐ	鄙	2805
bì	必	583
bì	壁	1186
bì	避	1187
bì	碧	1603
bì	币	1682
bì	毕	1708
bì	毙	1969
bì	蔽	2041
bì	弊	2044
bì	臂	2556
bì	闭	2626
biān	边	733
biān	编	1369
biān	鞭	2840
biǎn	扁	1367
biǎn	贬	2252

duān	端	966	fá	阀	2628	fēng	封	167	fù	妇	943
duǎn	短	1132	fǎ	法	676	fēng	风	1168	fù	父	1043
duàn	断	931	fān	番	1418	fēng	丰	1223	fù	附	1062
duàn	段	1388	fān	翻	1419	fēng	疯	1294	fù	赴	1671
duàn	锻	1389	fān	帆	1685	fēng	枫	2538	fù	覆	2616
duàn	缎	2813	fán	凡	62	fēng	锋	2583	fù	傅	2798
duī	堆	1764	fán	烦	173	fēng	蜂	2588	fù	缚	2799
duì	兑	499	fán	繁	2421	fēng	峰	2589	fù	咐	2998
duì	对	642	fǎn	反	656	féng	逢	2584			
duì	队	1067	fǎn	返	658	féng	缝	2585	**G**		
dūn	敦	1646	fàn	犯	1122	féng	冯	3007			
dūn	墩	1647	fàn	饭	1155	fěng	讽	1169	gā	嘎	1661
dūn	蹲	2479	fàn	贩	1897	fèng	奉	1232	gà	尬	2500
dūn	吨	2543	fàn	泛	2253	fèng	凤	2983	gāi	该	1198
dùn	盾	1896	fàn	范	2445	fó	佛	1021	gǎi	改	517
dùn	顿	2544	fāng	方	494	fǒu	否	992	gài	盖	1137
duō	多	116	fāng	芳	1729	fū	夫	726	gài	概	1159
duó	夺	1545	fáng	妨	495	fū	肤	1977	gài	溉	2527
duǒ	朵	1564	fáng	房	897	fū	孵	2429	gài	钙	2816
duǒ	躲	2293	fáng	防	1061	fū	敷	2796	gān	干	1277
duò	惰	1802	fáng	坊	1728	fú	福	904	gān	甘	1333
duò	舵	2823	fǎng	访	1730	fú	服	1103	gān	尴	2499
			fǎng	仿	2086	fú	辐	1625	gān	肝	2638
E			fǎng	纺	2382	fú	幅	1686	gān	竿	2645
			fàng	放	496	fú	蝠	1738	gǎn	感	576
é	额	313	fēi	飞	96	fú	扶	1978	gǎn	敢	722
é	蛾	1825	fēi	非	1267	fú	伏	2075	gǎn	赶	1280
é	俄	2097	fēi	啡	2992	fú	袱	2076	gǎn	淦	1731
é	鹅	2871	féi	肥	2726	fú	符	2099	gǎn	杆	2642
è	恶	1352	fěi	菲	2632	fú	拂	2277	gǎn	橄	2987
è	噩	1608	fěi	匪	2678	fú	浮	2431	gāng	冈	1170
è	鳄	2290	fèi	肺	420	fú	俘	2432	gāng	刚	1171
è	愕	2291	fèi	费	1020	fú	芙	2989	gāng	钢	2539
è	扼	2446	fèi	废	1303	fǔ	抚	612	gāng	纲	2541
è	饿	2526	fèi	沸	2276	fǔ	府	826	gāng	缸	2879
ēn	恩	570	fēn	分	694	fǔ	俯	827	gǎng	港	1357
ér	儿	56	fēn	芬	1944	fǔ	腐	845	gǎng	岗	2540
ér	而	962	fēn	纷	2385	fǔ	甫	1379	gàng	杠	1565
ěr	耳	717	fēn	氛	2835	fǔ	辅	1380	gāo	高	325
ěr	尔	798	fēn	吩	2997	fǔ	斧	2312	gāo	膏	1636
èr	二	2	fén	焚	1575	fù	负	64	gāo	糕	2040
èr	贰	1659	fén	坟	2713	fù	副	89	gǎo	搞	1848
			fěn	粉	779	fù	富	200	gǎo	稿	2008
F			fèn	份	796	fù	赋	386	gào	告	254
			fèn	奋	1522	fù	复	472	gē	哥	93
fā	发	1302	fèn	愤	1874	fù	腹	473	gē	戈	361
fá	乏	989	fèn	粪	2770	fù	付	825	gē	歌	476
fá	罚	1652							gē	割	1225
fá	伐	2079									

gē	胳	1630
gē	搁	2622
gē	鸽	2867
gé	格	310
gé	革	1407
gé	葛	2108
gé	隔	2351
gé	阁	2621
gè	个	258
gè	各	309
gěi	给	1084
gēn	跟	1143
gēn	根	1145
gēng	耕	2850
gěng	梗	1881
gěng	耿	1970
gèng	更	631
gōng	工	76
gōng	攻	339
gōng	公	696
gōng	功	742
gōng	弓	1013
gōng	供	1355
gōng	宫	2121
gōng	躬	2294
gōng	恭	2767
gǒng	巩	1513
gǒng	拱	2768
gòng	贡	81
gòng	共	1354
gōu	勾	1923
gōu	沟	1924
gōu	钩	1925
gǒu	狗	251
gǒu	苟	1581
gòu	够	117
gòu	购	686
gòu	构	687
gū	孤	1400
gū	咕	1502
gū	姑	1518
gū	估	2060
gū	辜	2551
gū	菇	2996
gǔ	古	16
gǔ	股	649
gǔ	谷	698

gǔ	骨	1053
gǔ	鼓	1134
gǔ	贾	1258
gù	故	342
gù	顾	523
gù	固	548
gù	雇	898
guā	瓜	1399
guā	刮	1515
guǎ	寡	1559
guà	挂	605
guāi	乖	1705
guǎi	拐	740
guài	怪	641
guān	冠	322
guān	观	639
guān	官	1041
guān	关	1469
guān	棺	2310
guǎn	管	1042
guǎn	馆	1157
guàn	贯	106
guàn	惯	582
guàn	罐	2881
guàn	灌	2882
guāng	光	130
guǎng	广	556
guàng	逛	299
guī	规	727
guī	归	2196
guī	瑰	2927
guī	龟	2941
guǐ	鬼	1472
guǐ	轨	1623
guǐ	诡	2457
guì	柜	2682
guì	贵	1340
guì	桂	1573
guì	跪	2458
gǔn	滚	1949
gùn	棍	1709
guō	锅	2365
guō	郭	2802
guó	国	549
guǒ	果	921
guǒ	裹	2182
guò	过	291

H

hā	哈	263
hái	孩	1196
hǎi	海	469
hài	亥	1194
hài	害	1224
hán	寒	1203
hán	含	1245
hán	韩	2593
hán	函	2720
hán	涵	2721
hǎn	喊	1666
hǎn	罕	2644
hàn	憾	577
hàn	汉	637
hàn	旱	1279
hàn	翰	1775
hàn	撼	1864
hàn	汗	2641
hàn	悍	2646
háng	行	754
háng	航	2822
háo	豪	1749
háo	毫	2848
hǎo	好	103
hào	浩	255
hào	号	1025
hào	耗	2849
hē	喝	851
hē	呵	1517
hé	河	153
hé	合	262
hé	禾	762
hé	和	764
hé	何	835
hé	核	1195
hé	荷	2101
hé	褐	2109
hé	盒	2489
hè	贺	750
hè	鹤	2868
hè	赫	2949
hēi	黑	182
hēi	嘿	1552
hén	痕	2672
hěn	很	1144

hěn	狠	2506
hèn	恨	2512
hēng	亨	1638
hēng	哼	1639
héng	横	1489
héng	恒	1797
héng	衡	2001
hōng	轰	1887
hōng	烘	2764
hóng	红	1089
hóng	虹	1737
hóng	宏	1906
hóng	弘	2268
hóng	洪	2763
hóng	鸿	2865
hōng	哄	2762
hóu	侯	1271
hóu	喉	2636
hóu	猴	2637
hǒu	吼	99
hòu	厚	124
hòu	后	659
hòu	候	1272
hū	忽	878
hū	乎	1163
hū	呼	1164
hú	胡	17
hú	湖	156
hú	糊	2029
hú	壶	2757
hú	狐	2828
hú	蝴	2975
hǔ	虎	1459
hǔ	唬	2911
hù	互	681
hù	户	896
hù	护	899
huā	花	833
huá	划	363
huá	华	831
huá	哗	832
huá	滑	1054
huá	猾	2335
huà	话	354
huà	化	830
huà	画	1173
huái	怀	997

lā	垃	1700	lí	篱	2549	liáo	僚	2696	lóu	楼	785
lǎ	喇	2652	lí	璃	2986	liáo	寥	2708	lǒu	搂	2046
là	辣	1288	lǐ	里	179	liào	料	969	lòu	漏	2141
là	腊	2240	lǐ	李	223	liě	咧	1967	lòu	陋	2343
là	蜡	2241	lǐ	理	276	liè	列	713	lú	卢	2134
lái	来	783	lǐ	礼	902	liè	烈	714	lú	炉	2155
lái	莱	2045	lǐ	哩	1549	liè	裂	1968	lú	芦	2156
lài	赖	2654	lǐ	鲤	1551	liè	劣	1984	lǔ	鲁	1538
lán	兰	533	lì	厉	123	liè	猎	2242	lǔ	虏	2912
lán	篮	1140	lì	丽	187	lín	林	203	lù	录	949
lán	蓝	1141	lì	立	444	lín	临	1010	lù	碌	950
lán	栏	1761	lì	力	732	lín	邻	2811	lù	路	1051
lán	拦	1860	lì	励	736	lín	麟	2916	lù	露	1052
lǎn	览	2264	lì	历	737	lín	磷	2917	lù	陆	1235
lǎn	揽	2265	lì	利	771	lín	琳	3017	lù	鹿	1462
lǎn	缆	2401	lì	例	816	lǐn	凛	2160	lǘ	驴	2903
lǎn	懒	2655	lì	粒	2039	lìn	淋	1574	lǚ	吕	865
lǎn	榄	2988	lì	隶	2225	líng	灵	942	lǚ	侣	866
làn	烂	534	lì	栗	2613	líng	零	1115	lǚ	旅	874
làn	滥	2498	lì	莉	3010	líng	陵	2346	lǚ	铝	2122
láng	郎	1385	liǎ	俩	1479	líng	菱	2348	lǚ	履	2145
láng	狼	2514	lián	连	301	líng	凌	2349	lǚ	屡	2147
láng	廊	2812	lián	莲	302	líng	玲	2437	lǚ	缕	2387
lǎng	朗	2513	lián	联	1471	líng	铃	2438	lǜ	律	755
làng	浪	1152	lián	廉	2219	líng	伶	2441	lǜ	绿	1093
lāo	捞	2127	lián	镰	2220	líng	龄	2547	lǜ	率	1320
láo	劳	868	lián	帘	2354	lǐng	领	1116	lǜ	虑	1460
láo	牢	1594	lián	怜	2439	lǐng	岭	2440	lǜ	氯	2837
lǎo	老	1029	liǎn	脸	1436	lìng	另	738	lǜ	滤	2914
lǎo	姥	2296	liǎn	敛	2859	lìng	令	1113	luǎn	卵	2428
le	了	101	liàn	练	1251	liū	溜	1108	luàn	乱	100
lēi	勒	1409	liàn	恋	1494	liú	流	684	lüè	略	311
léi	雷	426	liàn	链	1626	liú	留	1107	lüè	掠	1852
lěi	蕾	1691	liàn	炼	2609	liú	硫	1919	lún	轮	466
lěi	垒	1907	liáng	凉	434	liú	琉	1920	lún	沦	1712
lèi	类	782	liáng	良	1151	liú	榴	2433	lún	伦	2083
lèi	泪	1530	liáng	梁	2036	liú	瘤	2668	lùn	论	465
lèi	累	2418	liáng	粱	2037	liú	刘	2712	luó	罗	120
léng	棱	2347	liáng	粮	2515	liǔ	柳	1110	luó	萝	1583
lěng	冷	1114	liǎng	两	1478	liù	六	6	luó	锣	1616
lèng	愣	1813	liàng	量	180	lóng	龙	1474	luó	逻	1621
lí	离	1178	liàng	亮	329	lóng	隆	2571	luó	箩	2048
lí	厘	1550	liàng	谅	1654	lóng	胧	2931	luó	螺	2419
lí	狸	1589	liàng	辆	2939	lóng	聋	2936	luó	骡	2905
lí	梨	2020	liáo	聊	1109	lóng	笼	2937	luǒ	裸	2181
lí	犁	2021	liáo	辽	1620	lǒng	拢	2935	luò	洛	315
lí	黎	2024	liáo	疗	2658	lǒng	垄	2932	luò	落	316

luò	络	2375	méi	霉	1714	míng	明	21	nǎi	奶	626
luò	骆	2979	méi	眉	2149	míng	名	119	nài	奈	2158
			méi	媒	2732	míng	铭	285	nài	耐	2231
M			méi	煤	2733	míng	鸣	2864	nán	难	644
mā	妈	1454	měi	每	467	mìng	命	1105	nán	男	741
má	麻	561	měi	美	529	miù	谬	2709	nán	南	1259
mǎ	马	1453	mèi	妹	219	mō	摸	1844	náng	囊	2744
mǎ	码	2893	mèi	昧	1577	mó	模	232	náo	挠	1854
mǎ	玛	2895	mèi	媚	2150	mó	摩	586	nǎo	脑	1176
mǎ	蚂	2899	mèi	魅	2926	mó	魔	1473	nǎo	恼	1177
mà	骂	1456	mēn	闷	2625	mó	膜	1584	nào	闹	2623
ma	吗	1455	mén	门	1260	mó	磨	1785	ne	呢	884
ma	嘛	1784	men	们	1261	mǒ	抹	1843	nèi	内	840
mái	埋	181	méng	萌	1580	mó	蘑	2995	nèn	嫩	2656
mǎi	买	858	méng	朦	2126	mò	墨	183	néng	能	1464
mài	脉	139	méng	盟	2484	mò	末	216	ní	尼	883
mài	迈	292	měng	蒙	2125	mò	沫	217	ní	泥	885
mài	卖	859	měng	猛	2486	mò	莫	231	nǐ	你	799
mài	麦	1206	mèng	梦	205	mò	漠	233	nǐ	拟	2119
mán	馒	2523	mèng	孟	2485	mò	默	246	nì	腻	1660
mán	瞒	2940	mī	眯	2028	mò	寞	1586	nì	逆	1939
mán	蛮	2952	mí	迷	780	mò	陌	2337	nì	匿	2679
mǎn	满	1480	mí	谜	781	móu	谋	2734	nián	年	871
màn	曼	723	mí	弥	1015	mǒu	某	1334	nián	黏	2023
màn	慢	724	mǐ	米	778	mǔ	母	105	niàn	廿	976
màn	漫	725	mì	密	692	mǔ	亩	324	niàn	念	1246
màn	蔓	1976	mì	泌	1822	mǔ	姆	1520	niáng	娘	1153
máng	盲	491	mì	蜜	1824	mǔ	牡	1595	niàng	酿	2516
máng	忙	581	mì	觅	1900	mǔ	拇	1836	niǎo	鸟	1438
máng	芒	1724	mì	秘	2016	mù	目	15	niào	尿	2137
máng	茫	1727	mián	棉	418	mù	木	202	niē	捏	1841
máng	氓	2789	mián	眠	1378	mù	墓	234	nín	您	800
mǎng	莽	1871	mián	绵	2380	mù	幕	417	níng	宁	1558
māo	猫	1587	miǎn	免	1449	mù	暮	1585	níng	凝	2436
máo	矛	1002	miǎn	勉	2889	mù	牧	1644	nǐng	拧	1842
máo	毛	1421	miàn	面	1406	mù	慕	1818	niú	牛	252
máo	茅	2261	miáo	苗	235	mù	募	1985	niǔ	扭	1487
mào	冒	184	miáo	瞄	236	mù	穆	3014	niǔ	钮	2946
mào	茂	367	miáo	描	1845				niǔ	纽	2948
mào	帽	416	miǎo	渺	1534	**N**			nóng	农	408
mào	贸	1106	miǎo	秒	2005				nóng	浓	409
mào	貌	1903	miào	妙	127	ná	拿	587	nòng	弄	615
me	么	670	miào	庙	2171	nǎ	哪	1477	nú	奴	747
méi	梅	468	miè	灭	171	nà	呐	841	nǔ	努	748
méi	没	647	miè	蔑	1665	nà	那	1476	nù	怒	1990
méi	枚	1643	mín	民	1377	nà	纳	2389	nǚ	女	102
méi	玫	1645	mǐn	敏	1713	nà	娜	3015	nuǎn	暖	2395
						nǎi	乃	625			

qīng	卿	2511	rǎng	嚷	2562	sǎn	伞	1598	shē	奢	2304
qīng	氢	2836	ràng	让	349	sāng	丧	1427	shé	舌	40
qīng	蜻	2981	ráo	饶	2518	sāng	桑	2751	shé	蛇	513
qíng	情	1211	rǎo	扰	1847	sǎng	嗓	2752	shè	涉	381
qíng	晴	2566	rào	绕	2378	sāo	骚	2901	shè	设	648
qǐng	请	1210	rě	惹	1796	sǎo	扫	944	shè	社	901
qǐng	顷	1703	rè	热	603	sǎo	嫂	2965	shè	射	1027
qìng	庆	1783	rén	人	793	sè	色	1330	shè	舍	1599
qióng	穷	2356	rén	仁	820	sè	涩	1669	shè	摄	1973
qióng	琼	3016	rěn	忍	565	sè	瑟	1823	shéi	谁	540
qiū	秋	768	rèn	刃	84	sēn	森	204	shēn	申	918
qiū	丘	1077	rèn	认	794	sēng	僧	2088	shēn	伸	919
qiú	求	140	rèn	任	853	shā	砂	126	shēn	身	1026
qiú	球	268	rēng	扔	1878	shā	沙	146	shēn	深	1075
qiú	酋	1128	réng	仍	809	shā	杀	1167	shēn	呻	2174
qiú	囚	2089	rì	日	12	shā	纱	2374	shēn	绅	2391
qū	曲	967	róng	容	701	shā	刹	2537	shén	什	802
qū	区	1295	róng	溶	702	shá	啥	1600	shén	神	920
qū	屈	2143	róng	荣	867	shǎ	傻	2974	shěn	审	2176
qū	趋	2199	róng	榕	1953	shà	厦	1631	shěn	婶	2177
qū	躯	2689	róng	熔	1954	shà	煞	2198	shěn	沈	2501
qū	驱	2908	róng	融	2350	shāi	筛	2052	shèn	甚	1338
qú	渠	2683	róng	绒	2377	shài	晒	2610	shèn	慎	1801
qǔ	取	718	róng	蓉	2990	shān	山	688	shèn	肾	2266
qǔ	娶	1975	rǒng	冗	318	shān	杉	2700	shèn	渗	2705
qù	去	675	róu	柔	1003	shān	衫	2702	shēng	升	41
qù	趣	719	róu	揉	1004	shān	删	2783	shēng	生	1218
quān	圈	2449	ròu	肉	844	shān	珊	2785	shēng	声	1411
quán	泉	141	rú	如	104	shǎn	陕	2345	shēng	牲	2570
quán	全	275	rú	儒	964	shǎn	闪	2627	shéng	绳	2943
quán	拳	985	rǔ	乳	2430	shàn	善	870	shěng	省	132
quán	权	1884	rǔ	辱	2919	shàn	擅	1866	shèng	圣	634
quǎn	犬	239	rù	入	693	shàn	扇	2157	shèng	胜	1222
quàn	劝	1986	ruǎn	软	477	shāng	商	451	shèng	剩	1707
quàn	券	2248	ruì	瑞	965	shāng	伤	822	shèng	盛	2490
quē	缺	1444	ruì	锐	1736	shǎng	赏	703	shī	诗	355
què	却	1101	rùn	润	2620	shǎng	响	1556	shī	师	412
què	确	1363	ruò	若	226	shàng	上	45	shī	狮	413
què	雀	1763	ruò	弱	1017	shàng	尚	190	shī	失	729
què	鹊	2869				shang	裳	1955	shī	施	875
qún	裙	960		**S**		shāo	烧	377	shī	尸	882
qún	群	961	sǎ	撒	975	shāo	梢	1568	shī	湿	2759
			sǎ	洒	2611	shāo	捎	1837	shí	十	10
	R		sà	萨	2711	shāo	稍	2006	shí	石	125
rán	然	247	sài	赛	1204	sháo	勺	69	shí	时	168
rán	燃	1591	sài	塞	2564	shǎo	少	110	shí	实	857
rǎn	染	222	sān	三	3	shào	哨	1528	shí	食	1154
rǎng	壤	1202	sǎn	散	974	shào	绍	2373	shí	拾	1850

shí	蚀	2521	shū	舒	2263	sǒng	耸	2105	tāi	胎	1908
shǐ	史	630	shú	熟	327	sòng	送	1470	tái	台	672
shǐ	始	674	shú	赎	2116	sòng	宋	1572	tái	抬	1912
shǐ	使	838	shǔ	属	1500	sòng	颂	1947	tài	太	131
shǐ	矢	998	shǔ	暑	2299	sòng	讼	1948	tài	态	567
shǐ	屎	2146	shǔ	署	2301	sòng	诵	2444	tài	泰	1231
shì	世	28	shǔ	薯	2302	sōu	搜	2966	tài	汰	1535
shì	适	290	shǔ	鼠	2960	sōu	艘	2968	tān	摊	645
shì	士	334	shù	树	643	sòu	嗽	2653	tān	滩	1888
shì	识	353	shù	数	784	sū	苏	745	tān	贪	2607
shì	式	359	shù	术	1199	sū	稣	2007	tān	瘫	2663
shì	试	360	shù	述	1200	sú	俗	2095	tán	谈	358
shì	是	394	shù	束	1286	sù	诉	936	tán	坛	1693
shì	市	419	shù	恕	1790	sù	素	1207	tán	潭	2615
shì	室	679	shù	竖	2267	sù	速	1287	tán	痰	2659
shì	势	734	shuā	刷	2140	sù	溯	1940	tán	谭	3003
shì	示	900	shuǎ	耍	2230	sù	塑	1941	tǎn	坦	1539
shì	视	903	shuāi	摔	1321	sù	宿	2074	tǎn	毯	2847
shì	逝	934	shuāi	衰	1678	sù	肃	2211	tàn	探	1076
shì	事	953	shuǎi	甩	2777	suān	酸	2474	tàn	叹	1882
shì	氏	1371	shuài	帅	411	suàn	算	790	tàn	炭	1932
shì	释	1417	shuān	栓	1609	suàn	蒜	2166	tàn	碳	1933
shì	柿	1689	shuān	拴	1849	suī	虽	512	tāng	汤	527
shì	拭	1853	shuāng	霜	427	suí	随	1057	táng	堂	706
shì	侍	2071	shuāng	双	636	suǐ	髓	2336	táng	唐	954
shì	誓	2192	shuǎng	爽	2972	suì	岁	691	táng	糖	955
shì	嗜	2295	shuǐ	水	137	suì	遂	1752	táng	膛	1958
shì	饰	2519	shuì	睡	1243	suì	穗	2015	táng	塘	2224
shì	驶	2900	shuì	税	2012	suì	崇	2161	tǎng	淌	1557
shōu	收	1193	shùn	顺	136	suì	隧	2342	tǎng	倘	2073
shǒu	首	71	shùn	瞬	2915	suì	碎	2471	tǎng	躺	2292
shǒu	守	192	shuō	说	501	sūn	孙	112	tàng	趟	1672
shǒu	手	584	shuò	硕	1526	sǔn	损	1832	tàng	烫	1756
shòu	售	541	shuò	烁	1899	sǔn	笋	2229	tāo	涛	2577
shòu	受	667	sī	思	569	suō	缩	2388	tāo	掏	2885
shòu	授	668	sī	丝	1079	suō	梭	2475	tāo	滔	2962
shòu	兽	1509	sī	斯	1339	suǒ	所	926	táo	桃	238
shòu	寿	2575	sī	司	1391	suǒ	琐	1604	táo	逃	295
shòu	瘦	2967	sī	私	2017	suǒ	锁	1614	táo	陶	2883
shū	输	305	sī	嘶	2738	suǒ	索	2423	táo	淘	2884
shū	叔	653	sī	撕	2739				táo	萄	2994
shū	梳	685	sǐ	死	715		**T**		tǎo	讨	351
shū	枢	1296	sì	四	4				tào	套	1498
shū	书	1393	sì	寺	169	tā	它	462	tè	特	253
shū	淑	1894	sì	似	862	tā	她	506	téng	藤	2249
shū	疏	1921	sì	饲	2819	tā	他	810	téng	疼	2661
shū	蔬	1922	sì	肆	2957	tā	塌	1774	téng	腾	2904
shū	殊	1965	sōng	松	697	tǎ	塔	264	tī	梯	2280
						tà	踏	2319			

tī	踢	2326	tú	途	1285	wǎng	网	1172	wò	沃	1697
tí	题	395	tú	徒	1995	wǎng	枉	1606	wò	卧	1980
tí	提	598	tú	屠	2309	wàng	妄	492	wū	巫	850
tí	啼	1701	tú	涂	2648	wàng	望	493	wū	屋	886
tí	蹄	2322	tǔ	土	158	wàng	忘	564	wū	诬	2107
tǐ	体	813	tǔ	吐	163	wàng	旺	1602	wū	污	2286
tì	替	728	tù	兔	1447	wēi	威	371	wū	乌	2873
tì	惕	2133	tuán	团	622	wēi	微	759	wū	呜	2874
tì	屉	2135	tuī	推	600	wēi	危	1123	wú	吾	19
tì	剃	2278	tuí	颓	2004	wéi	维	1082	wú	吴	437
tì	涕	2281	tuǐ	腿	1148	wéi	韦	1227	wú	无	611
tiān	天	436	tuì	退	1147	wéi	围	1228	wǔ	五	5
tiān	添	1819	tūn	吞	1695	wéi	唯	1762	wǔ	武	385
tián	田	14	tún	屯	2542	wéi	惟	1816	wǔ	午	542
tián	填	162	tuō	脱	500	wéi	违	2594	wǔ	舞	1342
tián	甜	2729	tuō	托	1424	wěi	委	774	wǔ	伍	2054
tiáo	条	307	tuō	拖	1858	wěi	伪	797	wǔ	侮	2084
tiǎo	挑	1846	tuó	驼	2980	wěi	伟	1229	wù	误	439
tiào	跳	1050	tuǒ	妥	1901	wěi	尾	1422	wù	务	752
tiē	贴	53	tuò	拓	1833	wěi	萎	2022	wù	雾	753
tiě	铁	730	tuò	唾	2605	wěi	纬	2595	wù	勿	877
tiě	帖	1684				wèi	胃	29	wù	物	879
tīng	厅	122		**W**		wèi	未	215	wù	悟	1798
tīng	听	925	wā	哇	165	wèi	味	218			
tíng	亭	328	wā	蛙	1741	wèi	为	746		**X**	
tíng	停	818	wā	挖	2353	wèi	位	807	xī	夕	115
tíng	廷	854	wá	娃	1542	wèi	卫	1112	xī	息	574
tíng	庭	855	wǎ	瓦	2117	wèi	谓	1649	xī	吸	628
tíng	蜓	2982	wà	袜	1677	wèi	蔚	2164	xī	昔	971
tǐng	挺	2115	wāi	歪	2254	wèi	慰	2165	xī	希	1165
tǐng	艇	2825	wài	外	118	wèi	畏	2853	xī	稀	1166
tōng	通	1117	wān	弯	1492	wèi	喂	2854	xī	西	1253
tóng	同	185	wān	湾	1493	wèi	魏	3008	xī	熄	1821
tóng	铜	281	wán	丸	42	wēn	温	1138	xī	熙	1982
tóng	童	450	wán	顽	61	wén	闻	1266	xī	膝	2025
tóng	桐	1571	wán	完	193	wén	文	1315	xī	锡	2132
tǒng	统	1083	wán	玩	270	wén	蚊	1316	xī	犀	2138
tǒng	筒	2050	wǎn	晚	1450	wén	纹	2714	xī	析	2183
tǒng	桶	2443	wǎn	宛	2451	wěn	吻	2129	xī	晰	2184
tòng	痛	1293	wǎn	婉	2453	wěn	稳	2204	xī	惜	2238
tōu	偷	2077	wǎn	碗	2454	wèn	问	1263	xī	溪	2409
tóu	投	646	wǎn	挽	2888	wēng	翁	1950	xī	嘻	2482
tóu	头	856	wàn	万	65	wēng	嗡	1951	xī	牺	2614
tòu	透	776	wàn	腕	2452	wō	窝	2363	xī	悉	2846
tū	凸	32	wāng	汪	1605	wō	涡	2364	xí	习	545
tū	突	1072	wáng	王	265	wō	蜗	2367	xí	席	977
tū	秃	2003	wáng	亡	490	wǒ	我	588	xí	袭	1475
tú	图	555	wǎng	往	758	wò	握	887	xí	媳	1820

yán	盐	2487	yè	叶	18	yīn	殷	2817	yóu	邮	2807
yán	沿	2826	yè	页	60	yín	银	1142	yǒu	有	79
yǎn	眼	1150	yè	夜	872	yín	寅	1465	yǒu	友	635
yǎn	演	1466	yè	液	873	yín	淫	2113	yòu	右	78
yǎn	掩	1485	yè	业	1349	yín	吟	2606	yòu	又	633
yǎn	衍	2000	yī	一	1	yǐn	尹	957	yòu	诱	777
yàn	宴	198	yī	衣	400	yǐn	引	1014	yòu	佑	2063
yàn	厌	241	yī	依	815	yǐn	隐	2344	yòu	幼	2408
yàn	彦	1313	yī	伊	958	yǐn	饮	2520	yú	鱼	154
yàn	艳	1332	yī	医	1298	yǐn	瘾	2671	yú	渔	155
yàn	雁	1431	yí	移	767	yìn	荫	1060	yú	逾	306
yàn	验	1457	yí	遗	1341	yìn	印	1125	yú	娱	438
yàn	燕	2243	yí	怡	1910	yīng	英	1323	yú	于	1281
yàn	焰	2969	yí	夷	2269	yīng	应	1432	yú	余	1283
yāng	央	1322	yí	姨	2270	yīng	鹰	1440	yú	榆	1629
yāng	殃	2723	yí	疑	2435	yīng	婴	1519	yú	愉	1809
yāng	秧	2724	yí	仪	2550	yīng	樱	1567	yú	舆	2459
yáng	羊	528	yí	宜	2746	yīng	莺	2866	yú	愚	2877
yáng	洋	530	yǐ	乙	95	yíng	营	869	yǔ	语	356
yáng	阳	1058	yǐ	已	519	yíng	迎	1300	yǔ	雨	425
yáng	杨	1755	yǐ	以	861	yíng	赢	1723	yǔ	羽	544
yáng	扬	1859	yǐ	蚁	1182	yíng	萤	2123	yǔ	予	1005
yǎng	养	537	yǐ	椅	1566	yíng	莹	2124	yǔ	与	1032
yǎng	仰	1299	yǐ	倚	2068	yíng	盈	2494	yǔ	宇	1282
yǎng	痒	2662	yì	艺	228	yíng	蝇	2942	yǔ	屿	2298
yǎng	氧	2834	yì	意	572	yǐng	影	1305	yù	玉	266
yàng	样	532	yì	异	616	yǐng	颖	2010	yù	狱	350
yāo	夭	440	yì	易	880	yìng	硬	632	yù	育	683
yāo	腰	1255	yì	义	1180	yìng	映	2722	yù	浴	699
yāo	妖	1696	yì	议	1181	yō	哟	2402	yù	欲	700
yāo	邀	2400	yì	益	1401	yōng	拥	2775	yù	预	1007
yáo	尧	376	yì	逸	1448	yōng	佣	2776	yù	遇	1443
yáo	遥	1445	yì	亦	1491	yōng	庸	2778	yù	喻	1628
yáo	摇	1446	yì	忆	1805	yǒng	永	138	yù	域	1662
yáo	淆	2532	yì	毅	1889	yǒng	泳	143	yù	愈	1792
yáo	窑	2880	yì	役	1997	yǒng	勇	1118	yù	裕	1952
yáo	谣	2886	yì	亿	2066	yǒng	咏	1536	yù	御	2427
yáo	姚	3004	yì	译	2601	yǒng	涌	2442	yù	吁	2647
yǎo	咬	2313	yì	疫	2664	yòng	用	1361	yù	郁	2801
yào	药	1098	yì	抑	2691	yōu	忧	578	yù	誉	2857
yào	要	1254	yì	谊	2747	yōu	优	821	yù	寓	2876
yào	钥	1611	yì	翼	2766	yōu	悠	2090	yù	豫	2892
yào	耀	1776	yì	溢	2830	yōu	幽	2410	yuān	渊	2035
yē	耶	2806	yì	奕	2950	yóu	尤	240	yuān	冤	2887
yé	爷	2434	yīn	音	484	yóu	游	876	yuán	员	55
yě	也	505	yīn	因	551	yóu	由	913	yuán	元	59
yě	野	1008	yīn	阴	1059	yóu	油	915	yuán	原	142
yě	冶	1911	yīn	姻	1779	yóu	犹	1590	yuán	源	150

INDEX V

Key Words and Primitive Meanings

This Index contains a cumulative list of all the key words and primitive meanings used in Books 1 and 2. Key words are listed with their respective character and frame number. Primitive meanings are listed in italics and are followed only by the number of the volume and the page (also in italics) on which they are first introduced.

make	做	804	meat	肉	844	*miser*		*2.75*
make a present of	赠	504	meat, dried	腊	2240	miserable	凄	2209
make an			medicine	药	1098	misfortune	祸	2366
appointment	约	1090	mediocre	庸	2778	mislay	丢	1915
make			meditation	禅	2275	miss	念	1246
arrangements	筹	2580	meet with	遭	2235	*missile*		*1.220*
make the rounds	逻	1621	meeting	会	677	*mist*		*1.37*
makeup, put on	妆	243	*meeting*		*1.117*	mistaken	错	973
male	男	741	mellow wine	醇	2463	mix	混	458
male phoenix	凤	2983	melon	瓜	1399	mock	讽	1169
malicious	歹	712	melt	融	2350	model	范	2445
mama	妈	1454	membrane	膜	1584	modest	逊	298
man, elderly	翁	1950	Mencius	孟	2485	moisten	润	2620
man, young	郎	1385	*mending*		*1.157*	mold	型	619
manage	办	743	mentor	傅	2798	mom	娘	1153
mandala		*1.233*	merchant	贾	1258	*Mona Lisa*		*2.152*
maneuver	驶	2900	merely	仅	811	monarch	君	959
mango	芒	1724	merit	勋	1983	money, paper	钞	1613
manifest	彰	2703	*mesh, wire*		*1.312*	Mongolia	蒙	2125
mannered, well-	彬	2701	mess around	耍	2230	monk, Buddhist	僧	2088
many	多	116	messed up	糟	2236	monkey	猴	2637
maple	枫	2538	*metal*		*1.122*	*monkey*		*1.263*
march		*1.151*	method	法	676	*monks*		*1.89*
mark	标	905	meticulous	仔	2067	*(monk's) cowl*		*1.88*
market	市	419	metropolis	都	1383	*monocle*		*1.255*
marquis	侯	1271	mid-	仲	2058	month	月	13
marriage	婚	1374	middle	中	38	*moon*		*1.23*
married woman	妇	943	mien	貌	1903	moor	泊	1532
marrow	髓	2336	might	威	371	morality	德	761
marry	嫁	1753	*migrating ducks*		*2.149*	more, even	更	631
marsh	沼	145	mildew	霉	1714	more and more	愈	1792
marvelous	瑰	2927	mile	哩	1549	moreover	且	1343
massage	搓	1861	military	武	385	morning	晨	1468
master thief	盗	2492	milk	奶	626	*mortar*		*2.228*
mat	席	977	millet, fine	梁	2036	*mosaic*		*1.337*
matchmaker	媒	2732	milli-	毫	2848	*Moses, baby*		*1.226*
mate	伙	2072	million, one			mosquito	蚊	1316
material	料	969	hundred	亿	2066	most	最	720
maternal aunt	姨	2270	mimic	仿	2086	moth	蛾	1825
maternal			*mind, state of*		*1.207*	mother	母	105
grandmother	姥	2296	mine	矿	1782	mother's brother	舅	2961
Matteo	玛	2895	mingle	交	1044	mound	墩	1647
matter	事	953	minister	卿	2511	mountain	山	688
mausoleum	陵	2346	*Minuteclods*		*2.143*	*mountain goat*		*2.88*
meal	饭	1155	mirror	镜	488	mountain range	岭	2440
meaning	谓	1649	*mirror*		*1.184*	mourn	悼	1799
measuring cup		*1.272*	miscellaneous	杂	225	mouse	鼠	2960

voucher	券	2248	wealthy	富	200
vow	誓	2192	weapon	械	1869
vulture		*1.222*	wear at the waist	佩	2080
			weary	乏	989
W			*weather*		*1.169*
Waaah!	哇	165	weave	织	1080
wagon		*1.131*	web	络	2375
waist	腰	1255	weep	泣	445
waist, wear at the	佩	2080	weep aloud	啼	1701
wait	候	1272	Wei	魏	3008
waitress		*1.304*	weigh	称	801
walk	走	391	weight	衡	2001
walking legs		*1.133*	welcome	接	604
walking stick		*1.32*	well	井	1358
wall	墙	1780	well, wish	祝	2162
wall		*1.224*	well-behaved	乖	1705
wall paint	漆	2026	well-mannered	彬	2701
walls, city		*1.348*	west	西	1253
walls, outer	郭	2802	*West, Old*		*1.322*
wand, magic		*1.35*	wet	湿	2759
want	要	1254	wha?	啥	1600
war	战	362	whale	鲸	1640
war, civil		*1.353*	what?	什	802
ward off	防	1061	whatwhichwho-		
warehouse	库	558	wherewhy?	何	835
warm	暖	2395	wheat	麦	1206
warm by a fire	烘	2764	wheel	轮	466
warn	诫	1870	wheeze	喘	2232
warship	舰	2821	wherefore	由	913
wash	洗	257	which?	哪	1477
wash in a			whip	鞭	2840
container	淘	2884	whirl	旋	2128
wasteland	荒	1725	whirlpool	涡	2364
watchful	惕	2133	*whirlwind*		*1.137*
water	水	137	*whisk broom*		*2.151*
water caltrop	菱	2348	*whiskey bottle*		*1.300*
water lily		*1.306*	whistle	哨	1528
waterfall	瀑	2773	white	白	34
water's edge	滨	2369	*white bird*		*1.32*
waves	波	708	*white towel*		*1.166*
waves, large	涛	2577	who?	谁	540
wax	蜡	2241	whole	全	275
way	道	287	wholeheartedly	恳	2507
we (exclusive)	俺	2945	wicked	邪	2845
we (inclusive)	咱	1504	*wicker basket*		*1.338*
weak	弱	1017	wide	宽	230
wealth		*1.54*	widowed	寡	1559

width of cloth	幅	1686
wield	秉	2207
wife	妻	2208
wife, elder		
brother's	嫂	2965
wild	野	1008
wild dogs, pack of		*1.108*
wild goose	雁	1431
wild rice		*1.239*
willow	柳	1110
wilt	萎	2022
wily	刁	2814
win	赢	1723
wind	风	1168
wind		*1.42*
wind around	缠	2383
winded, long-	絮	2422
winding	宛	2451
window	窗	1483
windstorm		*1.307*
wind-up teeth		*1.111*
wine, mellow	醇	2463
wine, pour	酌	2460
wings	翼	2766
wings		*1.202*
winter	冬	435
wipe away	拭	1853
wire, razor		*1.368*
wire mesh		*1.312*
wisdom	智	1001
wish	愿	571
wish, as you	随	1057
wish well	祝	2162
witch	巫	850
withdraw	却	1101
withered	枯	210
without haste	悠	2090
withstand	御	2427
witted, quick-	敏	1713
wolf	狼	2514
woman	女	102
woman, married	妇	943
woman, old	婆	709
wonderful	妙	127
wood		*1.94*
wood pulp		*2.140*
wooden leg		*1.286*

collected in *Journey to America* (New Haven, CT: Yale University Press, 1960).

64. Alexis and Marie de Tocqueville to Francis Lieber (July 22, 1846), *Tocqueville in America after 1840: Letters and Other Writings*, eds. Aurelian Craiutu and Jeremy Jennings (New York: Cambridge University Press, 2009), 85.

65. Francis Lieber to Alexis de Tocqueville (September 25, 1846), *Tocqueville in America after 1840*, 87–88.

66. Ibid., 87.

67. A related point that Lieber added to his analysis concerns the rugged individualism, independence, and penchant for isolation of American settlers. While the Frenchman "loves his coffee house with all the buzz of talk and clicking of the domino," Americans have "no objection to settle separately, but they prefer it, because economically speaking it is preferable and they have perfect independence. They dot a country and consequently subdue it easier"; Francis Lieber to Alexis de Tocqueville (Sept. 25, 1846), *Tocqueville in America after 1840*, 88.

68. Francis Lieber, *On Civil Liberty and Self-Government* (Philadelphia: J. B. Lippincott, 1874 [1853]), 21. It is important to note that Lieber's own racial views were more complicated than a simple endorsement of Anglo-Saxon supremacy. He did not restrict Anglican liberty to the Anglo-Saxon race: "We call this liberty Anglican freedom, not because we think that it ought to be restricted to the Anglican race . . . but because it has been evolved first and chiefly by this race" (*Civil Liberty*, 52–53). By 1850 Lieber became repelled by the chauvinistic racialism used to justify slavery and westward expansion; Horsman, *Race and Manifest Destiny*, 171–173.

69. Lieber, *Civil Liberty*, 70, 281.

70. Francis Lieber to Alexis de Tocqueville (September 25, 1846), *Tocqueville in America after 1840*, 88.

71. Ibid.

72. Tocqueville, "Essay on Algeria," *Writings on Empire and Slavery*, 70–71.

73. Margaret Kohn, "Empire's Law: Tocqueville on Colonialism and the State of Exception," *Canadian Journal of Political Science* 41, no. 2 (June 2008): 256.

74. Francis Lieber to Alexis de Tocqueville (September 25, 1846), *Tocqueville in America after 1840*, 89.

75. Tocqueville, "Essay on Algeria," 81.

76. Ibid., 97–98.

77. Ibid., 110.

78. Tocqueville, *Democracy*, 393–394; Francis Fukuyama, "The March of Equality," *Journal of Democracy* 11, no. 1 (January 2000): 11–17.

79. Sheldon Wolin, *Tocqueville between Two Worlds* (Princeton, NJ: Princeton University Press, 2004), 241.

Chapter 4: Manifest Destiny and the Safety Valve of Colonization

1. Ernest Lee Tuveson, *Redeemer Nation: The Idea of America's Millennial Role* (Chicago: University of Chicago Press, 1968).

2. Walt Whitman, *The Gathering of the Forces*, vol. 1 (New York: G. P. Putnam's Sons, 1920), 27, 246.

3. Stephanson, *Manifest Destiny*.

4. Classic works on manifest destiny include Albert Weinberg, *Manifest Destiny: A Study of Nationalist Expansionism in American History* (Chicago: Quadrangle Press, 1935); Merk, *Manifest Destiny and Mission in American History*; and Horsman, *Race and Manifest Destiny*. Also see Norman Graebner, *Manifest Destiny* (Indianapolis: Bobbs-Merrill, 1968).

5. On the political theology of manifest destiny, see Adam Gomez, "Deus Vult:

John L. O'Sullivan, Manifest Destiny, and American Democratic Messianism," *American Political Thought* 1, no. 2 (September 2012): 236–262.

6. Thomas Hietala, *Manifest Design: American Exceptionalism and Empire*, rev. ed. (Ithaca, NY: Cornell University Press, 2003), 4, 255. This tendency to neglect manifest destiny and the safety valve as substantive expressions of democratic thought likely stems from the "myth and symbol school" of American studies. In his famous study of "virgin land," for instance, Henry Nash Smith argued that "the safety valve" trope was part of a symbolic structure of the "myth of empire"; *Virgin Land: The American West As Symbol and Myth* (Cambridge, MA: Harvard University Press, 1950).

7. There were significant critics of the Mexican-American War. For instance, Whig leader Joshua Giddings attributed the war to the "democratic doctrine," which prioritized the "arbitrary will of an irresponsible majority"; "My Country, Right or Wrong" (May 1846), in *Great Debates in American History: Foreign Relations*, vol. 2, part 1, ed. Marion Miller (New York: Current Literature, 1913), 354, 356. Yet what is important in these criticisms is that Whig critics almost invariably criticized the war and colonization as defects of democracy, not as violations of democratic principles. Despite a vibrant debate about conquest and colonization during this period, my focus will thus be on thinkers who blended democratic theory with theories of settler colonization.

8. John O'Sullivan, "Annexation," *Democratic Review* 17, no. 85 (July-August 1845): 5. On the origins of manifest destiny in the writings of O'Sullivan, see Julius Pratt, "The Origins of Manifest Destiny," *American Historical Review* 32 (1927): 795–798.

9. John O'Sullivan, "The True Title," *New York Morning News*, December 27, 1845.

10. Stephanson, *Manifest Destiny*, xii.

11. Edward Widmer, *Young America: The Flowering of Democracy in New York City* (New York: Oxford University Press, 1999), 28–29; Robert Sampson, *John O'Sullivan and His Times* (Kent, OH: Kent State University Press, 2003), 15–17; Stephanson, *Manifest Destiny*, 39.

12. John O'Sullivan, "The Democratic Principle—The Importance of Its Assertion, and Application to Our Political System and Literature," *United States Magazine and Democratic Review* 1, no. 1 (October 1837): 14.

13. Ibid., 1.

14. Ibid., 2–3.

15. Ibid., 7.

16. Ibid., 4.

17. Madison, "Federalist #10," *The Federalist Papers*, 126.

18. O'Sullivan, "The Democratic Principle," 9.

19. Stephanson, *Manifest Destiny*, 5.

20. John O'Sullivan, "The Great Nation of Futurity," *United States Magazine and Democratic Review* 6, no. 3 (November 1839): 426.

21. Ibid., 427–428.

22. Ibid., 427.

23. Ibid., 427, 429.

24. Wai-Chee Dimock, *Empire for Liberty: Melville and the Poetics of Individualism* (Princeton, NJ: Princeton University Press, 1991), 102–103.

25. Stephanson, *Manifest Destiny*, 18. Tuveson similarly defines *translatio imperii* as the idea that "in any given period one nation or people will exercise the imperium of civilization, culturally and politically. . . . After some centuries, 'empire' will move to another state"; *Redeemer Nation*, 95.

26. Hegel, *Philosophy of History*, 86. There is a subtext beneath Hegel's pronouncement of American ascendance that troubles progressive narratives of American destiny. America was not simply a space of promise and possibility but was also the geographic area where the "burden of world history revealed itself." Every historical epoch, according to Hegel, breeds its contradictions, and the American era would be no different. In calling America "evening land," Hegel speculates about the new social and political tensions that would arise in North America and then come to be generalized on a global scale.

27. Russell Hanson, *The Democratic Imagination in America* (Princeton, NJ: Princeton University Press, 1985), 124–125.

28. My understanding of republican temporality and cyclical conceptions of history is deeply indebted to J. G. A. Pocock, *The Machiavellian Moment: Florentine Political Thought and the Atlantic Republican Tradition* (Princeton, NJ: Princeton University Press, 1975).

29. Angela Miller, *Empire of the Eye: Landscape Representation and American Cultural Politics, 1825–1875* (Ithaca, NY: Cornell University Press, 1993), 143–144; G. Edward White, *The Marshall Court and Cultural Change, 1815–1835* (New York: Oxford University Press, 1991), 50–52, 69. The *translatio* concept builds off Adam Ferguson's *Essay on the History of Civil Society* (New York: Cambridge University Press, 1995 [1767]), in which he offered a stadial view of history characterized by the cyclical temporality of rise and decline. Ferguson used the language of civic virtue and corruption to critique the rise of commercial principles as the primary means of organizing civil

society. Although commercial society was dominant, Ferguson held that the unchecked assertion of self-interest over civic virtue would result in corruption and social decay. As one nation sinks into decline, the laws of history dictate that another nation will rise to claim the mantle of imperial sovereignty over the world (198).

30. John O'Sullivan, "The Course of Civilization," *United States Magazine and Democratic Review* 6, no. 19 (September 1839): 208.

31. Ibid., 209.

32. Ibid., 210.

33. Ibid., 210–211.

34. Ibid., 211.

35. Ibid., 213.

36. Sohui Lee, "Manifest Empire: Anglo-American Rivalry and the Shaping of U.S. Manifest Destiny," in *Romantic Border Crossings*, eds. Jeffrey Cass and Larry Peer (Burlington, VT: Ashgate, 2008), 183.

37. John O'Sullivan, "One of the Problems of the Age," *United States Magazine and Democratic Review* 14, no. 67 (February 1844): 160.

38. John O'Sullivan, "Legislative Embodiment of Public Opinion," *United States Magazine and Democratic Review* 19, no. 98 (August 1846): 86.

39. O'Sullivan, "One of the Problems of the Age," 167.

40. Quoted in Slotkin, *Fatal Environment*, 118.

41. Hietala, *Manifest Design*, 99–100.

42. Twenty-First Congress, Sess. I, Ch. 119, Statute 1 (June 22, 1838), 420–421.

43. My use of Hegel here is not intended to suggest that he directly influenced O'Sullivan (despite significant overlap in their thinking), but to use the similarities in Hegel and O'Sullivan's theories of colonization to illuminate how

democracy and settler colonization were blended together in antebellum thought.

44. Hegel, The Philosophy of History, 85–86.

45. Frederick Jackson Turner, The Frontier in American History (New York: Holt, 1920).

46. Hegel, The Philosophy of History, 84.

47. Ibid., 81–82.

48. John O'Sullivan, "Territorial Aggrandizement," United States Magazine and Democratic Review 17, no. 88 (October 1845): 243, 245–246.

49. Sunil Agnani, Hating Empire Properly: The Two Indies and the Limits of Enlightenment Anticolonialism (New York: Fordham University Press, 2013), 26. Also see Adam Dahl, "Commercial Conquest: Empire and Property in the Early U.S. Republic," American Political Thought 5, no. 3 (Summer 2016): 421–445.

50. US Congress, "Indian Removal Act," in Major Problems in American Foreign Relations, vol. 1, eds. Dennis Merrill and Thomas Paterson (Boston: Wadsworth, 2010), 178.

51. Rogin, Fathers and Children, 227–228; US Congress, "Treaty of Dancing Rabbit," in Indian Affairs: Laws and Treaties, vol. 2, ed. Charles Kappler (Washington, DC: Government Printing Office, 1904), 313. The 1830 Treaty with the Chickasaw similarly states, "The reservations secured under this article, shall be granted in fee simple, to those who choose to remain, and become subject to the laws of the whites"; Indian Affairs, vol. 2, 1036.

52. Rogin, Fathers and Children, 309. An article from the New York Evening Post (December 24, 1847) similarly racialized Mexicans as indigenous in asserting, "The Mexicans are Indians—Aboriginal Indians. . . . They do not possess the elements of an independent national existence. . . .

The Mexicans are Aboriginal Indians, and they must share the destiny of their race"; quoted in Merk, Manifest Destiny and Mission in American History, 158.

53. John O'Sullivan, "The Popular Movement," New York Morning News, May 24, 1845. Quoted in Merk, Manifest Destiny and Mission in American History, 23.

54. O'Sullivan, "Territorial Aggrandizement," 243, 245–246.

55. John O'Sullivan, "Occupation of Mexico" (November 1847), in Graebner's Manifest Destiny, 202–203, 205.

56. US Congress, "Treaty of Guadalupe Hidalgo," in Foreigners in Their Native Land: Historical Roots of the Mexican Americans, ed. David Weber (Albuquerque: University of New Mexico Press, 2003), 163–164.

57. David Kazanjian, The Colonizing Trick: National Culture and Imperial Citizenship in Early America (Minneapolis: University of Minnesota Press), 177.

58. Kazanjian, The Colonizing Trick, 12. For a similar postcolonial critique of the Treaty of Guadalupe Hidalgo, see Kevin Bruyneel, "Hierarchy and Hybridity: The Internal Postcolonialism of Mid-Nineteenth-Century American Expansionism," in Race and American Political Development, eds. Joe Lowndes, Julie Novkov, and Dorian Warren (New York: Routledge, 2008).

59. US Congress, "Treaty of Guadalupe Hidalgo," 165.

60. Weinberg, Manifest Destiny, 19.

61. John O'Sullivan, "Emerson's Essays," United States Magazine and Democratic Review 16, no. 84 (June 1845): 5, 591.

62. Cheryl Bohde, "Young America," in American History through Literature, 1820–1870, vol. 3, eds. Janet Gabler-Hover and Robert Sattelmeyer (New York: Charles Scribner's Sons, 2006), 1265–1269.

63. Evert Duyckinck, "Nationality in

Literature," *United States Magazine and Democratic Review* 20, no. 103 (March 1847): 267, 272.

64. Yonatan Eyal, *The Young America Movement and the Transformation of the Democratic Party, 1828–1861* (New York: Cambridge University Press, 2007), 2.

65. George Henry Evans, "Vote Yourself a Farm" (1846), in *The Radical Reader: A Documentary History of the American Radical Tradition*, eds. Timothy McCarthy and John McMillan (New York: New Press, 2011), 228. Mark Lause, *Young America: Land, Labor, and Republican Community* (Urbana-Champaign: University of Illinois Press, 2005), 61.

66. Eric Hobsbawm, *The Age of Revolutions, 1789–1848* (New York: New American Library, 1962), 163–165; Michael Rogin, *Subversive Genealogy: The Politics and Art of Herman Melville* (New York: Alfred A. Knopf, 1983), 71.

67. Wald, *Constituting Americans*, 116.

68. George Sanders quoted in Rogin, *Subversive Genealogy*, 73.

69. Emerson provided an anemic criticism of the Mexican War. Although he expressed anxiety about the war in his journals, he never publicly condemned the war. For instance, speaking to an audience of no one, Emerson wrote in his journals that we must "resist the annexation tooth and nail"; *Journals of Ralph Waldo Emerson*, vol. 6 (Boston: Houghton Mifflin, 1909), 495. Due to the inevitable spread of slavery that attended the annexation of Texas, Emerson also lamented that "the United States will conquer Mexico, but it will be as the man swallows the arsenic, which brings him down in turn. Mexico will poison us"; *Journals*, vol. 7, 206.

70. In this way, my interpretation of Emerson substantially differs from those that focus on how amoral and atomistic

individualism authorized the acquisitive commercial ethos that in turn drove settler expansion; see Quentin Anderson, *The Imperial Self: An Essay in American Literary and Cultural History* (New York: Alfred A. Knopf, 1971); Wilson Carey McWilliams, *The Idea of Fraternity in America* (Berkeley: University of California Press, 1973); and John Diggins, *The Lost Soul of American Politics: Virtue, Self-Interest, and the Foundations of Liberalism* (New York: Basic Books, 1984). These critics, following the Vietnam War, blasted Emerson as standing for the "embodiment of the irresponsible frontier mentality" exemplified by the atomistic individualism of the "imperial self"; Alan Levine and Daniel Malachuk, "Introduction," in *A Political Companion to Ralph Waldo Emerson*, eds. Levine and Malachuk (Lexington: University Press of Kentucky, 2011), 19. Instead, I emphasize how the moral bonds that tie individuals together in a democratic community cohere around regimes of land appropriation and ideologies of settler colonialism. By focusing on land and indigeneity rather than just race and slavery, my interpretation also challenges those that see in Emerson an ethics of democratic citizenship and reformist impulse emphasizing the ethical obligations citizens have to confront racial injustice; see George Kateb, *The Inner Ocean: Individualism and Democratic Culture* (Ithaca, NY: Cornell University Press, 1992); Len Gougeon, *Virtue's Hero: Emerson, Antislavery, and Reform* (Athens: University of Georgia Press, 1990); Jack Turner, *Awakening to Race: Individualism and Social Consciousness in America* (Chicago: University of Chicago Press, 2012); and Neal Dolan, *Emerson's Liberalism* (Madison: University of Wisconsin Press, 2009).

71. Ralph Waldo Emerson, "The Young American," *The Complete Works of Ralph*

Waldo Emerson, vol. 1 (Boston: Houghton Mifflin, 1904), 365.

72. Emerson, *Complete Works*, vol. 11, 383, 386.

73. Emerson, "The Young American," 368, 378.

74. Ibid., 370–371.

75. Ibid., 365–366.

76. Emerson, *Journals*, vol. 3, 389–390.

77. Emerson, "The Young American," 369.

78. Ibid., 370.

79. Emerson, "Nature," *Essays: First and Second Series* (New York: Vintage, 1990), 315–316, 318. On the distinction between Emerson's two conceptions of nature, see Carolyn Merchant, *Reinventing Eden: The Fate of Nature in Western Culture* (New York: Routledge, 2003), 120–121.

80. Emerson, "Politics," *Essays: First and Second Series*, 336.

81. Emerson, "The Young American," 371.

82. Emerson, "Fate," *Complete Works*, vol. 6, 32, 35–36.

83. Emerson, "The Young American," 364.

84. Emerson, "The Anglo-American," *Later Lectures of Ralph Waldo Emerson, 1843–1871*, vol. 1 (Athens: University of Georgia Press, 2010), 294. Also see Emerson's speech, "The Genius and National Character of the Anglo-Saxon Race," *Later Lectures*, vol. 1.

85. Emerson, "Spirit of the Times," *Later Lectures*, vol. 1, 107.

86. Daniel Walker Howe, *What Hath God Wrought? The Transformation of America, 1843–1848* (New York: Cambridge University Press, 2007), 343–344.

87. Emerson, Letter to Martin Van Buren (1836), *Complete Works*, vol. 11, 90.

88. Elias Boudinot, "An Address to the Whites," in *Cherokee Editor: The Writings of Elias Boudinot*, ed. Theda Perdue (Athens: University of Georgia Press, 1983), 71, 78.

89. Rogin, "Herman Melville: State, Civil Society, and the American 1848," *Yale Review*, 69 (1979): 73.

Chapter 5: Slavery and the Empire of Free Soil

1. Walter Johnson, *River of Dark Dreams: Slavery and Empire in the Cotton Kingdom* (Cambridge, MA: Harvard University Press, 2013).

2. Sean Wilentz, *The Rise of American Democracy: Jefferson to Lincoln* (New York: Norton, 2005), 637–640.

3. Susan Grant, *North over South: Northern Nationalism and American Identity in the Antebellum Era* (Lawrence: University Press of Kansas, 2000), 35. James Cobb, *Away Down South: A History of Southern Identity* (New York: Oxford University Press, 2005), 3.

4. Tocqueville, *Democracy*, 43.

5. Ibid., 30–31. Michael Morrison, *Slavery and the American West: The Eclipse of Manifest Destiny and the Coming of the Civil War* (Chapel Hill: University of North Carolina Press, 1997), 110–120.

6. Roediger, *The Wages of Whiteness*, 44.

7. While these choices might seem peculiar in a work focused on democratic theory, I follow Kari Palonen in reading politicians as political theorists. Ideas are neither epiphenomenal to nor regulative discourses for political action but are the medium of politics itself. By providing the languages and discourses within which policies and practices are justified and legitimated, political ideas constitute those policies and practices. Rather than *ex post facto* rationalizations of political action, political ideas and discourses provide the horizon of intelligibility within which politics is understood; "Political

Theorizing as a Dimension of Political Life," *European Journal of Political Theory* 4, no. 4 (October 2005): 351–366.

8. Betsy Erkkila, *Whitman the Political Poet* (New York: Cambridge University Press, 1989), 52.

9. Free Soil Party, "Free Soil Party Platform" (1848), in *National Party Platforms, 1840–1972*, 5th ed., eds. Donald Johnson and Kirk Porter (Urbana-Champaign: University of Illinois Press, 1973), 13–14.

10. William Wilson, *The Great American Question, Democracy vs. Doulocracy* (Cincinnati: E. Shepard's Steam Press, 1848), 17, 24.

11. Morrison, *Slavery and the American West*, 166, 171.

12. G. A. Grow, *Man's Right to the Soil* (Washington, DC: Congressional Globe Office, 1852), 1.

13. Ibid., 4.

14. Ibid., 6.

15. Ibid., 4.

16. Ibid., 6–7.

17. Ibid., 7.

18. Throughout the seventeenth and eighteenth centuries, Locke's theory of property was continually taken up by defenders of English colonization. See Barbara Arneil, "The Wild Indian's Venison: Locke's Theory of Property and English Colonialism in America," *Political Studies* 44, no. 1 (March 1996): 60–74.

19. *Johnson & Graham's Lessee v. M'Intosh*, 21 U.S. 573–574 (1823).

20. Grow, *Man's Right to the Soil*, 5–6.

21. Ibid., 7–8.

22. Abraham Lincoln cites this language from the Kansas-Nebraska Act in the "House Divided Speech" in Springfield, IL (June 16, 1858), *The Portable Abraham Lincoln*, ed. Andrew Delbanco (New York: Penguin, 2009), 102.

23. Lincoln, "Speech on the Kansas-Nebraska Act at Peoria, Illinois" (October 16, 1854), *Portable Abraham Lincoln*, 42–43.

24. Ibid., 50, 74.

25. Ibid., 65, 71.

26. Lincoln, "Address to the Wisconsin State Agricultural Society" (September 30, 1859), *Portable Abraham Lincoln*, 188.

27. James Hammond, "Cotton Is King," *Selections from the Letters and Speeches of the Honorable James H. Hammond of South Carolina* (New York: John F. Trow, 1866), 317–318.

28. Lincoln, "Address to the Wisconsin State Agricultural Society," 188–189 (emphasis added).

29. Lincoln, "Message to Congress in Special Session" (July 4, 1861), *Portable Abraham Lincoln*, 253.

30. Lincoln, "Address to the Wisconsin State Agricultural Society," 185.

31. Slotkin, *The Fatal Environment*, 239.

32. "Speech on the Dred Scott Decision" (June 26, 1857), *Portable Abraham Lincoln*, 99–100.

33. Barbara Arneil has also emphasized how Lincoln continually promoted a program of "domestic colonization" by which freed slaves would settle labor colonies within the United States in places such as Florida and Texas. The purpose of domestic labor colonies was threefold. First, *racial segregation* was an essential component of domestic colonization because Lincoln believed white and black could not live together on terms of equality because of both white prejudice and black inferiority. Second, the principle of *agrarian labor* emphasized the ethical and economic benefits that freed slaves received from domestic colonization, specifically undisputed title to land. Third, the principle of *improvement* saw domestic colonization and agrarian

labor as a necessary path to republican and productive citizenship; "Domestic Colonies in America: Labour, Utopian, and Farm Colonies" (paper presented at the American Political Science Association annual meeting, San Francisco, CA, September 3–6, 2015).

34. Lincoln, "Address on Colonization to a Committee of Colored Men," *Portable Abraham Lincoln*, 266.

35. For a further exploration of these themes, see Robert Nichols, "Tocqueville, Beaumont, and the Dialectic of Race and Place" (paper presented at the American Political Science Association annual meeting, Chicago, IL, August 29–September 1, 2013).

36. Ernst Paolinio, *The Foundations of American Empire: William Henry Seward and U.S. Foreign Policy* (Ithaca, NY: Cornell University Press, 1973).

37. Quoted in Eric Sundquist, *Empire and Slavery in American Literature, 1820–1865* (Oxford: University of Mississippi Press, 1995), 64; William Seward, "Freedom in the New Territories" (1850), *Works of William Seward*, vol. 1 (Boston: Houghton Mifflin, 1884), 58.

38. Seward also noted that the primary "political law" of human history has been that "empire has, for the last three thousand years, so long as we have records of civilization, made its way constantly westward, and that it must continue to move on westward until the tides of the renewed and of the decaying civilizations of the world meet on the shores of the Pacific Ocean"; "Democracy the Chief Element of Government" (1860), *Works*, vol. 4, 319.

39. Seward, "Freedom in the New Territories," 57.

40. Seward, "Democracy the Chief Element of Government," 320.

41. Seward, "The Physical, Moral, and Intellectual Development of the American People," *Works*, vol. 4, 168–169.

42. Seward, "Democracy the Chief Element of Government," 321.

43. Seward, "The National Idea," *Works*, vol. 4, 348.

44. J. H. Elliott, *Empires of the Atlantic World: Britain and Spain in America, 1492–1830* (New Haven, CT: Yale University Press, 2006), 77–79.

45. Seward, "The Irrepressible Conflict" (1858) *Works*, vol. 4, 290.

46. Wakefield, *England and America*, 203–204.

47. Ibid., 219.

48. George Fredrickson notes that this basic sociological principle explains why regimes of involuntary labor emerge in some contexts and not others. In societies where land is open, owners of capital seek to impose coerced systems of labor to maintain profitability of their economic ventures. Conversely, where labor is plentiful and land is more scare, it becomes more profitable to seek temporary modes of employment at low wages rather than bonded labor for permanent employment; *White Supremacy: A Comparative Study in American and South African History* (New York: Oxford University Press, 1981), 55.

49. Quoted in Walter Grünzweig, "Imperialism," *A Companion to Walt Whitman*, ed. Donald Kummings (Malden, MA: Blackwell Publishing, 2009), 152. For an excellent example of Whitman's reception among Latin American radicals, see José Martí, "The Poet Walt Whitman," *Selected Writings*, ed. Esther Allen (New York: Penguin, 2002), 183–194.

50. Mauricio Gonzales de la Garza, *Walt Whitman: Racista, Imperialista, Antimexicano* (Mexico City: Colección Málaga, 1971); Grünzweig, "Imperialism"; Jason Frank, "Aesthetic Democracy: Walt

Whitman and the Poetry of the People," *Review of Politics* 69, no. 3 (Summer 2007): 402–430; Alan Trachtenberg, "Whitman's Visionary Politics," *Mickle Street Review* 10 (1988): 15–31.

51. On these points, I have drawn on Molesworth, "Whitman's Political Vision," *Raritan* 12, no. 1 (Summer 1992): 98–113; and Heidi Kim, "From Language to Empire: Walt Whitman in the Context of Nineteenth-Century Popular Anglo-Saxonism," *Walt Whitman Quarterly Review* 24, no. 1 (Summer 2006): 1–19.

52. Erkkila, *Whitman the Political Poet*, 45; Whitman, *The Gathering of the Forces*, vol. 1, 187.

53. Whitman, *Gathering of Forces*, 17–18.

54. Ibid., 25–26.

55. Erkkila, *Whitman the Political Poet*, 130.

56. Whitman, "The Eighteenth Presidency!," *Poetry and Prose* (New York: Penguin, 1982), 1331.

57. Ibid., 1334.

58. Ibid., 1340.

59. Phyllis McBride, "Feudalism," in *Walt Whitman: An Encyclopedia*, eds. J. R. LeMaster and Donald Kummings (New York: Garland Publishing, 1998), 223.

60. Walt Whitman, "Facing West from California's Shores," *Poetry and Prose*, 266; cf. Erkkila, *Whitman the Political Poet*, 178.

61. Whitman, "A Broadway Pageant," *Poetry and Prose*, 387.

62. Whitman, "Eighteen Sixty-One," *Poetry and Prose*, 418–419.

63. Whitman, "The Eighteenth Presidency!," 1347–1348.

64. Whitman, "Starting from Paumanok," *Poetry and Prose*, 176.

65. Whitman, "Pioneers! O Pioneers!," *Poetry and Prose*, 372.

66. Whitman, "Starting from Paumanok," 177.

67. Ibid., 186.

68. Ed Folsom, *Walt Whitman's Native Representations* (New York: Cambridge University Press, 1994), 93.

69. Whitman, "The Spanish Element in Our Nationality," *Poetry and Prose*, 1171.

70. Whitman, "Indian Life and Customs," *Gathering of Forces*, vol. 2, 137–138.

71. Ibid., 138–139.

72. Whitman, Preface to "Leaves of Grass," *Poetry and Prose*, 5.

73. Anna Johnston and Alan Lawson, "Settler Colonies," in *A Companion to Postcolonial Studies*, eds. Henry Schwarz and Sangeeta Ray (Malden, MA: Blackwell Publishing 2008), 369.

74. Byrd, *The Transit of Empire*, xx.

75. George Santayana, *Interpretations of Poetry and Religion* (New York: Harper and Row, 1957), 182.

76. Whitman, "Democratic Vistas," *Poetry and Prose*, 1038, 1219.

77. Ibid., 954.

78. Ibid., 959.

79. Ibid., 1028–1029.

80. Whitman, "Nationality—(And Yet)," *Poetry and Prose*, 1074.

81. Whitman, "Democratic Vistas," 987, 989.

82. Whitman, "Nationality," 1074–1075.

83. Whitman, "Democratic Vistas," 1000–1001.

84. Benjamin Barber, "Whitman's Song of Democracy," in *Walt Whitman, Where the Future Becomes Present*, eds. David Blake and Michael Robertson (Iowa City: University of Iowa Press, 2008), 100.

85. Whitman, "Democratic Vistas," 955–956.

86. Ibid., 986.

87. A few pages before, Whitman outlined the geographic contours of his imperial vision: "Long ere the second

centennial arrives, there will be some forty to fifty great States, among them Canada and Cuba. When the present century closes, our population will be sixty or seventy millions. The Pacific will be ours, and the Atlantic mainly ours. There will be daily electric communication with every part of the globe. What an age! What a land!" Ibid., 1005–1006, 1014.

88. Ibid., 954, 1014.

Chapter 6: William Apess and the Paradox of Settler Sovereignty

1. Joshua Foa Dienstag, "A Storied Shooting: Liberty Valance and the Paradox of Sovereignty," Political Theory 40, no. 3 (June 2012): 291; Bonnie Honig, "Between Decision and Deliberation: Political Paradox in Democratic Theory," American Political Science Review 101 (February 2007): 1–17; Connolly, Ethos of Pluralization; and Chantal Mouffe, The Democratic Paradox (New York: Verso, 2000).

2. Diego Von Vacano's recent review vividly shows that comparative political theory has largely failed to engage indigenous political thinkers; "The Scope of Comparative Political Theory," Annual Review of Political Science 18 (2015): 1–16.

3. David Carlson, Sovereign Selves: American Indian Autobiography and the Law (Urbana-Champaign: University of Illinois Press, 2006), 106; and Armin Mattes, Citizens of a Common Intellectual Homeland: The Transatlantic Origins of American Democracy and Nationhood (Charlottesville: University of Virginia Press, 2015), S206–207.

4. Michel Foucault, Security, Territory, and Population (New York: Picador, 2009). Also see Robert Nichols, "Of First and Last Men: Contract and Colonial Historicality in Foucault," in The Ends of History: Questioning the Stakes of Historical Reason, eds.

Amy Swiffen and Joshua Nichols (New York: Routledge, 2013).

5. Jacques Rancière, "Ten Theses on Politics," Theory and Event 5 (2001). Available at: http://muse.jhu.edu/journals/theory_and_event/v005/5.3ranciere.html.

6. Robert Nichols, "Contract and Usurpation: Enfranchisement and Racial Governance in Settler-Colonial Contexts," in Theorizing Native Studies, eds. Audra Simpson and Andrea Smith (Durham, NC: Duke University Press, 2014).

7. Mouffe, The Democratic Paradox, 4.

8. Caroline Elkins and Susan Pedersen, Introduction, Settler Colonialism in the Twentieth Century, eds. Elkins and Pedersen (New York: Routledge, 2005), 4.

9. Frantz Fanon, Wretched of the Earth (New York: Grove Press, 1965), 36.

10. Glen Coulthard, Red Skin, White Masks: Rejecting the Colonial Politics of Recognition (Minneapolis: University of Minnesota Press, 2014); Joanne Barker, Native Acts: Law, Recognition, and Cultural Authenticity (Durham, NC: Duke University Press, 2011).

11. Kennan Ferguson, "Refusing Settler Colonialism: Simpson's Mohawk Interruptus," Theory & Event 18 (2005). Available at: https://muse.jhu.edu/article/595847.

12. Audra Simpson, Mohawk Interruptus: Political Life across the Borders of Settler States (Durham, NC: Duke University Press, 2014).

13. This analysis significantly moves beyond that of William Connolly, who focuses on a hypothetical encounter between Thoreau and Apess to show how an ethical sensibility of "critical responsiveness" might emerge out of the colonial politics of the period; The Ethos of Pluralization, 175–178. Connolly's points are mildly productive, but his cursory treatment of Apess lacks systematic analysis.

14. Donald Nielsen, "The Mashpee Indian Revolt of 1833," *New England Quarterly* 58, no. 3 (September 1985): 400–420.

15. Jack Campisi, *The Mashpee Indians* (Syracuse, NY: Syracuse University Press, 1990), 82–84.

16. Campisi, *The Mashpee Indians*, 86–91.

17. William Apess, "Indian Nullification of the Unconstitutional Laws of Massachusetts Relative to the Marshpee Tribe; or, The Pretended Riot Explained," *On Our Own Ground: The Complete Writings of William Apess, a Pequot*, ed. Barry O'Connell (Amherst: University of Massachusetts Press, 1992), 169–173, 175–179.

18. Ibid., 175.

19. Ibid., 180–184.

20. Maureen Konkle, *Writing Indian Nations: Native Intellectuals and the Politics of Historiography, 1827–1863* (Chapel Hill: University of North Carolina Press, 2004).

21. Barry O'Connell, Introduction to "Indian Nullification," *On Our Own Ground*, 164.

22. Ibid., 167.

23. Ibid., 195.

24. Ibid., 166.

25. Sharon Korman, *The Right of Conquest: The Acquisition of Territory by Force in International Law and Practice* (New York: Oxford University Press, 1996), 8–10.

26. Yves Winter, "Conquest," *Political Concepts: A Critical Lexicon* 1 (December 2011). Available at: http://www.political concepts.org/conquest-winter-finished/.

27. Pateman and Mills, "The Settler Contract." Charles Mills also writes of the "white settler state": "the establishment of society thus implies the denial that a society already existed"; *The Racial Contract*, 13. I also draw here on the work of Lisa Ford, who argues that the "moment of settler sovereignty" emerged when "the legal obliteration of indigenous customary law

became the litmus test of settler statehood." Settler sovereignty arose when settlers destroyed aboriginal customary law by imposing territorial jurisdiction on native peoples; *Settler Sovereignty: Jurisdiction and Indigenous People in America and Australia, 1788–1836* (Cambridge, MA: Harvard University Press, 2010), 2.

28. On the "paradox of conquest," see Winter, "Conquest."

29. Daniel Webster, "First Settlement of New England," *The Works of Daniel Webster*, vol. 1 (Boston: Little & Brown, 1851), 7.

30. Ibid., 20–21.

31. Ibid., 22, 35.

32. Daniel Webster, "The Bunker Hill Monument," *Works of Daniel Webster*, vol. 1, 77.

33. Jill Lepore, *The Name of War: King Philip's War and the Origins of American Identity* (New York: Alfred A. Knopf, 1998), 76–81.

34. Thomas Jefferson, "Draft of the Kentucky Resolutions," in *Liberty and Order: The First American Party Struggle*, ed. Lance Banning (Indianapolis: Liberty Fund Press, 2004), 234–235.

35. John Calhoun, "Exposition and Protest," *Union and Liberty: The Political Philosophy of John C. Calhoun* (Indianapolis: Liberty Fund Press, 1993), 350.

36. Daniel Webster, "Speech on the Force Bill," *Works of Daniel Webster*, vol. 3, 453.

37. Andrew Jackson, "Proclamation Regarding Nullification," *The Avalon Project: Documents in Law, History, and Diplomacy*, Yale Law School, 1832. Available at the Yale Avalon Project: http://avalon.law .yale.edu/19th_century/jack01.asp.

38. Calhoun, "Exposition and Protest," 340.

39. Richard Latner, "The Nullification Crisis and Republican Subversion," *Journal*

of Southern History 43, no. 1 (February 1977): 30. Also see David Ericson, "The Nullification Crisis, American Republicanism, and the Force Bill Debate," Journal of Southern History 61, no. 2 (May 1995): 249–270.

40. Webster, "Speech on the Force Bill," 486.

41. Ibid., 431.

42. On the distinctions between Jackson and Webster, see Richard Ellis, The Union at Risk: Jacksonian Democracy, States' Rights, and the Nullification Crisis (New York: Oxford University Press, 1987).

43. Jefferson, "Draft of the Kentucky Resolutions," 234–235.

44. Cherokee Nation v. Georgia, 30 U.S. 5 Pet. 2 (1831).

45. Vicki Hsueh, Hybrid Constitutions: Challenging Legacies of Law, Privilege, and Culture in Colonial North America (Durham, NC: Duke University Press, 2010), 4, 10.

46. Apess did not frame his efforts in terms of the assertion of "native sovereignty." As a concept that originated in European legal discourse to denote complete territorial control, Taiaiake Alfred notes that the term "sovereignty" does not adequately capture the diverse and different ways of conceptualizing the relationship between land and power in native modes of governance; Peace, Power, Righteousness: An Indigenous Manifesto (New York: Oxford University Press, 1999), 55–72. Nevertheless, I retain the term not as a way of characterizing the positive features of native systems of governance but as a categorical stand-in denoting those modes of governance that settler sovereignty seeks to eliminate.

47. "Indian Nullification," 175 (emphasis added).

48. Ibid., 179–180.

49. Ibid., 204.

50. Ibid., 183.

51. Priscilla Wald, "Terms of Assimilation: Legislating Subjectivity in the Emerging Nation," boundary 2 19, no. 3 (Autumn 1992): 86.

52. Jacques Rancière, Disagreement: Politics and Philosophy (Minneapolis: University of Minnesota Press, 2004), 25.

53. Apess, "A Son of the Forest," On our Own Ground, 4.

54. Campisi, The Mashpee Indians, 82.

55. Wolfe, "Settler Colonialism and the Elimination of the Native," 388.

56. Apess, "Indian Nullification," 212–214.

57. Rogin, Fathers and Children, 165–205.

58. Rancière, Disagreement, 25–26.

59. Fred Lee, "The Racial Constitution of the Public: Four Exercises in Historicizing the American Polity" (PhD dissertation, University of California, Los Angeles, 2010), ch. 3.

60. Apess, "Indian Nullification," 190.

61. Ibid., 196.

62. Ibid., 198; Gayatri Spivak, A Critique of Postcolonial Reason (Cambridge, MA: Harvard University Press, 1999).

63. In a similar instance, Apess contends, "But the crimes committed against our race cannot be enumerated here below. They will each and all, however, be judged at the bar of God, and it must be the comfort of the poor and oppressed, who cry for justice, and find it not, that there is one who sees and knows and will do right"; "Indian Nullification," 192, 197–198.

64. Rancière, "Ten Theses on Politics."

65. Kenneth Burke, The Grammar of Motives (New York: Prentice-Hall, 1945).

66. Wald, Constituting Americans, 16–18.

67. Francis Jennings, The Invasion of America (New York: Norton, 1976), 127, 146; Slotkin, The Fatal Environment, 53.

68. William Apess, "Eulogy on King Phillip," On Our Own Ground, 278, 296.

69. Apess, "Indian Nullification," 180–181.

70. In making this argument, I draw on Cheryl Walker's distinction between transpositional and subjugated discourses. In the former, the speaker transposes each element in a political relation (i.e., settler and native) into its opposite in a horizontal sense in an effort to stress the equality of the two poles. Thus, in transpositional discourse of Emerson and Boudinot, the state of being civilized is transposed from settlers onto the Cherokee. Subjugated discourses flip the valence of group differences in a vertical sense. Where settlers cast their superiority to natives in civilizational terms, Apess recasts this superiority and supposed civilization as savagery; Indian Nation: Native American Literature and Nineteenth-Century Nationalisms (Durham, NC: Duke University Press, 1997), 16–17.

71. Apess, "Eulogy," 283.

72. Drew Lopenzina, "What to the American Indian Is the Fourth of July? Moving beyond Abolitionist Rhetoric in Apess's Eulogy on King Philip," American Literature 82, no.4 (2010): 689.

73. Apess, "Eulogy," 306.

74. Ibid., 308.

75. Tocqueville, Democracy, 34.

76. Apess, "Eulogy," 306.

77. Ibid., 286.

78. Cherokee Nation v. Georgia, 30 U.S. 5 Pet. 22–23.

79. "Treaty of Hopewell," Indian Affairs: Laws and Treaties, vol. 2, ed. Charles Kappler (Washington, DC: Government Printing Office, 1902), 10.

80. Apess, "Eulogy," 307.

Afterword: Decolonizing the Democratic Tradition

1. Mamdani, "Settler Colonialism: Then and Now," 602–603.

2. Angélica Maria Bernal, Beyond Origins: Rethinking Founding in a Time of Constitutional Democracy (Oxford University Press, 2017).

3. Hartz, The Founding of New Societies.

4. Samuel Huntington, Who Are We? The Challenges to America's National Identity (New York: Simon & Schuster, 2004), 246.

5. Ibid., xv, 38–46.

6. Ibid., 40–41. Huntington goes on: "In its origin and its continuing core, America is thus a colonial society, in the strict and original sense of the word 'colony,' that is, a settlement created by people who leave a mother country and travel elsewhere to establish a new society on distant turf." The definition of "colony" here only focuses on the transfer of culture and people between metropolis and settler colony, and thus erases colonial dispossession.

7. Smith, "Beyond Tocqueville, Myrdal and Hartz, 549–566; and Civic Ideals: Conflicting Visions of Citizenship in US History (New Haven, CT: Yale University Press, 1999).

8. Rana, Two Faces of American Freedom, 7, 23.

9. Ibid., 181.

10. Although Rana's Two Faces of American Freedom, to some extent, engages in the reclamation of settler colonial traditions, his later essays propose a more dramatic rupture with those traditions by recovering decolonial perspectives in the black radical thought of Stokely Carmichael and the Black Panther Party. Drawing on historical perspectives offered by these figures, Rana criticizes creedal narratives of civic inclusion for erasing the

constitutively settler-colonial structure of the American past and polity. Rana, "Constitutional Memory," and "Race and the American Creed: Recovering Black Radicalism," *n+1* 24, (Winter 2016). Available at: https://nplusonemag.com/issue-24/politics/race-and-the-american-creed/.

11. Cocks, *On Sovereignty and Other Political Delusions*, 3.

12. Ibid., 23, 30.

13. Ibid., 43–45.

14. Quoted in ibid., 71.

15. Cocks further argues, "traditional native philosophies of life are in fundamental respects at odds with sovereign power as the Western tradition understands the term," ibid., 76.

16. Alfred, *Peace, Power, Righteousness*, 21.

17. Ibid., 25, 42.

18. Christine Keating, *Decolonizing Democracy: Transforming the Social Contract in India* (State College, PA: Penn State University Press, 2012), 9.

19. Enrique Dussel, *The Invention of the Americas: Eclipse of "The Other" and the Myth of Modernity* (New York: Continuum International, 1995), 10–11.

20. Enrique Dussel, "Transmodernity and Interculturality: An Interpretation from the Perspective of Philosophy of Liberation," *Transmodernity: Journal of Peripheral Cultural Production of the Luso-Hispanic World* 1, no. 3 (2012): 50.

21. Iris Marion Young, "Hybrid Democracy: Iroquois Federalism and the Postcolonial Project," *Global Challenges: War, Self-Determination, and Responsibility for Justice* (Cambridge: Polity Press, 2007), 16, 32.

22. Ibid., 18–19. See Donald Grinde and Bruce Johansen's *Exemplar of Liberty: Native America and the Evolution of Democracy* (Los Angeles: American Indian Studies Center, 1991).

23. Young, "Hybrid Democracy," 19.

24. Ibid., 21; Grinde and Johansen, *Exemplar of Liberty*, Ch. 6.

25. Quoted in ibid., 66.

26. Young, "Hybrid Democracy," 20.

27. I will note, however, that I agree with Young that critics of the influence thesis exclusively focus on the constitutional debates, thereby ignoring the broader range of historical evidence supporting the thesis. For instance, see Elisabeth Tooker, "The United States Constitution and the Iroquois League," *Ethnohistory* 35, no. 4 (Autumn 1988): 305–336. For a more extensive refutation of Tooker's rejection of the influence thesis, see Donald Grinde, "Iroquois Political Theory and Roots of American Democracy," in *Exiled in the Land of the Free: Democracy, Indian Nations, and the U.S. Constitution*, eds. Oren Lyons and John Mohawk (Santa Fe, NM: Clear Light Publishers, 1992), 277–278.

28. Lolomi is a Hopi term meaning "perfect goodness be upon you"; "Our Democracy and the American Indian," in *American Philosophies: An Anthology*, eds. Leonard Harris, Scott L. Pratt, and Anne S. Waters (Malden, MA: Blackwell, 2002), 426.

29. Ibid., 423.

30. Ibid., 424–425.

31. Young, "Hybrid Democracy," 24.

BIBLIOGRAPHY

Adams, John. *Works of John Adams*, 10 vols. Boston: Little, Brown, 1850–1856.
———. *The Political Writings of John Adams*. Indianapolis: Hackett, 2003.
Adams, Willi Paul. *The First American Constitutions: Republican Ideology and the Making of the State Constitutions in the Revolutionary Era*. Chapel Hill: University of North Carolina Press, 1980.
Agnani, Sunil. *Hating Empire Properly: The Two Indies and the Limits of Enlightenment Anti-colonialism*. New York: Fordham University Press, 2013.
Alfred, Taiaiake. *Peace, Power, Righteousness: An Indigenous Manifesto*. New York: Oxford University Press, 1999.
Anderson, Fred. *The Crucible of War: The Seven Years' War and the Fate of Empire in British North America*. New York: Random House, 2007.
Anderson, Fred, and Andrew Cayton. *The Dominion of War: Empire and Liberty in North America, 1500–2000*. New York: Penguin, 2005.
Anderson, Quentin. *The Imperial Self: An Essay in American Literary and Cultural History*. New York: Alfred A. Knopf, 1971.
Apess, William. *On Our Own Ground: The Complete Writings of William Apess, a Pequot*, ed. Barry O'Connell. Amherst: University of Massachusetts Press, 1992.
Appleby, Joyce. "Commercial Farming and the 'Agrarian Myth' in the Early Republic." *Journal of American History* 68, no. 4 (March 1982): 833–849.
———. *Liberalism and Republicanism in the Historical Imagination*. Cambridge, MA: Harvard University Press, 1992.
Arendt, Hannah. *The Origins of Totalitarianism*. New York: Harcourt, 1976.
———. "Reflections on Little Rock." In *The Portable Hannah Arendt*, ed. Peter Baehr. New York: Penguin, 2003, 231–246.
———. *On Revolution*. New York: Penguin, 2006.
Armitage, David. "John Locke, Carolina, and the Two Treatises of Government." *Political Theory* 32, no. 5 (October 2004): 602–627.
Arneil, Barbara. *John Locke and America: The Defense of English Colonialism*. New York: Oxford University Press, 1996.
———. "The Wild Indian's Venison: Locke's Theory of Property and English Colonialism in America." *Political Studies* 44, no. 1 (March 1996): 60–74.
———. "Domestic Colonies in America: Labour, Utopian, and Farm Colonies." Paper presented at the American Political Science Association annual meeting, San Francisco, CA, September 3–6, 2015.
Ashcraft, Richard. "Political Theory and the Problem of Ideology." *Journal of Politics* 42, no. 3 (August 1980): 687–705.
Banner, Stuart. *How the Indians Lost Their Land: Law and Power on the Frontier*. Cambridge, MA: Harvard University Press, 2007.
Barber, Benjamin. "Whitman's Song of Democracy." In *Walt Whitman, Where the Future*

Becomes Present, eds. David Blake and Michael Robertson. Iowa City: University of Iowa Press, 2008.

Barker, Joanne. *Native Acts: Law, Recognition, and Cultural Authenticity*. Durham, NC: Duke University Press, 2011.

Barlow, Joel. *Vision of Columbus*. London: J. Stockdale, 1787.

Behdad, Ali. *A Forgetful Nation: On Immigration and Cultural Identity in the United States*. Durham, NC: Duke University Press, 2005.

Belich, James. *Replenishing the Earth: The Settler Revolution and the Rise of the Anglo World, 1783–1939*. New York: Oxford University Press, 2011.

Bell, Duncan. *The Idea of Greater Britain: Empire and the Future of World Order, 1860–1900*. Princeton, NJ: Princeton University Press, 2009.

———. "John Stuart Mill on Colonies." *Political Theory* 38, no. 1 (February 2010): 34–64.

———. *Remaking the World: Essays on Liberalism and Empire*. Princeton, NJ: Princeton University Press, 2016.

Benjamin, Walter. "Critique of Violence." In *Reflections: Essays, Aphorisms, Autobiographical Writings*. New York: Schocken Books, 1986, 277–300.

Berkeley, George. *The Works of George Berkeley*, vol. 2. Boston: John Exshaw, 1784.

Bernal, Angélica Maria. *Beyond Origins: Rethinking Founding in a Time of Constitutional Democracy*. New York: Oxford University Press, 2017.

Black Hawk. *Life of Black Hawk, or Ma-ka-tai-me-she-kia-kiak*. New York: Penguin, 2008.

Blackstone, William. *Commentaries on the Laws of England*, vol. 1. Philadelphia: J. B. Lippincott, 1893.

Bland, Richard. "The Colonel Dismounted." In *Pamphlets of the American Revolution, 1750–1776*, ed. Bernard Bailyn. Cambridge, MA: Belknap Press, 1965.

———. "An Inquiry into the Rights of the British Colonies." In *American Political Writings during the Founding Era: 1760–1805*, vol. 1, eds. Charles Hyneman and Donald Lutz. Indianapolis: Liberty Fund, 1983.

Boesche, Roger. "The Dark Side of Tocqueville: On War and Emoire." *Review of Politics* 67, no. 4 (Autumn 2005): 737–752.

Bohde, Cheryl. "Young America." In *American History through Literature, 1820–1870*, vol. 3, eds. Janet Gabler-Hover and Robert Sattelmeyer. New York: Charles Scribner's Sons, 2006, 1265–1270.

Bouchard, Gerard. *The Making of the Nations and Cultures of the New World*. Montreal: McGill-Queen's Press, 2008.

Boudinot, Elias. "An Address to the Whites." In *Cherokee Editor: The Writings of Elias Boudinot*, ed. Theda Perdue. Athens: University of Georgia Press, 1983, 65–84.

Boyd, Richard. "Imperial Fathers and Favorite Sons: J. S. Mill, Alexis de Tocqueville, and Nineteenth-Century Visions of Empire." In *Feminist Interpretations of Alexis de Tocqueville*, eds. Jill Locke and Eileen Hunt-Botting. State College, PA: Penn State Press, 2010, 225–252.

Bruyneel, Kevin. *The Third Space of Sovereignty: The Postcolonial Politics of U.S.-Indigenous Relations*. Minneapolis: University of Minnesota Press, 2007.

———. "Hierarchy and Hybridity: The Internal Postcolonialism of Mid-

Nineteenth-Century American Expansionism." In *Race and American Political Development*, eds. Joe Lowndes, Julie Novkov, and Dorian Warren. New York: Routledge, 2008, 106–124.

———. "The American Liberal Colonial Tradition." *Settler Colonial Studies* 3, no. 3-04 (2013): 311–321.

Burbank, Jane, and Frederick Cooper. *Empires in World History: Power and the Politics of Difference*. Princeton, NJ: Princeton University Press, 2011.

Burke, Kenneth. *The Grammar of Motives*. New York: Prentice-Hall, 1945.

Byrd, Jodi. *The Transit of Empire: Indigenous Critiques of Colonialism*. Minneapolis: University of Minnesota Press, 2011.

Calhoun, John. *Union and Liberty: The Political Philosophy of John C. Calhoun*. Indianapolis: Liberty Fund Press, 2003.

Campisi, Jack. *The Mashpee Indians*. Syracuse, NY: Syracuse University Press, 1990.

Carlson, David. *Sovereign Selves: American Indian Autobiography and the Law*. Urbana-Champaign: University of Illinois Press, 2006.

Chakrabarty, Dipesh. *Provincializing Europe: Postcolonial Thought and Historical Difference*. Princeton, NJ: Princeton University Press, 2009.

Cobb, James. *Away Down South: A History of Southern Identity*. New York: Oxford University Press, 2005.

Cocks, Joan. "Foundational Violence and the Politics of Erasure." *Radical Philosophy Review* 15, no. 1 (2012): 103–126.

———. *On Sovereignty and Other Political Delusions*. New York: Bloomsbury, 2014.

Connolly, William. *Ethos of Pluralization*. Minneapolis: University of Minnesota Press, 1995.

Coulthard, Glen. *Red Skin, White Masks: Rejecting the Colonial Politics of Recognition*. Minneapolis: University of Minnesota Press, 2014.

Crèvecœur, J. Hector St. John de. *Letters from an American Farmer*. New York: Penguin, 1986.

Dahl, Adam. "Commercial Conquest: Empire and Property in the Early American Republic." *American Political Thought* 5, no. 3 (Summer 2016): 421–445.

Dienstag, Joshua Foa. "A Storied Shooting: Liberty Valance and the Paradox of Sovereignty." *Political Theory* 40, no. 3 (June 2012): 290–318.

Diggins, John. *The Lost Soul of American Politics: Virtue, Self-Interest, and the Foundations of Liberalism*. New York: Basic Books, 2012.

Dimock, Wai-Chee. *Empire for Liberty: Melville and the Poetics of Individualism*. Princeton, NJ: Princeton University Press, 1991.

Disch, Lisa. "Democratic Representation and the Constituency Paradox," *Perspectives on Politics* 10, no. 3 (September 2012): 599–616.

Dolan, Neal. *Emerson's Liberalism*. Madison: University of Wisconsin Press, 2009.

Drinnon, Richard. *Facing West: The Metaphysics of Indian-Hating and Empire-Building*. Norman: University of Oklahoma Press, 1997.

Du Bois, W. E. B. *Black Reconstruction in America*. New York: Free Press, 1992.

Dussel, Enrique. *The Invention of the Americas: Eclipse of "The Other" and the Myth of Modernity*. New York: Continuum International, 1995.

———. "Transmodernity and Interculturality: An Interpretation from the Perspective of Philosophy of Liberation." *Transmodernity: Journal of Peripheral Cultural Production of the Luso-Hispanic World* 1, no. 3 (2012): 28–59.

Duyckinck, Evert. "Nationality in Literature." *United States Magazine and Democratic Review* 20, no. 103 (March 1847): 264–272.

Egnal, Mark. *Mighty Empire: The Origins of the American Revolution.* Ithaca, NY: Cornell University Press, 1988.

Elazar, Daniel. *Covenant and Constitutionalism: The Great Frontier and the Matrix of Federal Democracy.* New Brunswick: Transaction Publishers, 1998.

Elkins, Caroline, and Susan Pedersen, eds. *Settler Colonialism in the Twentieth Century.* New York: Routledge, 2005.

Elliott, J. H. *Empires of the Atlantic World: Britain and Spain in America, 1492–1830.* New Haven, CT: Yale University Press, 2006.

Ellis, Richard. *The Union at Risk: Jacksonian Democracy, States' Rights, and the Nullification Crisis.* New York: Oxford University Press, 1987.

Emerson, Ralph Waldo. *The Complete Works of Ralph Waldo Emerson,* 12 vols. Boston: Houghton Mifflin, 1903–1906.

———. *Journals of Ralph Waldo Emerson,* 10 vols. Boston: Houghton Mifflin, 1909.

———. *Essays: First and Second Series.* New York: Vintage Books, 1990.

———. *Later Lectures of Ralph Waldo Emerson, 1843–1871,* vols. 1 & 2. Athens: University of Georgia Press, 2001.

Ericson, David. "The Nullification Crisis, American Republicanism, and the Force Bill Debate." *Journal of Southern History* 61, no. 2 (May 1995): 249–270.

Erkkila, Betsy. *Whitman the Political Poet.* New York: Cambridge University Press, 1989.

Evans, George Henry. "Vote Yourself a Farm." In *The Radical Reader: A Documentary History of the American Radical Tradition,* eds. Timothy McCarthy and John McMillan. New York: New Press, 2011, 227–229.

Eyal, Yonatan. *The Young America Movement and the Transformation of the Democratic Party, 1828–1861.* New York: Cambridge University Press, 2007.

Fanon, Frantz. *Wretched of the Earth.* New York: Grove Press, 1965.

Farrand, Max, ed. *Records of the Federal Convention,* 3 vols. New Haven, CT: Yale University Press, 1911.

Ferguson, Adam. *Essay on the History of Civil Society.* New York: Cambridge University Press, 1995.

Ferguson, Kennan. "Refusing Settler Colonialism: Simpson's *Mohawk Interruptus.*" *Theory & Event* 18, no. 4 (2015). Available at: https://muse.jhu.edu/article/595847.

———. "Why Does Political Science Hate American Indians?" *Perspectives on Politics* 14, no. 4 (December 2016): 1029–1038.

Fieldhouse, D. K. *The Colonial Empires: A Comparative Study from the Eighteenth Century.* London: Weidenfeld and Nicolson, 1966.

Finkelman, Paul. *Slavery and the Founders: Race and Liberty in the Age of Jefferson.* Armonk, NY: M. E. Sharpe, 2001.

Fischer, Sibylle. *Modernity Disavowed: Haiti and the Cultures of Slavery in the Age of Revolution.* Durham, NC: Duke University Press, 2004.

Foley, Tadhg. "An Unknown and Feeble Body: How Settler Colonialism Was Theorized in the Nineteenth Century." In *Studies in Settler Colonialism: Politics, Identity, and Culture*, ed. Fiona Bateman and Lionel Pilkington. New York: Palgrave MacMillan, 2011.

Folsom, Ed. *Walt Whitman's Native Representations*. New York: Cambridge University Press, 1994.

Foner, Eric. *Free Soil, Free Labor, Free Men: The Ideology of the Republican Party before the Civil War*. New York: Oxford University Press, 1971.

Foner, Philip S., ed. *The Complete Writings of Thomas Paine*, vol. 2. Westport, CT: Greenwood Press, 1945.

———. *The Democratic-Republican Societies, 1790–1800: A Documentary Sourcebook of Constitutions, Declarations, Addresses, Resolutions, and Toasts*. Westport, CT: Greenwood Press, 1976.

Ford, Lisa. *Settler Sovereignty: Jurisdiction and Indigenous People in America and Australia, 1788–1836*. Cambridge, MA: Harvard University Press, 2010.

Foucault, Michel. *Security, Territory, and Population*. New York: Picador, 2009.

Frank, Jason. "Aesthetic Democracy: Walt Whitman and the Poetry of the People." *Review of Politics* 69, no. 3 (Summer 2007): 402–430.

———. *Constituent Moments: Enacting the People in Postrevolutionary America*. Durham, NC: Duke University Press, 2009.

Franklin, Benjamin. *The Interest of Great Britain Considered, with Regard to her Colonies and the Acquisitions of Canada and Guadaloupe*. Philadelphia: William Bradford, 1760.

———. *Works of Benjamin Franklin*, vol. 3. New York: G. P. Putnam's Sons, 1904.

———. *Autobiography and Other Writings*. New York: Cambridge University Press, 2004.

Fredrickson, George. *White Supremacy: A Comparative Study in American and South African History*. New York: Oxford University Press, 1981.

———. *The Arrogance of Race: Historical Perspectives on Slavery, Racism, and Social Inequality*. Middletown, CT: Wesleyan University Press, 1989.

Free Soil Party. "Free Soil Party Platform." In *National Party Platforms, 1840–1972*, 5th ed., eds. Donald Johnson and Kirk Porter. Urbana-Champaign: University of Illinois Press, 1973, 13–14.

Friedrich-Walling, Karl. *Republican Empire: Alexander Hamilton on War and Free Government*. Lawrence: University Press of Kansas, 1999.

Frymer, Paul. "Building an American Empire: Territorial Expansion in the Antebellum Era." *UC Irvine Law Review* 1 (2011): 913–954.

———. "A Rush and a Push and the Land Is Ours: Territorial Expansion, Land Policy, and U.S. State Formation." *Perspectives on Politics* 12, no. 1 (March 2014): 119–144.

Fukuyama, Francis. "The March of Equality." *Journal of Democracy* 11, no. 1 (January 2000): 11–17.

Garnett, Richard. *Edward Gibbon Wakefield: The Colonization of South Australia and New Zealand*. London: T. Fisher Unwin, 1898.

Garza, Mauricio Gonzales de la. *Walt Whitman: Racista, Imperialista, Antimexicano*. Mexico City: Colección Málaga, 1971.

Gibbon, Edward. *The History of the Decline and Fall of the Roman Empire*, vol. 1. Dublin: William Hallhead, 1776.

Giddings, Franklin. *Democracy and Empire*. New York: MacMillan, 1900.

Giddings, Joshua. "My Country, Right or Wrong." In *Great Debates in American History: Foreign Relations*, vol. 2, part 1, ed. Marion Miller. New York: Current Literature, 1913.

Go, Julian. *Patterns of Empire: The British and American Empires, 1688 to the Present*. New York: Cambridge University Press, 2011.

Goldberg, Chad. "Social Citizenship and a Reconstructed Tocqueville." *American Sociological Review* 66, no. 2 (April 2001): 289–315.

Goldstein, Alyosha. "Where the Nation Takes Place: Proprietary Regimes, Antistatism, and U.S. Settler Colonialism." *South Atlantic Quarterly* 107, no. 4 (Fall 2008): 833–861.

Gomez, Adam. "Deus Vult: John L. O'Sullivan, Manifest Destiny, and American Democratic Messianism." *American Political Thought* 1, no. 2 (September 2012): 236–262.

Gougeon, Len. *Virtue's Hero: Emerson, Antislavery, and Reform*. Athens: University of Georgia Press, 1990.

Gourevitch, Alex. *From Slavery to the Cooperative Commonwealth: Labor and Republican Liberty in the Nineteenth Century*. New York: Cambridge University Press, 2015.

Graebner, Norman. *Manifest Destiny*. Indianapolis: Bobbs-Merrill, 1968.

Grant, Susan. *North over South: Northern Nationalism and American Identity in the Antebellum Era*. Lawrence: University Press of Kansas, 2000.

Greene, Jack P. "The Imperial Roots of American Federalism." *This Constitution* 6 (1985): 4–11.

———. *Peripheries and Center: Constitutional Development in the Extended Polities of the British Empire and the United States, 1607–1788*. Athens: University of Georgia Press, 1986.

Griffin, Patrick. *American Leviathan: Empire, Nation, and Revolutionary Frontier*. New York: MacMillan, 2008.

Grinde, Donald. "Iroquois Political Theory and Roots of American Democracy." In *Exiled in the Land of the Free: Democracy, Indian Nations, and the U.S. Constitution*, eds. Oren Lyons and John Mohawk. Santa Fe, NM: Clear Light Publishers, 1992, 227–280.

Grinde, Donald, and Bruce Johansen. *Exemplar of Liberty: Native America and the Evolution of Democracy*. Los Angeles: American Indian Studies Center, 1991.

Grow, G. A. *Man's Right to the Soil*. Washington, DC: Congressional Globe Office, 1852.

Grünzweig, Walter. "Imperialism." *A Companion to Walt Whitman*, ed. Donald Kummings. Malden, MA: Blackwell Publishing, 2006.

Gustafson, Sandra. "Histories of Democracy and Empire." *American Quarterly* 59, no. 1 (March 2007): 107–133.

Hall, Anthony. *American Empire and the Fourth World*. Montreal: McGill-Queens Press, 2005.

Hämäläinen, Pekka. *Comanche Empire*. New Haven, CT: Yale University Press, 2009.

Hammond, James. "Cotton Is King." *Selections from the Letters and Speeches of the Honorable James H. Hammond of South Carolina*. New York: John F. Trow, 1866.

Hanson, Russell. *The Democratic Imagination in America*. Princeton, NJ: Princeton University Press, 1985.

Hartz, Louis. *The Liberal Tradition in America*. New York: Harcourt, 1955.

———. *The Founding of New Societies*. Boston: Houghton Mifflin, 1969.

Hayne, Robert. *The Webster-Hayne Debate on the Nature of the Union: Selected Documents*, ed. Herman Belz. Indianapolis: Liberty Fund Press, 2000.

Hegel, G. W. F. *The Philosophy of History*. New York: Colonial Press, 1899.

———. *Elements of the Philosophy of Right*. New York: Cambridge University Press, 1991.

Heiskell, S. G. *Andrew Jackson and Early Tennessee History*. Nashville: Ambrose Printing Company, 1920.

Hendrickson, David. *Peace Pact: The Lost World of the American Founding*. Lawrence: University Press of Kansas, 2003.

———. *Union, Nation, or Empire: The American Debate over International Relations*. Lawrence: University Press of Kansas, 2009.

Heumann, Stefan. "The Tutelary Empire: State- and Nation-Building in the 19th Century United States." PhD dissertation, University of Pennsylvania, 2009.

Hietala, Thomas. *Manifest Design: American Exceptionalism and Empire*. Ithaca, NY: Cornell University Press, 2003.

Hill, Robert. "Federalism, Republicanism, and the Northwest Ordinance." *Publius: The Journal of Federalism* 18, no. 4 (Autumn 1988): 41–52.

Hill, William. *The Vermont State Constitution*. New York: Oxford University Press, 2011.

Hinderaker, Eric. *Elusive Empires: Constructing Colonialism in the Ohio Valley, 1673–1800*. New York: Cambridge University Press, 1999.

Hobsbawm, Eric. *The Age of Revolutions, 1789–1848*. New York: New American Library, 1962.

Holland, Catherine. *The Body Politic: Foundings, Citizenship, and Difference in the American Political Imagination*. New York: Routledge, 2001.

Honig, Bonnie. "Between Decision and Deliberation: Political Paradox in Democratic Theory." *American Political Science Review* 101 (February 2007): 1–17.

Hopkins, Samuel. "Rights of Colonies Examined." In *Pamphlets of the American Revolution, 1750–1776*, ed. Bernard Bailyn. Cambridge, MA: Belknap Press, 1965, 507–522.

Horsman, Reginald. *Race and Manifest Destiny: The Origins of American Racial Anglo-Saxonism*. Cambridge, MA: Harvard University Press, 1981.

Howe, Daniel Walker. *What Hath God Wrought? The Transformation of America, 1843–1848*. New York: Cambridge University Press, 2007.

Hsueh, Vicki. *Hybrid Constitutions: Challenging Legacies of Law, Privilege, and Culture in Colonial North America*. Durham, NC: Duke University Press, 2010.

Hulsebosch, Daniel. *Constituting Empire: New York and the Transformation of Constitutionalism in the Atlantic World, 1664–1830*. Chapel Hill: University of North Carolina Press, 2005.

Huntington, Samuel. *Who Are We? The Challenges to America's National Identity*. New York: Simon & Schuster, 2004.

Jackson, Andrew. "First Annual Message." *The American Presidency Project*, 1829. Available at: http://www.presidency.ucsb.edu/ws/?pid=29471.

———. "Second Annual Message." *The American Presidency Project*, 1830. Available at: http://www.presidency.ucsb.edu/ws/?pid=29472.

———. "Proclamation Regarding Nullification." *The Avalon Project: Documents in Law,*

History, and Diplomacy, Yale Law School, 1832. Available at: http://avalon.law.yale. edu/19th_century/jack01.asp.

James, C. L. R. *The Black Jacobins.* New York: Random House, 1963.

Janara, Laura. "Brothers and Others: Tocqueville and Beaumont, U.S. Genealogy, Democracy, and Racism." *Political Theory* 32, no. 6 (December 2004): 773–800.

Jefferson, Thomas. *The Works of Thomas Jefferson,* 12 vols. New York: G. P. Putnam's Sons, 1904–1905.

———. *Political Writings.* New York: Cambridge University Press, 1999.

———. "Draft of the Kentucky Resolutions." In *Liberty and Order: The First American Party Struggle,* ed. Lance Banning. Indianapolis: Liberty Fund Press, 2004, 233–236.

Jennings, Francis. *The Invasion of America.* New York: Norton, 1976.

———. *The Creation of America: Through Revolution to Empire.* New York: Cambridge University Press, 2000.

Jensen, Merrill, ed. *The Documentary History of the Ratification of the Constitution,* 26 vols. Madison: State Historical Society of Wisconsin, 1976.

Johnson, Samuel. *Political Writings.* Indianapolis: Liberty Fund Press, 2000.

Johnson, Walter. *River of Dark Dreams.* Cambridge, MA: Harvard University Press, 2013.

Johnston, Anna, and Alan Lawson. "Settler Colonies." In *A Companion to Postcolonial Studies,* eds. Henry Schwarz and Sangeeta Ray. Malden, MA: Blackwell Publishing, 2008, 360–376.

Jones, Dorothy. *License for Empire: Colonialism by Treaty in Early America.* Chicago: University of Chicago Press, 1982.

Jordan, Winthrop. *The White Man's Burden: Historical Origins of Racism in the United States.* New York: Oxford University Press, 1974.

Kagan, Robert. *Dangerous Nation: America's Foreign Policy from Its Earliest Days to the Dawn of the Twentieth Century.* New York: Alfred A. Knopf, 2006.

Kalyvas, Andreas. "Popular Sovereignty, Democracy, and the Constituent Power." *Constellations* 12, no. 2 (June 2005): 223–244.

———. "Constituent Power," *Political Concepts: A Critical Lexicon* 3, no. 1 (Fall 2013). Available at: http://www.politicalconcepts.org/constituentpower/.

Kammen, Michael. "The Meaning of Colonization in American Revolutionary Thought," *Journal of the History of Ideas* 31, no. 3 (July-September 1970): 337–358.

Kateb, George. *The Inner Ocean: Individualism and Democratic Culture.* Ithaca, NY: Cornell University Press, 1992.

Kazanjian, David. *The Colonizing Trick: National Culture and Imperial Citizenship in Early America.* Minneapolis: University of Minnesota Press, 2003.

Keating, Christine. *Decolonizing Democracy: Transforming the Social Contract in India.* State College, PA: Penn State University Press, 2012.

Kellogg, Laura Cornelius. "Our Democracy and the American Indian." In *American Philosophies: An Anthology,* eds. Leonard Harris, Scott L. Pratt, and Anne S. Waters. Malden, MA: Blackwell, 2002, 423–432.

Kim, Heidi. "From Language to Empire: Walt Whitman in the Context of Nineteenth-Century Popular Anglo-Saxonism." *Walt Whitman Quarterly Review* 24, no. 1 (Summer 2006): 1–19.

King George III. "The Proclamation of 1763." In *Documents of American History*, vol. 1, ed. Henry Steele Commager. New York: F. S. Crofts, 1946, 47–50.

Klausen, Jimmy Casas. "Room Enough: America, Natural Liberty, and Consent in Locke's *Second Treatise*." *Journal of Politics* 69, no. 3 (August 2007): 760–769.

Klusmeyer, Douglas. "Hannah Arendt's Case for Federalism." *Publius: The Journal of Federalism* 40, no. 1 (Winter 2010): 31–58.

Knox, Henry. "Report on the Northwestern Indians" (June 15, 1789). In US Congress, *American State Papers: Documents, Legislative and Executive, of the Congress of the United States*, vol. 4, eds. Walter Lowrie and Matthew Clarke. Washington, DC: Gales and Seaton, 1832.

———. "Report on Indian Affairs." *Journals of the Continental Congress*, vol. 33. Washington, DC: Government Printing Office, 1904.

Kohn, Margaret. "The Other America: Tocqueville and Beaumont on Race and Slavery." *Polity* 35, no. 2 (Winter 2002): 169–193.

———. "Empire's Law: Tocqueville on Colonialism and the State of Exception." *Canadian Journal of Political Science* 41, no. 2 (June 2008): 255–278.

Konkle, Maureen. *Writing Indian Nations: Native Intellectuals and the Politics of Historiography, 1827–1863*. Chapel Hill: University of North Carolina Press, 2004.

———. "Indigenous Ownership and the Emergence of U.S. Liberal Imperialism." *American Indian Quarterly* 32, no. 3 (Summer 2008): 297–323.

Korman, Sharon. *The Right of Conquest: The Acquisition of Territory by Force in International Law and Practice*. New York: Oxford University Press, 1996.

LaCroix, Alison L. "The Labor Theory of Empire." *Common-Place* 12, no. 3 (April 2012). Available at: http://www.common-place.org/vol-12/no-03/reviews/lacroix.shtml.

Lafeber, Walter. *The American Age: United States Foreign Policy at Home and Abroad*. New York: Norton, 1989.

Lake, Marilyn, and Henry Reynolds. *Drawing the Global Color Line: White Men's Countries and the International Challenge of Racial Equality*. New York: Cambridge University Press, 2008.

Latner, Richard. "The Nullification Crisis and Republican Subversion." *Journal of Southern History* 43, no. 1 (February 1977): 19–38.

Lause, Mark. *Young America: Land, Labor, and Republican Community*. Urbana-Champaign: University of Illinois Press, 2005.

Lieber, Francis. *On Civil Liberty and Self-Government*. Philadelphia: J. B. Lippincott, 1874.

Lincoln, Abraham. *The Portable Abraham Lincoln*, ed. Andrew Delbanco. New York: Penguin, 2009.

Lipset, Seymour Martin, and Jason Lakin. *The Democratic Century*. Norman: University of Oklahoma Press, 2004.

Lee, Fred. "The Racial Constitution of the Public: Four Exercises in Historicizing the American Polity." PhD dissertation, University of California, Los Angeles, 2010.

Lee, Sohui. "Manifest Empire: Anglo-American Rivalry and the Shaping of U.S. Manifest Destiny." In *Romantic Border Crossings*, eds. Jeffrey Cass and Larry Peer. Burlington, VT: Ashgate, 2008, 181–190.

Lefebvre, Henri. *The Production of Space*. Malden, MA: Blackwell Publishing, 1991.

Lepore, Jill. *The Name of War: King Philip's War and the Origins of American Identity*. New York: Alfred A. Knopf, 1998.

Levine, Alan, and Daniel Malachuk. "Introduction." In *A Political Companion to Ralph Waldo Emerson*, eds. Levine and Malachuk. Lexington: University Press of Kentucky, 2011, 1–41.

Locke, John. *Second Treatise of Government*. Indianapolis: Hackett Publishing, 1980.

Lopenzina, Drew. "What to the American Indian Is the Fourth of July? Moving beyond Abolitionist Rhetoric in Apess's *Eulogy on King Philip*." *American Literature* 82, no. 4 (2010): 673–699.

Losurdo, Domenico. *Liberalism: A Counter-History*. New York: Verso, 2011.

Lummis, Charles Fletcher. *The Land of Poco Tiempo*. New York: Charles Scribner's Sons, 1897.

Madison, James. *Writings of James Madison*. New York: G. P. Putnam's Sons, 1900–1910.

———. "Political Observations." *Liberty and Order: The First American Party Struggle*, ed. Lance Banning. Indianapolis: Liberty Fund Press, 2004.

Madison, James, Alexander Hamilton, and John Jay. *The Federalist Papers*, ed. Isaac Kramnick. New York: Penguin, 1987.

Maier, Charles. *Among Empires: American Ascendancy and Its Predecessors*. Cambridge, MA: Harvard University Press, 2009.

Maloy, J. S. *The Colonial American Origins of Modern Democratic Thought*. New York: Cambridge University Press, 2008.

Mamdani, Mahmood. "Settler Colonialism: Then and Now." *Critical Inquiry* 41, no. 3 (Spring 2015): 596–614.

Mantena, Karuna. *Alibis of Empire: Henry Maine and the Ends of Liberal Imperialism*. Princeton, NJ: Princeton University Press, 2010.

Martí, José. "The Poet Walt Whitman." In *Selected Writings*, ed. Esther Allen. New York: Penguin, 2002, 183–194.

Mattes, Armin. *Citizens of a Common Intellectual Homeland: The Transatlantic Origins of American Democracy and Nationhood*. Charlottesville: University of Virginia Press, 2015.

McBride, Phyllis. "Feudalism." In *Walt Whitman: An Encyclopedia*, eds. J. R. LeMaster and Donald Kummings. New York: Garland Publishing, 1998.

McCoy, Drew. *Elusive Republic: Political Economy in Jeffersonian America*. Chapel Hill: University of North Carolina Press, 1980.

McWilliams, Wilson Carey. *The Idea of Fraternity in America*. Berkeley: University of California Press, 1973.

Mehta, Uday. *Liberalism and Empire: A Study in Nineteenth-Century British Liberal Thought*. Chicago: University of Chicago, 1999.

Merchant, Carolyn. *Reinventing Eden: The Fate of Nature in Western Culture*. New York: Routledge, 2003.

Merk, Frederick. *Manifest Destiny and Mission in American History*. Cambridge, MA: Harvard University Press, 1963.

Mill, John Stuart. "Essay on Government." *Collected Works of John Stuart Mill, Vol. XVIII*. Toronto: University of Toronto Press, 1977.

———. *On Liberty and Other Essays*. New York: Oxford University Press, 1991.

Miller, Angela. *Empire of the Eye: Landscape Representation and American Cultural Politics, 1825–1875*. Ithaca, NY: Cornell University Press, 1993.

Miller, Robert et al. *Discovering Indigenous Lands: The Doctrine of Discovery in the English Colonies*. New York: Oxford University Press, 2010.

Mills, Charles. *The Racial Contract*. Ithaca, NY: Cornell University Press, 1997.

Molesworth, Charles. "Whitman's Political Vision." *Raritan* 12, no. 1 (Summer 1992): 98–113.

Morgan, Edmund. "Slavery and Freedom: The American Paradox." *Journal of American History* 59, no. 1 (June 1972): 5–29.

———. *American Slavery, American Freedom: The Ordeal of Colonial Virginia*. New York: Norton, 1975.

———. *Inventing the People: The Rise of Popular Sovereignty in England and America*. New York: Norton, 1989.

Morrison, Michael. *Slavery and the American West: The Eclipse of Manifest Destiny and the Coming of the Civil War*. Chapel Hill: University of North Carolina Press, 1997.

Morse, Jedediah. *The American Geography*, 2nd ed. London: J. Stockdale, 1792.

Mouffe, Chantal. *The Democratic Paradox*. New York: Verso, 2009.

Moyn, Samuel. "Fantasies of Federalism." *Dissent Magazine*, Winter 2015. Available at http://www.dissentmagazine.org/article/fantasies-of-federalism.

Münkler, Herfried. *Empires: The Logic of World Domination from Ancient Rome to the United States*. Cambridge, UK: Polity Press, 2007.

Nash, Gary. *The Unknown American Revolution: The Unruly Birth of Democracy and the Struggle to Create America*. New York: Penguin, 2006.

Negri, Antonio. *Insurgencies: Constituent Power and the Modern State*. Minneapolis: University of Minnesota Press, 1999.

Nelson, Eric. *The Greek Tradition in Republican Thought*. New York: Cambridge University Press, 1998.

Nichols, Robert. "Realizing the Social Contract: The Case of Colonialism and Indigenous Peoples." *Contemporary Political Theory* 4, no. 1 (February 2005): 42–62.

———. "Of First and Last Men: Contract and Colonial Historicality in Foucault." In *The Ends of History: Questioning the Stakes of Historical Reason*, eds. Amy Swiffen and Joshua Nichols. New York: Routledge, 2013, 64–83.

———. "Tocqueville, Beaumont, and the Dialectic of Race and Place." Paper presented at the American Political Science Association annual meeting, Chicago, IL, August 29–September 1, 2013.

———. "Contract and Usurpation: Enfranchisement and Racial Governance in Settler-Colonial Contexts." In *Theorizing Native Studies*, eds. Audra Simpson and Andrea Smith. Durham, NC: Duke University Press, 2014, 99–121.

Nielsen, Donald. "The Mashpee Indian Revolt of 1833." *New England Quarterly* 58, no. 3 (September 1985): 400–420.

North Carolina Constitution. *The Avalon Project: Documents in Law, History, and Diplomacy*, Yale Law School, 1776. Available at: http://avalon.law.yale.edu/18th_century/nc07.asp.

Nugent, Walter. *Habits of Empire: A History of American Expansion*. New York: Vintage, 2009.

O'Brien, Jean. *Dispossession by Degrees: Indian Land and Identity in Natick, Massachusetts, 1650–1790.* Lincoln: University of Nebraska Press, 2003.

———. *Firsting and Lasting: Writing Indians Out of Existence in New England.* Minneapolis: University of Minnesota Press, 2010.

Ochoa Espejo, Paulina. "Paradoxes of Popular Sovereignty: A View from Spanish America." *Journal of Politics* 74, no. 4 (October 2012): 1053–1065.

Olson, Joel. *The Abolition of White Democracy.* Minneapolis: University of Minnesota Press, 2004.

Onuf, Peter. "State-Making in Revolutionary America: Independent Vermont as a Case Study." *Journal of American History* 67, no. 4 (March 1981): 797–815.

———. *The Origins of the Federal Republic: Jurisdictional Controversies in the United States, 1775–1787.* Philadelphia: University of Pennsylvania Press, 1983.

———. *Statehood and Union: A History of the Northwest Ordinance.* Bloomington: Indiana University Press, 1987.

———. *Jefferson's Empire: The Language of American Nationhood.* Charlottesville: University Press of Virginia, 2000.

O'Shaughnessy, Andrew Jackson. *An Empire Divided: The American Revolution and the British Caribbean.* Philadelphia: University of Pennsylvania Press, 2000.

Ostler, Jeffrey. *The Plains Sioux and U.S. Colonialism.* New York: Cambridge University Press, 2004.

O'Sullivan, John. "The Democratic Principle—And the Importance of Its Assertion, and Application to Our Political System and Literature." *United States Magazine and Democratic Review* 1, no. 1 (October 1837): 1–15.

———. "The Course of Civilization." *United States Magazine and Democratic Review* 6, no. 19 (September 1839): 208–217.

———. "The Great Nation of Futurity." *United States Magazine and Democratic Review* 6, no. 23 (November 1839): 426–430.

———. "One of the Problems of the Age." *United States Magazine and Democratic Review* 14, no. 67 (February 1844): 156–167.

——— "The Popular Movement." *New York Morning News,* May 24, 1845.

———. "Emerson's Essays," *United States Magazine and Democratic Review* 16, no. 84 (June 1845): 589–602.

———. "Annexation." *United States Magazine and Democratic Review* 17, no. 85 (July–August 1845): 5–10.

———. "Territorial Aggrandizement." *United States Magazine and Democratic Review* 17, no. 88 (October 1845): 243–247.

———. "The True Title." *New York Morning News,* December 27, 1845.

———. "Legislative Embodiment of Public Opinion." *United States Magazine and Democratic Review* 19, no. 98 (August 1846): 83–89.

Pagden, Anthony. *Lords of All the World: Ideologies of Empire in Spain, Britain, and France c. 1500–c. 1800.* New Haven, CT: Yale University Press, 1995.

Paine, Thomas. *The Writings of Thomas Paine,* 4 vols. New York: G. P. Putnam's Sons, 1906.

Palonen, Kari. "Political Theorizing As a Dimension of Political Life." *European Journal of Political Theory* 4, no. 4 (October 2005): 351–366.

Paolinio, Ernst. *The Foundations of American Empire: William Henry Seward and U.S. Foreign Policy.* Ithaca, NY: Cornell University Press, 1973.

Paquette, Gabriel. "Colonies and Empire in the Political Thought of Hegel and Marx." In *Empire and Modern Political Thought,* ed. Sankar Muthu. New York: Cambridge University Press, 2012, 292–323.

Pateman, Carole, and Charles Mills. "The Settler Contract." In *Contract and Domination.* Cambridge, UK: Polity Press, 2007, 35–78.

Pease, Donald. "American Studies after American Exceptionalism? Toward a Comparative Analysis of Imperial State Exceptionalisms." In *Globalizing American Studies,* eds. Brian T. Edwards and Dilip Parameshwar Gaonkar. Chicago: University of Chicago Press, 2010.

Pennsylvania Constitution. *The Avalon Project: Documents in Law, History, and Diplomacy.* Yale Law School, 1776. Available at: http://avalon.law.yale.edu/18th_century/pa08.asp.

Pierson, George. *Tocqueville and Beaumont in America.* New York: Oxford University Press, 1938.

Pitts, Jennifer. "Empire and Democracy: Tocqueville and the Algeria Question." *Journal of Political Philosophy* 8, no. 3 (September 2000): 295–318.

———. *A Turn to Empire: The Rise of Imperial Liberalism in Britain and France.* Princeton, NJ: Princeton University Press, 2005.

———. "Political Theory of Empire and Imperialism." *Annual Review of Political Science* 13 (2010): 211–235.

Pocock, J. G. A. *The Machiavellian Moment: Florentine Political Thought and the Atlantic Republican Tradition.* Princeton, NJ: Princeton University Press, 1975.

Pownall, Thomas. *The Administration of the Colonies,* 3rd ed. London: J. Dodsley, 1766.

Pratt, Julius. "The Origins of Manifest Destiny." *American Historical Review* 32, no. 4 (July 1927): 795–798.

Prucha, Francis Paul. *The Great Father: The United States Government and the American Indians.* Lincoln: University of Nebraska Press, 1984.

Quijano, Anibal. "Coloniality of Power, Eurocentrism, and Social Classification." In *Coloniality at Large: Latin America and the Postcolonial Debate,* eds. Mabel Moraña, Enrique Dussel, and Carlos Jáuregui. Durham, NC: Duke University Press, 2008, 181–224.

Rana, Aziz. *The Two Faces of American Freedom.* Cambridge, MA: Harvard University Press, 2011.

———. "Colonialism and Constitutional Memory." *UC Irvine Law Review* 5 (2015): 263–288.

———. "Race and the American Creed: Recovering Black Radicalism." *n+1* 24 (Winter 2016). Available at: https://nplusonemag.com/issue-24/politics/race-and-the-american-creed/.

Rancière, Jacques. *Disagreement: Politics and Philosophy.* Minneapolis: University of Minnesota Press, 1999.

———. "Ten Theses on Politics." *Theory and Event* 5 (2001). Available at: http://muse.jhu.edu/journals/theory_and_event/v005/5.3ranciere.html.

———. *Hatred of Democracy.* New York: Verso, 2006.

Razack, Sherene. *Race, Space, and the Law: Unmapping a White Settler Society*. Toronto: Between the Lines, 2002.

Reinhardt, Mark. *The Art of Being Free: Taking Liberties with Tocqueville, Marx, and Arendt*. Ithaca, NY: Cornell University Press, 1997.

Rifkin, Mark. "Documenting Tradition: Territoriality and Textuality in Black Hawk's Narrative." *American Literature* 80, no. 4 (2008): 677–705.

———. *Manifesting America: The Imperial Construction of U.S. National Space*. New York: Oxford University Press, 2009.

Riker, William. *The Development of American Federalism*. Boston: Kluwer, 1987.

Roebuck, John Arthur. *The Colonies of England: A Plan for the Government of Some Portion of Our Colonial Possessions*. London: John W. Parker, 1849.

Roediger, David. *Wages of Whiteness: Race and the Making of the American Working Class*. New York: Verso, 1999.

Rogin, Michael. *Fathers and Children: Andrew Jackson and the Subjugation of the American Indian*. New York: Vintage Books, 1976.

———. "Herman Melville: State, Civil Society, and the American 1848." *Yale Review*, 69, 1 (October 1979): 72–88.

———. *Subversive Genealogy: The Politics and Art of Herman Melville*. New York: Alfred A. Knopf, 1983.

———. "Liberal Society and the Indian Question." In *Ronald Reagan, the Movie: And Other Episodes in American Political Demonology*. Berkeley: University of California Press, 1988, 134–168.

Roosevelt, Theodore. *The Winning of the West*, vol. 1: *From the Alleghenies to the Mississippi, 1769–1776*. New York: G. P. Putnam's Sons, 1889.

———. *The Winning of the West*, vol. 2: *From the Alleghenies to the Mississippi, 1776–1783*. New York: G. P. Putnam's Sons, 1896.

Rousseau, Jean-Jacques. *On the Social Contract*. Indianapolis: Hackett, 1987.

Said, Edward. *Culture and Imperialism*. New York: Alfred A. Knopf, 1993.

Saler, Bethel. *The Settlers' Empire: Colonialism and State Formation in America's Old Northwest*. Philadelphia: University of Pennsylvania Press, 2015.

Sampson, Robert. *John O'Sullivan and His Times*. Kent, OH: Kent State University Press, 2003.

Santayana, George. *Interpretations of Poetry and Religion*. New York: Harper and Row, 1957.

Savelle, Max. *Empires to Nations: Expansion in America, 1713–1824*. Minneapolis: University of Minnesota Press, 1974.

Saxton, Alexander. *The Rise and Fall of the White Republic: Class Politics and Mass Culture in Nineteenth-Century America*. New York: Verso, 2003.

Schlesinger, Arthur, Jr. *Cycles of American History*. Boston: Houghton Mifflin, 1998.

Schneck, Stephen Frederick. "Habits of the Head: Tocqueville's America and Jazz." *Political Theory* 17, no. 4 (November 1989): 643–647.

Seward, William. *Works of William Seward*, 4 vols. Boston: Houghton Mifflin, 1884.

Shapiro, Michael. *Deforming American Political Thought: Ethnicity, Facticity, and Genre*. Lexington: University Press of Kentucky, 2006.

Shaw, Karena. *Indigeneity and Political Theory*. New York: Routledge, 2008.

Simpson, Audra. *Mohawk Interruptus: Political Life across the Borders of Settler States.* Durham, NC: Duke University Press, 2014.

Skinner, Quentin. *Visions of Politics, Vol. 1.* New York: Cambridge University Press, 2002.

Slotkin, Richard. *Regeneration through Violence: The Mythology of the American Frontier, 1600–1860.* Norman: University of Oklahoma Press, 1973.

———. *The Fatal Environment: The Myth of the Frontier in the Age of Industrialization, 1800–1890.* Norman: University of Oklahoma Press, 1985.

———. *Gunfighter Nation: The Myth of the Frontier in Twentieth-Century America.* Norman: University of Oklahoma Press, 1992.

Smith, Henry Nash. *Virgin Land: The American West As Symbol and Myth.* Cambridge, MA: Harvard University Press, 1950.

Smith, Rogers. "Beyond Tocqueville, Myrdal and Hartz: The Multiple Traditions in America." *American Political Science Review* 87, no. 3 (September 1993): 549–566.

———. *Civic Ideals: Conflicting Visions of Citizenship in US History.* New Haven, CT: Yale University Press, 1999.

———. *Stories of Peoplehood: The Politics and Morals of Political Membership.* New York: Cambridge University Press, 2003.

Spivak, Gayatri. *A Critique of Postcolonial Reason.* Cambridge, MA: Harvard University Press, 1999.

Stephanson, Anders. *Manifest Destiny: American Expansionism and the Empire of Right.* New York: Hill and Wang, 1995.

———. "An American Story? Second Thoughts on Manifest Destiny." In *Manifest Destinies and Indigenous Peoples,* eds. David Maybury-Lewis et al. Cambridge, MA: Harvard University Press, 2009, 21–49.

Sundquist, Eric. *Empire and Slavery in American Literature, 1820–1865.* Oxford: University of Mississippi Press, 1995.

Tecumseh. Speech to Governor W. H. Harrison. *The Portable North American Indian Reader,* ed. Frederick Turner. New York: Viking Press, 1977, 245–247.

Temin, David. "Custer's Sins: Vine Deloria Jr. and the Settler-Colonial Politics of Civic Inclusion." *Political Theory,* forthcoming. Available at http://journals.sagepub.com /doi/abs/10.1177/0090591717712151.

Tocqueville, Alexis de. *Journey to America.* New Haven, CT: Yale University Press, 1960.

———. *Selected Letters on Politics and Society.* Berkeley: University of California Press, 1985.

———. *Democracy in America.* Chicago: University of Chicago Press, 2000.

———. *Writings on Empire and Slavery,* ed. Jennifer Pitts. Baltimore: Johns Hopkins University Press, 2001.

———. "Two Weeks in the Wilderness." In *Democracy in America and Two Essays on America.* New York: Penguin, 2003.

———. *Tocqueville in America after 1840: Letters and Other Writings,* eds. Aurelian Craiutu and Jeremy Jennings. New York: Cambridge University Press, 2009.

Tomlins, Christopher. *Freedom Bound: Law, Labor, and Civic Identity in Colonizing English America, 1580–1865.* New York: Cambridge University Press, 2010.

Tooker, Elisabeth. "The United States Constitution and the Iroquois League." *Ethnohistory* 35, 4 (Autumn 1988): 305–336.

Trachtenberg, Alan. "Whitman's Visionary Politics." *Mickle Street Review* 10 (1988): 15–31.

Tuck, Richard. *The Rights of War and Peace: Political Thought and the International Order from Grotius to Kant.* New York: Oxford University Press, 1999.

Tully, James. *An Approach to Political Philosophy: Locke in Contexts.* New York: Cambridge University Press, 1993.

———. *Strange Multiplicity: Constitutionalism in an Age of Diversity.* New York: Cambridge University Press, 1995.

———. *Public Philosophy in a New Key: Volume 1, Democracy and Civic Freedom.* New York: Cambridge University Press, 2009.

———. *Public Philosophy in a New Key: Volume II, Imperialism and Civic Freedom.* New York: Cambridge University Press, 2009.

Turner, Frederick Jackson. "Western State-Making in the Revolutionary Era." *American Historical Review* 1, no. 1 (October 1895): 70–87.

———. "Western State-Making in the Revolutionary Era, II." *American Historical Review* 1, no. 2 (January 1896): 251–269.

———. *The Frontier in American History.* New York: Holt, 1920.

Turner, Jack. *Awakening to Race: Individualism and Social Consciousness in America.* Chicago: University of Chicago Press, 2012.

Tuveson, Ernest Lee. *Redeemer Nation: The Idea of America's Millennial Role.* Chicago: University of Chicago Press, 1968.

Tyrrell, Ian. "Beyond the View from Euro-America: Environment, Settler Societies, and the Internationalization of American History." In *Rethinking American History in a Global Age*, ed. Thomas Bender. Berkeley: University of California Press, 2002.

US Congress. "Treaty of Dancing Rabbit Creek." In *Indian Affairs: Laws and Treaties*, vol. 2, ed. Charles Kappler. Washington, DC: Government Printing Office, 1902, 310–319.

———. "Treaty of Hopewell." *Indian Affairs: Laws and Treaties*, vol. 2, ed. Charles Kappler. Washington, DC: Government Printing Office, 1902, 8–11.

———. "Resolution on Public Lands." *Journals of the Continental Congress*, vol. 18. Washington, DC: Government Printing Office, 1980.

———. "Objection to the Louisiana Purchase." In *Issues of Westward Expansion*, ed. Mitchel Roth. Westport, CT: Greenwood Press, 2002, 21–26.

———. "Treaty of Guadalupe Hidalgo." In *Foreigners in Their Native Land: Historical Roots of the Mexican Americans*, ed. David Weber. Albuquerque: University of New Mexico Press, 2003, 162–168.

———. "Indian Removal Act." In *Major Problems in American Foreign Relations, Volume I*, ed. Dennis Merrill and Thomas Paterson. Boston: Wadsworth, 2010, 178–179.

Veracini, Lorenzo. *Settler Colonialism: A Theoretical Overview.* New York: Palgrave Mac-Millan, 2010.

Vermont Constitution. *The Avalon Project: Documents in Law, History, and Diplomacy.* Yale Law School, 1777. Available at: http://avalon.law.yale.edu/18th_century/vt01.asp.

Virginia Declaration of Rights. *The Avalon Project: Documents in Law, History, and Diplomacy.* Yale Law School, 1776. Available at: http://avalon.law.yale.edu/18th_century/virginia.asp.

Von Vacano, Diego. "The Scope of Comparative Political Theory." *Annual Review of Political Science* 18 (2015): 1–16.

Wakefield, Edward Gibbon. *A Statement of the Principles and Objects of a Proposed National Society, for the Cure and Prevention of Pauperism, by Means of Systematic Colonization.* London: James Ridgway, 1830.

———. *England and America: A Comparison of the Social and Political State of Both Nations.* New York: Harper & Brothers, 1834.

Wald, Priscilla. "Terms of Assimilation: Legislating Subjectivity in the Emerging Nation." *boundary 2* 19, no. 3 (Autumn 1992): 77–104.

———. *Constituting Americans: Cultural Anxiety and Narrative Form.* Durham, NC: Duke University Press, 1995.

Walker, Cheryl. *Indian Nation: Native American Literature and Nineteenth-Century Nationalisms.* Durham, NC: Duke University Press, 1997.

Ward, John Manning. *Colonial Self-Government: The British Experience, 1759–1856.* Toronto: University of Toronto Press, 1976.

Warner, Michael. "What's Colonial about Colonial America?" In *Possible Pasts: Becoming Colonial in Early America,* ed. Robert Blair St. George. Ithaca, NY: Cornell University Press, 2000.

Washington, George. *A Collection.* Indianapolis: Liberty Fund Press, 1988.

Webster, Daniel. *The Works of Daniel Webster,* vol. 1. Boston: Little & Brown, 1851.

———. *The Works of Daniel Webster,* vol. 3. Boston: Little & Brown, 1851.

Weinberg, Albert. *Manifest Destiny: A Study of Nationalist Expansionism in American History.* Chicago: Quadrangle Press, 1935.

Welch, Cheryl. "Colonial Violence and the Rhetoric of Evasion: Tocqueville on Algeria." *Political Theory* 31, no. 2 (April 2003): 235–264.

White, G. Edward. *The Marshall Court and Cultural Change, 1815–1835.* New York: Oxford University Press, 1991.

Whitman, Walt. *The Gathering of the Forces,* vols. 1 and 2. New York: G. P. Putnam's Sons, 1920.

———. *Poetry and Prose.* New York: Penguin, 1982.

Widmer, Edward. *Young America: The Flowering of Democracy in New York City.* New York: Oxford University Press, 1999.

Wilentz, Sean. *The Rise of American Democracy: Jefferson to Lincoln.* New York: Norton, 2005.

Williams, Raymond. *Keywords: A Vocabulary of Culture and Society.* New York: Oxford University Press, 1985.

Williams, Robert. *The American Indian in Western Legal Thought: The Discourse of Conquest.* New York: Oxford University Press, 1990.

Williams, Samuel Cole. *History of the Lost State of Franklin.* Boone, NC: Watauga Press, 1924.

Williams, William Appleman. "The Age of Mercantilism: An Interpretation of the American Political Economy, 1763–1828." *William and Mary Quarterly* 15, no. 4 (October 1958): 419–437.

———. *Empire As Way of Life.* New York: Oxford University Press, 1980.

Wilson, William. *The Great American Question, Democracy vs. Doulocracy.* Cincinnati: E. Shepard's Steam Press, 1848.

Winter, Yves. "Conquest." *Political Concepts: A Critical Lexicon* 1 (December 2011). Available at: http://www.politicalconcepts.org/conquest-winter-finished/.

Wolfe, Patrick. *Settler Colonialism and the Transformation of Anthropology: The Politics and Poetics of an Ethnographic Event.* New York: Bloomsbury, 1999.

———. "Land, Labor, and Difference: Elementary Structures of Race." *American Historical Review* 106, no. 3 (June 2001): 866–905.

———. "Settler Colonialism and the Elimination of the Native." *Journal of Genocide Research* 8, no. 4 (December 2006): 387–409.

———. "Race and the Trace of History." *Studies in Settler Colonialism: Politics, Identity, and Culture,* eds. Fiona Bateman and Lionel Pilkington. New York: Palgrave Mac-Millan, 2011.

Wolin, Sheldon. *The Presence of the Past: Essays on the State and the Constitution.* Baltimore: Johns Hopkins University Press, 1989.

———. *Tocqueville between Two Worlds.* Princeton, NJ: Princeton University Press, 2001.

———. *Politics and Vision.* Princeton, NJ: Princeton University Press, 2004.

———. *Democracy Incorporated: Managed Democracy and the Specter of Inverted Totalitarianism.* Princeton, NJ: Princeton University Press, 2008.

Wood, Ellen Meiksins. *Empire of Capital.* New York: Verso, 2003.

———. *Liberty and Property: A History of Western Political Thought from the Renaissance to the Enlightenment.* New York: Verso, 2012.

Wood, Gordon. *The Creation of the American Republic, 1776–1787.* Chapel Hill: University of North Carolina Press, 1969.

———. *The Radicalism of the American Revolution.* New York: Vintage, 1991.

———. *Empire of Liberty: A History of the Early Republic, 1789–1815.* New York: Oxford University Press, 2009.

Yirush, Craig. *Settlers, Liberty, and Empire: The Roots of Early American Political Theory, 1675–1775.* New York: Cambridge University Press, 2011.

———. "The Idea of Rights in the Imperial Crisis." *Social Philosophy and Policy* 29, no. 2 (July 2012): 82–103.

Young, Iris Marion. *Global Challenges: War, Self-Determination, and Responsibility for Justice.* Cambridge, UK: Polity Press, 2007.

Young, Richard, and Jeffrey Meiser. "Race and the Dual State in the Early American Republic." In *Race and American Political Development,* ed. Joe Lowndes, Julie Novkov, and Dorian Warren. New York: Routledge, 2008, 31–58.

Young, Thomas. "To the Inhabitants of Vermont, a Free and Independent State, Bounding on the River Connecticut and Lake Champlain." Reprinted in Zadock Thompson, *A History of Vermont, Natural, Civil, and Statistical.* Burlington, VT: Chauncey Goodrich, 1842.aristocracyfeudalism

INDEX

absent-feudalism trope, 77, 78, 87, 93–94
accommodation, indigenous resistance to, 68–69
Adams, John, 27
Adams, Willi Paul, 50
"Address to the Whites" (Boudinot), 125
"Address to the Wisconsin State Agricultural Society" (Lincoln), 136
African Americans
  Jefferson's racial views and, 71–72
  Lincoln's racial views and, 138–139
  Tocqueville's account of race in America, 89–91
  See also slavery
Albany Plan (1754), 28, 192
Alfred, Taiaiake, 188–189
Algeria, 15–16, 94–99, 159–160
Alien and Sedition Acts, 168
American Creed, 185, 186
American democracy
  absent-feudalism trope, 77, 78, 87, 93–94
  decolonizing the democratic tradition, 184–194
  Indian nullification and, 158–159, 168–170 (see also Indian nullification)
  notions of democratic empire and, 7–10 (see also democratic empire)
  poetic dispossession in Whitman's democratic theory, 149–153
  representations of land and, 78–79
  safety-valve theory of colonization and, 102–104 (see also safety-valve theory of colonization)
  slavery expansion and free-soil

ideology (see free-soil ideology; slavery expansion)
  Tocqueville's account of race in America, 89–95
  Tocqueville's external configuration of North America, 79–85
  transnational history and, 15–16
  Whitman's theory of democratic development, 151–153
  William Apess's counter-narrative of the founding of, 176–182
American exceptionalism, 102
American federalism. See federalism
American founding, counter-narrative of, 176–182
American identity, 185–186
American Revolution, 34, 37–38, 50
Amos, Blind Joe, 163
apartheid, 16
Apess, William
  appropriation of US constitutionalism, 170–173
  counter-narrative of the American founding, 176–182
  critique of the treaty system, 181–182
  Indian nullification, 158–159, 160 (see also Indian nullification)
  "Eulogy on King Philip," 158, 176–179, 180–182
  "Indian Nullification," 158, 163, 164, 176, 178
  Mashpee Revolt of 1833 and, 160–164
Arabs, 97, 98
Arendt, Hannah, 23–24, 47–48
aristocracy
  absent-feudalism trope, 77, 78, 87, 93–94

9 780700 626076